First World War
and Army of Occupation
War Diary
France, Belgium and Germany

29 DIVISION
87 Infantry Brigade
Border Regiment
1st Battalion
2 April 1916 - 3 April 1919

WO95/2305/1

The Naval & Military Press Ltd
www.nmarchive.com
Published in association with The National Archives

Published by

The Naval & Military Press Ltd

Unit 10 Ridgewood Industrial Park,

Uckfield, East Sussex,

TN22 5QE England

Tel: +44 (0) 1825 749494

www.naval-military-press.com

www.nmarchive.com

This diary has been reprinted in facsimile from the original. Any imperfections are inevitably reproduced and the quality may fall short of modern type and cartographic standards.

Contents

Document type	Place/Title	Date From	Date To
Heading	WO/95/2305/1		
Heading	1st Bn. Border Regt Apr 1916 Apr 1919		
Heading	1st Battalion The Border Regiment April 1916		
War Diary	Amplier	02/04/1916	02/04/1916
War Diary	Beauval	02/04/1916	02/04/1916
War Diary	Acheux	03/04/1916	03/04/1916
War Diary	Firing Line	04/04/1916	05/04/1916
War Diary	Amplier	02/04/1916	02/04/1916
War Diary	Beauval	02/04/1916	02/04/1916
War Diary	Acheux	03/04/1916	03/04/1916
War Diary	Firing Line	04/04/1916	13/04/1916
War Diary	Acheux	15/04/1916	30/04/1916
Heading	1st Battalion The Border Regiment May 1916		
War Diary	Front Line	01/05/1916	04/05/1916
War Diary	Englebelmer	05/05/1916	11/05/1916
War Diary	Front Line	14/05/1916	18/05/1916
War Diary	Louvencourt	19/05/1916	28/05/1916
War Diary	Englebelmer	28/05/1916	31/05/1916
Heading	1st Battalion The Border Regiment June 1916		
War Diary	Englebelmer	01/06/1916	01/06/1916
War Diary	Englebelmer	05/06/1916	05/06/1916
War Diary	Front Line	07/06/1916	15/06/1916
War Diary	Louvencourt	16/06/1916	23/06/1916
War Diary	Acheux	26/06/1916	27/06/1916
Heading	1st Battalion The Border Regiment July 1916		
Heading	War Diary Of 1st Div Border Regiment For July 1916		
War Diary	Front Line	01/07/1916	08/07/1916
War Diary	Acheux	09/07/1916	15/07/1916
War Diary	Mailly	07/07/1916	19/07/1916
War Diary	Front Line	22/07/1916	22/07/1916
War Diary	Bus	24/07/1916	24/07/1916
War Diary	Amplier	25/07/1916	29/07/1916
War Diary	Proven	30/07/1916	31/07/1916
War Diary	1st Battalion The Border Regiment August 1916		
Heading	War Diary From August 1st 1916 To August 31st 1916		
War Diary	Proven	01/08/1916	16/08/1916
War Diary	Flanders	19/08/1916	23/08/1916
War Diary	Canal	24/08/1916	29/08/1916
Heading	1st Battalion The Border Regiment September 1916		
Heading	War Diary 1st Bn Border Regiment From 1-9-16 To 30-9-16		
War Diary	Firing Line	01/09/1916	01/09/1916
War Diary	Kaaie Salient	02/09/1916	08/09/1916
War Diary	'A' Camp	10/09/1916	10/09/1916
War Diary	Brandhoek	11/09/1916	18/09/1916
War Diary	Canal Bank	19/09/1916	22/09/1916
War Diary	Canal Bank (Ypres)	23/09/1916	23/09/1916
War Diary	Firing Line	24/09/1916	29/09/1916
War Diary	Canal Bank	30/09/1916	30/09/1916

Miscellaneous	General Notes On The Recent Raid Carried Out In The Salient.		
Miscellaneous	Lessons From The Raid		
Diagram etc			
Miscellaneous	R.B. 116		
Miscellaneous	Report on Raid made by 1st Border Regiment on night 30th Sept. 1916		
War Diary	1st Battalion The Border Regiment October 1916		
Heading	War Diary Of 1st Bn Border Regiment. From-1st October 1916 To 31st October 1916		
War Diary	Canal Bank Ypres	01/10/1916	03/10/1916
War Diary	J Camp	04/10/1916	04/10/1916
War Diary	International Corner	05/10/1916	07/10/1916
War Diary	Longeau	08/10/1916	08/10/1916
War Diary	Buire	10/10/1916	12/10/1916
War Diary	Fricourt Camp	13/10/1916	15/10/1916
War Diary	Bernafay Wood	19/10/1916	20/10/1916
War Diary	Firing Line Guedecourt	21/10/1916	21/10/1916
War Diary	Firing Line	22/10/1916	31/10/1916
Heading	1st Battalion The Border Regiment November 1916		
Heading	War Diary Of 1st Bn The Border Regiment From 1st November 1916 To 30 November 1916		
War Diary	Albert	01/11/1916	03/11/1916
War Diary	Allery	04/11/1916	14/11/1916
War Diary	Carnoy	15/11/1916	15/11/1916
War Diary	Les Boeuf	16/11/1916	18/11/1916
War Diary	Firing Line	19/11/1916	19/11/1916
War Diary	Lesboeufs Ox Trench	20/11/1916	20/11/1916
War Diary	Mametz	21/11/1916	25/11/1916
War Diary	Or Trench	27/11/1916	27/11/1916
War Diary	Firing Line	28/11/1916	29/11/1916
War Diary	Guillemont	30/11/1916	30/11/1916
Heading	1st Battalion The Border Regiment December 1916		
Heading	War Diary Of 1st Batt The Border Regt From 1st December 1916 To 31st December 1916 Volume 21		
Miscellaneous	Extract From Army Routine Orders.		
War Diary	Mansel Camp	02/12/1916	03/12/1916
War Diary	Guillemont	06/12/1916	06/12/1916
War Diary	Firing Line	08/12/1916	09/12/1916
War Diary	Carnoy Camp	10/12/1916	10/12/1916
War Diary	Corbie	11/12/1916	11/12/1916
War Diary	Conde	12/12/1916	12/12/1916
War Diary	Picquigny	13/12/1916	17/12/1916
War Diary	Hangest	18/12/1916	31/12/1916
War Diary	War Diary Of 1st Battalion Border Regiment From January 1st 1917 To January 31st 1917 Volume No 22		
War Diary	Hangest	01/01/1917	12/01/1917
War Diary	Mericourt	12/01/1917	12/01/1917
War Diary	Bresle	13/01/1917	14/01/1917
War Diary	Meaulte	15/01/1917	15/01/1917
War Diary	Carnoy	15/01/1917	16/01/1917
War Diary	Guillemont	17/01/1917	17/01/1917
War Diary	Firing Line	18/01/1917	19/01/1917
War Diary	Carnoy	20/01/1917	21/01/1917
War Diary	Firing Line	22/01/1917	22/01/1917
War Diary	Carnoy	23/01/1917	26/01/1917

War Diary	Firing Line	27/01/1917	28/01/1917
War Diary	Carnoy	29/01/1917	31/01/1917
War Diary	Guillemont	01/02/1917	01/02/1917
War Diary	Firing Line	02/02/1917	03/02/1917
War Diary	Carnoy	04/02/1917	06/02/1917
War Diary	Meaulte	07/02/1917	18/02/1917
War Diary	Combles	19/02/1917	19/02/1917
War Diary	Firing Line	20/02/1917	21/02/1917
War Diary	Combles	22/02/1917	22/02/1917
War Diary	Bronfay	23/02/1917	24/02/1917
War Diary	Combles	25/02/1917	25/02/1917
War Diary	Firing Line	26/02/1917	27/02/1917
War Diary	Fregicourt	28/02/1917	28/02/1917
War Diary	Bronfay	01/03/1917	01/03/1917
War Diary	Ville	02/03/1917	02/03/1917
War Diary	Bussy	03/03/1917	19/03/1917
War Diary	Hangest	20/03/1917	31/03/1917
War Diary	Fieffs	01/04/1917	01/04/1917
War Diary	Boisbergue	02/04/1917	02/04/1917
War Diary	Lucheux	03/04/1917	05/04/1917
War Diary	Liencourt	06/04/1917	07/04/1917
War Diary	Grand Rullecourt	08/04/1917	08/04/1917
War Diary	Bavincourt	09/04/1917	12/04/1917
War Diary	Maison Rouge	13/04/1917	13/04/1917
War Diary	Brown Line	14/04/1917	18/04/1917
War Diary	Firing Line	19/04/1917	19/04/1917
War Diary	Arras	20/04/1917	23/04/1917
War Diary	Trenches	23/04/1917	24/04/1917
War Diary	Arras	25/04/1917	25/04/1917
War Diary	Duisans	25/04/1917	26/04/1917
War Diary	Noyellette	26/04/1917	27/04/1917
War Diary	Saulty	27/04/1917	01/05/1917
War Diary	Wanquetin	01/05/1917	02/05/1917
Map			
Heading	War Diary Of 1st Battalion The Border Regiment From 1st May 1917 To 31st May 1917 Volume 27		
War Diary	Wanquetin	01/05/1917	01/05/1917
War Diary	Arras	02/05/1917	03/05/1917
War Diary	Trenches	03/05/1917	04/05/1917
War Diary	Arras	05/05/1917	07/05/1917
War Diary	Duisans	07/05/1917	12/05/1917
War Diary	Arras	13/05/1917	13/05/1917
War Diary	Duisans	13/05/1917	13/05/1917
War Diary	Arras	14/05/1917	14/05/1917
War Diary	Trenches	15/05/1917	16/05/1917
War Diary	Trenches at Monchy Le Preux	17/05/1917	17/05/1917
War Diary	Trenches	18/05/1917	19/05/1917
War Diary	East Of Monchy Le Preux	19/05/1917	20/05/1917
War Diary	Monchy Le Preux	19/05/1917	20/05/1917
War Diary	Arras	21/05/1917	31/05/1917
Map			
War Diary	Monchy Le Preux	01/06/1917	01/06/1917
War Diary	Arras	02/06/1917	04/06/1917
War Diary	Candas	05/06/1917	26/06/1917
War Diary	Proven & Canal Bank	27/06/1917	30/06/1917
War Diary	Trenches	30/06/1917	30/06/1917

Heading	War Diary Of 1st Battalion The Border Regiment From 1st July 1917 To 31st July 1917 Volume 28		
War Diary	Canal Bank	01/07/1917	01/07/1917
War Diary	Nr Boesinghe	02/07/1917	05/07/1917
War Diary	Suez Camp	06/07/1917	06/07/1917
War Diary	Nr Crombeke	07/07/1917	13/07/1917
War Diary	Rivoli Farm near Woesten	13/07/1917	13/07/1917
War Diary	Hounslow Camp	14/07/1917	18/07/1917
War Diary	Proven	19/07/1917	19/07/1917
War Diary	Lancashire Camp	20/07/1917	28/07/1917
War Diary	Proven	28/07/1917	31/07/1917
War Diary	War Diary Of 1st Battalion The Border Regiment From 1-8-17 To 31-8-17 Volume No 29		
War Diary	De Wippe Cabaret	01/08/1917	01/08/1917
War Diary	Nr Elverdinghe	02/08/1917	02/08/1917
War Diary	Proven	03/08/1917	03/08/1917
War Diary	Penton Camp	04/08/1917	06/08/1917
War Diary	Proven	07/08/1917	07/08/1917
War Diary	Nr Elverdinghe	08/08/1917	08/08/1917
War Diary	Ballantine Wood	09/08/1917	11/08/1917
War Diary	Trenches Steenbeek Sector	11/08/1917	11/08/1917
War Diary	Trenches	12/08/1917	13/08/1917
War Diary	Front Line Trenches	13/08/1917	15/08/1917
War Diary	East of Steenbeek	16/08/1917	16/08/1917
War Diary	E Of Steenbeek Ne Of Langemarck	16/08/1917	18/08/1917
War Diary	De Wippe Corner	19/08/1917	19/08/1917
War Diary	Elverdinghe	20/08/1917	26/08/1917
War Diary	Trenches	27/08/1917	28/08/1917
War Diary	Charterhouse Camp	29/08/1917	29/08/1917
War Diary	Pollhill Camp Near Haandekot	30/08/1917	31/08/1917
Map			
Miscellaneous	Message Pad.		
Map			
War Diary	War Diary Of 1st Bn The Border Regiment From 1st Sept 1917 To 30th Sept 1917 Volume 30		
War Diary	Pollhill Camp	01/09/1917	11/09/1917
War Diary	Near Hanndekot	12/09/1917	14/09/1917
War Diary	Elverdinghe Michel Fm	14/09/1917	18/09/1917
War Diary	Pollhill Camp	19/09/1917	19/09/1917
War Diary	Henley Camp (Forest Area)	20/09/1917	29/09/1917
War Diary	War Diary Of 1st Battalion The Border Regiment From 1st October 1917 To 31st October 1917 Volume 31		
War Diary	Charterhouse Camp	01/10/1917	02/10/1917
War Diary	Trenches	03/10/1917	05/10/1917
War Diary	Charterhouse Camp	05/10/1917	06/10/1917
War Diary	Dublin Cam	07/10/1917	09/10/1917
War Diary	Piddington Camp	10/10/1917	15/10/1917
War Diary	Bailleulmont	16/10/1917	31/10/1917
War Diary	War Diary Of 1st Battalion The Border Regiment From 1st Nov 1917 To 30st Nov 1917 Vol 39		
War Diary	Bailleulmont	01/11/1917	16/11/1917
War Diary	Haut Allaines	17/11/1917	17/11/1917
War Diary	Fins	18/11/1917	18/11/1917
War Diary	Dessart Wood	19/11/1917	20/11/1917
War Diary	Marcoing	20/11/1917	30/11/1917

War Diary	War Diary Of 1st Battalion The Border Regiment From 1st December 1917 To 31st December 1917		
War Diary	Trenches Marcoing	01/12/1917	02/12/1917
War Diary	Trenches Marcoing Ribecourt	03/12/1917	03/12/1917
War Diary	Hindenburg Support Line At Ribecourt	04/12/1917	07/12/1917
War Diary	Grand Rullecourt	08/12/1917	16/12/1917
War Diary	Flers	17/12/1917	17/12/1917
War Diary	Azincourt	18/12/1917	18/12/1917
War Diary	Crequy	19/12/1917	30/12/1917
War Diary	Remilly Werquin	31/12/1917	31/12/1917
War Diary	War Diary Of 1st Battalion The Border Regiment From 1st Jan 1918 To 31st Jan 1918		
War Diary	La Crosse	01/01/1918	01/01/1918
War Diary	Zermezeele	02/01/1918	02/01/1918
War Diary	Herzeele	03/01/1918	03/01/1918
War Diary	Proven	04/01/1918	10/01/1918
War Diary	Caribou Camp	11/01/1918	17/01/1918
War Diary	Brandhoek	18/01/1918	25/01/1918
War Diary	Wieltje	26/01/1918	31/01/1918
Operation(al) Order(s)	87th. Infantry Brigade Order No. 70	01/01/1918	01/01/1918
Operation(al) Order(s)	87th. Infantry Brigade Order No. 72	14/01/1918	14/01/1918
Operation(al) Order(s)	87th. Infantry Brigade Order No. 73	25/01/1918	25/01/1918
War Diary	War Diary Of 1st Battalion The Border Regiment From 1st February 1918 To 28th February 1918		
War Diary	Wieltje	01/02/1918	02/02/1918
War Diary	Passchendaele	03/02/1918	05/02/1918
War Diary	Bellevue	06/02/1918	08/02/1918
War Diary	Passchendaele	09/02/1918	11/02/1918
War Diary	Watou	12/02/1918	28/02/1918
Heading	War Diary Of 1st Battalion The Border Regiment From 1st March 1918 To 31st March 1918		
War Diary	Poperinghe	01/03/1918	05/03/1918
War Diary	Wieltje	06/03/1918	08/03/1918
War Diary	Passchendale	09/03/1918	15/03/1918
War Diary	Wieltje	16/03/1918	22/03/1918
War Diary	Vlamertinghe	23/03/1918	30/03/1918
War Diary	Passchendaele	31/03/1918	31/03/1918
Heading	1st Battalion The Border Regiment April 1918		
Heading	War Diary Of 1st Bn. The Border Regiment. From 1st April 1918 To 30th April 1918		
War Diary	Passchendaele	01/04/1918	06/04/1918
War Diary	Wieltje	06/04/1918	07/04/1918
War Diary	St Jan Der Biezen	08/04/1918	09/04/1918
War Diary	Neuf Berquin	10/04/1918	12/04/1918
War Diary	Vieux Berquin	13/04/1918	13/04/1918
War Diary	St Sylvestre Cappel	14/04/1918	17/04/1918
War Diary	Courte Croix	17/04/1918	20/04/1918
War Diary	La Brearde	20/04/1918	30/04/1918
War Diary	Sec Bois	01/05/1918	06/05/1918
War Diary	Le Grand	06/05/1918	06/05/1918
War Diary	Hasard	07/05/1918	13/05/1918
War Diary	Swartenbrouch	14/05/1918	27/05/1918
War Diary	Le Grand Hasard	27/05/1918	05/06/1918
War Diary	Swartenbrouch	05/06/1918	15/06/1918
War Diary	Grand Hasard	15/06/1918	20/06/1918
War Diary	Eyk Haut Casteel	21/06/1918	21/06/1918

War Diary	Racquinghem	22/06/1918	11/07/1918
War Diary	Hazebrouck	12/07/1918	13/07/1918
War Diary	Tiflis House Strazeele	14/07/1918	14/07/1918
War Diary	Tiflis House	14/07/1918	18/07/1918
War Diary	Blaringhem	19/07/1918	21/07/1918
War Diary	St Marie Cappel	22/07/1918	31/07/1918
Miscellaneous	D.A.G. 3rd Echelon		
Heading	War Diary Serial No 40 For The March Of August 1918		
War Diary	St Marei Cappel	01/08/1918	03/08/1918
War Diary	La Kreule Area	03/08/1918	05/08/1918
War Diary	La Kreule	06/08/1918	14/08/1918
War Diary	Strazeele Sector	14/08/1918	18/08/1918
War Diary	Outter Steene	18/08/1918	20/08/1918
War Diary	'Z' Line	20/08/1918	23/08/1918
War Diary	Z Line Strazeele	23/08/1918	24/08/1918
War Diary	L'Hoffand	24/08/1918	26/08/1918
War Diary	Gerbedofn Fm	26/08/1918	27/08/1918
War Diary	'Y' Line Hoogenacker Mill Sector	27/08/1918	29/08/1918
War Diary	Hoogenacker Mill Sector	29/08/1918	30/08/1918
War Diary	Dook Fm.	31/08/1918	01/09/1918
Miscellaneous	1st Battalion The Border Regiment Appendix 1		
Miscellaneous	1st Battalion The Border Regiment.		
Miscellaneous	H.Q. 1st Inf Bde	11/10/1918	11/10/1918
Heading	War Diary For Month Of September 1918 Volume No 41		
War Diary	Dook House Near Bailleul	01/09/1918	01/09/1918
War Diary	Steenwerck	01/09/1918	01/09/1918
War Diary	Steenje	01/09/1918	09/09/1918
War Diary	Fletre	10/09/1918	11/09/1918
War Diary	Wallon Cappel	12/09/1918	16/09/1918
War Diary	Road Camp	16/09/1918	18/09/1918
War Diary	Orillia Camp	19/09/1918	23/09/1918
War Diary	Road Camp	24/09/1918	25/09/1918
War Diary	Poperinghe	26/09/1918	28/09/1918
War Diary	Menin Road	28/09/1918	28/09/1918
War Diary	Gheluvelt	29/09/1918	30/09/1918
War Diary	Kruiseeke	30/09/1918	30/09/1918
War Diary	Near Gheluwe	30/09/1918	30/09/1918
Heading	1st Bn The Border Regt War Diary For Month Ended 31st Oct 1918 Serial 42		
War Diary	Near Gheluwe	01/10/1918	01/10/1918
War Diary	Kruiseeck	02/10/1918	04/10/1918
War Diary	Westhoek	05/10/1918	06/10/1918
War Diary	Ypres.	07/10/1918	10/10/1918
War Diary	Becelaere	10/10/1918	10/10/1918
War Diary	Potterijebrug	11/10/1918	11/10/1918
War Diary	Before Covrtrai	12/10/1918	16/10/1918
War Diary	Salines	17/10/1918	22/10/1918
War Diary	Steenbrugge	23/10/1918	26/10/1918
War Diary	Mouscron	27/10/1918	27/10/1918
War Diary	St. Andre.	28/10/1918	31/10/1918
Miscellaneous	1st Battn. The Border Regt	19/10/1918	19/10/1918
War Diary			
War Diary	St Andre	01/11/1918	06/11/1918
War Diary	Tourcoing	07/11/1918	08/11/1918

War Diary	Petit Tourcoing	08/11/1918	08/11/1918
War Diary	Dries	09/11/1918	09/11/1918
War Diary	Near Celles	10/11/1918	13/11/1918
War Diary	St Sauveur	14/11/1918	14/11/1918
War Diary	Ogy	15/11/1918	17/11/1918
War Diary	Isieres	18/11/1918	20/11/1918
War Diary	Horrues	21/11/1918	21/11/1918
War Diary	Hautittre	22/11/1918	23/11/1918
War Diary	Sclage	24/11/1918	24/11/1918
War Diary	Walhain St Paul	25/11/1918	25/11/1918
War Diary	Grand Leez	26/11/1918	27/11/1918
War Diary	Seron	28/11/1918	28/11/1918
War Diary	Stree	29/11/1918	29/11/1918
War Diary	Comblain-Au-Pont	30/11/1918	30/11/1918
Heading	1st Bn The Border Regiment War Diary For Month Ending December 1918 Volume 44		
War Diary	Basse Desnie	01/12/1918	01/12/1918
War Diary	Mista Area	02/12/1918	04/12/1918
War Diary	Elsenborn	05/12/1918	05/12/1918
War Diary	Mountjoie	06/12/1918	06/12/1918
War Diary	Boich	07/12/1918	07/12/1918
War Diary	Gladbach	08/12/1918	08/12/1918
War Diary	Bruggen	09/12/1918	09/12/1918
War Diary	Kriel	10/12/1918	13/12/1918
War Diary	Berg Gladbach	13/12/1918	15/12/1918
War Diary	Hilgen	16/12/1918	31/12/1918
Heading	Southern (Late 29th) Divn. 87th Infy Bde 1st Bn Border Regt Jan-Apr 1919		
War Diary	Hilgen	01/01/1919	31/01/1919
Miscellaneous	Volume 45 War Diary Appendix A		
War Diary	Hilgen	03/01/1919	27/03/1919
War Diary	Mulheim	28/03/1919	30/03/1919
War Diary	Dunkirk	31/03/1919	03/04/1919

WO/95/2305 /1

1 Battalion Border Regiment

Apr 16 - Apr 19

29TH DIVISION
87TH INFY BDE

1ST BN BORDER REGT

APR 1916-~~DEC 1918~~ APR 1919

To UK

29th Division.

87th Infantry Brigade.

1st BATTALION

THE BORDER REGIMENT

A P R I L 1 9 1 6

29

87/29

Army Form C. 2118.

Instructions regarding War Diaries and Intelligence Summaries are contained in F. S. Regs., Part II. and the Staff Manual respectively. Title pages will be prepared in manuscript.

1 Border Regt

Vol I BEF

[illegible] Battn The BORDER REGIMENT

Place	Date	Hour	[illegible]ion	Remarks and references to Appendices
AMPLIER	2nd April	1345	Battalion paraded and [illegible]	ER
BEAUVAL	-	1505	Marched past Gen Sir A.H[illegible] [illegible]xpressed his pleasure at the march	
			discipline of the men t[illegible] [illegible]eyed to all ranks.	ER
ACHEUX		1720	arrived and billetted in [illegible]	ER.
	3rd	1710	Battn. left for ENGLEBEL[illegible] [illegible]RE Regt in Firing line	ER
		1925	arrived ENGLEBELMER	
		2005	Platoons leave at 5" interva[illegible] [illegible]nsport + Qr Mr remained at ENGLEBELMER	ER
FIRING LINE	4th	0100	Relief of 10th E YORKSHIRE [illegible]	ER
			Enemy Trench mortars act[illegible] [illegible]e done by them, and not	ER.
			definitely located by [illegible]	
		1145	Telephonic communica[illegible]	
		1730	— do –	ER
			Work of deepening the [illegible] [illegible]cedes during day	ER
	5th		Enemy Trench Mortors [illegible] during the afternoon	ER
			Fire trench deepened [illegible] partially and opening up of	
			"C" "D" + "E" streets, ESSE[illegible] [illegible]ed	ER
			[illegible] Roissell 2 Lieut [illegible] Adj. 1st Border Regt	

13.K
2 sheets

Army Form C. 2118.

87/29

Instructions regarding War Diaries and Intelligence Summaries are contained in F. S. Regs., Part II. and the Staff Manual respectively. Title pages will be prepared in manuscript.

or

~~INTELLIGENCE~~ SUMMARY.

(Erase heading not required.) 1st Battn The BORDER REGIMENT

Place	Date	Hour	Summary of Events and Information	Remarks and references to Appendices
AMPLIER	2nd April	1345	Battalion paraded and marched from AMPLIER	E.R.
BEAUVAL	-	1505	Marched past Gen Sir A. HUNTER WESTON (G.O.C. 8th Corps) who expressed his pleasure at the march discipline of the men to Brigadier Comdg Bde, to be conveyed to all ranks.	E.R.
ACHEUX		1720	arrived and billetted in ACHEUX wood	E.R.
	3rd	1710	Battn. left for ENGLEBELMER prior to relieving 10th E. YORKSHIRE Regt in Firing line	E.R.
		1925	arrived ENGLEBELMER	E.R.
		2005	Platoons leave at 5" interval for the front line. "D" Coy, Transport + Qr Mr remain at ENGLEBELMER	
FIRING LINE	4th	0100	Relief of 10th E. YORKSHIRE Regt completed.	E.R.
			Enemy Trench mortars active during the day. no damage done by them, and not definitely located by us.	E.R.
		1145	Telephone communication with Bde interrupted	E.R.
		1730	— do — — do — restored	
			work of deepening the communication trenches proceeds during day	E.R.
	5th		Enemy Trench Mortars and artillery show activity during the afternoon	E.R.
			Fire trench deepened in places, parapet rebuilt partially and opening up of "C" "D" + "E" streets, ESSEX Street, and ROONEYS sap commenced	E.R.

G. W. Rowsell 2nd Lieut
a/Adjt. 1st Border Regt

1577 Wt. W10791/1773 500,000 1/15 D. D. & L. A.D.S.S./Forms/C. 2118.

Army Form C. 2118.

Instructions regarding War Diaries and Intelligence Summaries are contained in F. S. Regs., Part II. and the Staff Manual respectively. Title pages will be prepared in manuscript.

WAR DIARY
or
~~INTELLIGENCE SUMMARY.~~
(Erase heading not required.) 1st Battn. The BORDER REGIMENT

Place	Date	Hour	Summary of Events and Information	Remarks and references to Appendices
FIRING LINE	6th April		Reopening of BROADWAY Communication Trench between POMPADOUR and ESSEX Street completed	GR
			a Patrol of 5 other Ranks under 2Lt E.A. CROSSLAND 13th DURHAM LIGHT INFTY (attached) which left our trenches at 2130 on the 5th did not return till dawn on the 6th. 2Lt E.A. CROSSLAND and one other rank failed to return.	GR
			Enemy artillery show activity. 'D' Coy ordered to join Battalion tonight	GR
		2050	a Party of the enemy attempted to Bomb ROONEYS Sap.	GR
		2055	Heavy Bombardment opened by enemy on communication trenches in our sector	GR
			Enemy machine Guns also show activity	GR
		2115	Capt MEIKLEJOHN reports enemy's infantry not attacking our front	GR
		2117	our artillery retaliate, machine Gun fire increases both enemy and our own	GR
		2147	All Companys report no infantry attack	GR
		2153	Communication with Brigade by telephone interrupted	GR
		2159	Bombardment of our communication trenches decreases slightly	GR
		2204	'A' Coy report although Bombardment is heavy - no casualties so far	GR
		2205	Enemy machine Gun fire increases	GR
		2228	Bombardment decreases appreciably	GR
		2230	—do— ceases altogether	GR

G.W.N. Rowsell 2Lt
a/adj 1st Border Regt

1577 Wt. W10791/1773 500,000 1/15 D. D. & L. A.D.S.S./Forms/C. 2118.

Instructions regarding War Diaries and Intelligence Summaries are contained in F. S. Regs., Part II. and the Staff Manual respectively. Title pages will be prepared in manuscript.

Army Form C. 2118.

WAR DIARY

or

~~INTELLIGENCE SUMMARY.~~

(*Erase heading not required.*) 1st Battn. The BORDER REGIMENT

Place	Date	Hour	Summary of Events and Information	Remarks and references to Appendices
FIRING LINE	7th	0015	Considerable damage done to our Parapet at Q 16-7, Q 16-8, Q 16-9, Q 16-2, + Q 16-3	SR
			and to our wire by last nights bombardment, and work of repairing same commenced	SR
			Evacuation of casualties very difficult owing to narrowness of trenches	SR
			Traverses commenced in DONEGAL PASS, BLOMFIELD SANDYROW 'C, D,' & E Streets and 1st AVENUE ~~commenced~~ SR	SR
		1015	Telephone communication with Brigade re-established	SR
			Water supply cut off, pipes damaged by bombardment	SR
	8th	2115	~~It~~ Enemy transport heard on the BEAUMONT-BEAUCOURT Road. Work of repairing damage of Bombardment continues	SR
			Casualties officers:- 2nd Lt E.A. CROSSLAND 13th D.L.I. missing 5/4/16. 2nd Lt. J.B. SINCLAIR 10th BORDER Regt wounded 6/4/16 To Hospital 7/4/16. Other Ranks:- Killed 11, died of wounds 2, Wounded 14,	SR
			suffering shell shock 3, wounded and Prisoner 1, sick to Hospital 35, rejoined from Hospital 38.	SR
			2nd Lt F.T. WILKINS 15th N. Fus. and 12 other Ranks proceeded to VALHEUREUX for Trench Mortar Course	SR
			2nd Lt W. de H. ROBINSON 3rd Border assumed duties as Town Commandant MAILLY MAILLET 3/4/16	SR
	9th		Re opening of original trench sector C Street to B Street continues. Parapet improved in places. ESSEX Street FETHARD Street + UXBRIDGE Road being prepared as fire trenches	SR
		0600	Capt J.W. STREATER + 2nd Lt CARGILL left to examine our wire in vicinity of ROONEYS SAP. discovered an enemys' sniper, and in attempting to capture him Capt STREATER was wounded, the sniper escaped in the mist, but believed to be wounded.	SR

[illegible] Rowsell Lt
a/Adjt 1st Border Regt

1577 Wt. W10791/1773 500,000 1/15 D. D. & L. A.D.S.S./Forms/C. 2118.

Instructions regarding War Diaries and Intelligence Summaries are contained in F. S. Regs., Part II. and the Staff Manual respectively. Title pages will be prepared in manuscript.

WAR DIARY
or
~~INTELLIGENCE SUMMARY.~~
(*Erase heading not required.*)

Army Form C. 2118.

1st Battn The BORDER REGIMENT

Place	Date	Hour	Summary of Events and Information	Remarks and references to Appendices
FIRING LINE	10th		Listening Patrols report enemy working during night 9th–10th. Work on CLONMEL Street begins.	ER
			Hostile anti aircraft gun believed to be located in front of Q10·5. about 1000x yards distant	ER
			Fire step & Parapet finished in ESSEX Street and FETHARD Road	ER
		2045	Enemy transport heard on BEAUMONT–BEAUCOURT Road	ER
		2215	our Patrols report "all clear" in "No mans Land"	ER
	11th		Bombing traverse completed in 'E' Street, work connecting 'X' and 'Y' Street progressing	ER
			'D' + 'E' Street finished. all work hampered by Rain.	ER
	12th	0135	Enemys artillery fired about 12 Rounds H.E. in vicinity of CLONMEL Street	ER
			Rain continued at intervals throughout the day.	ER
			our aircraft active, also enemys anti aircraft Guns, during day	ER
			Preparations made to hand over ~~relief~~ trenches tonight to 1st R Dublin Fus.	ER
		2015	Relief commences 2015. Lewis Guns "all clear"	ER
		2210	"B" Coy report 'all Clear"	ER
		2245 ~~2045~~ ER	"A" Coy report 'all Clear"	ER
	13th	0015	"C" Coy report 'all Clear"	ER
		0330	"D" Coy failed to Report, no trace of Coy. Report to Brigade relief complete. Coys marched independently to billets in ACHEUX	ER

G. W. N. Rowsell 2Lt
A/adj, 1st Border Regt

1577 Wt. W10791/1773 500,000 1/15 D. D. & L. A.D.S.S./Forms/C. 2118.

Instructions regarding War Diaries and Intelligence Summaries are contained in F. S. Regs., Part II. and the Staff Manual respectively. Title pages will be prepared in manuscript.

WAR DIARY
or
~~INTELLIGENCE SUMMARY.~~
(Erase heading not required.)

Army Form C. 2118.

1st Battn. The BORDER REGIMENT

Place	Date	Hour	Summary of Events and Information	Remarks and references to Appendices
			Casualties week ending 15th April:- Officers. 2Lt (Temp Capt) J. W. STREATER wounded 9-4-16	GR
			Lt J. B. SINCLAIR from Hospital 13/4/16. Other Ranks to Hospital 33. Rejoined from Hospital 20. Wounded (Self Inflicted) 1 Other Rank	GR
			Lt Col. A. E. St V. POLLARD to Senior Officers Course (FLEXICOURT) 10-4-16	GR
			87 Other Ranks joined from EGYPT 10-4-16	GR
			67 — — do — — do — ENGLAND 11-4-16	GR
ACHEUX	15th		2 Officers + 20 O. Ranks commence course of Bombing. 3 Officers + 28 O. Ranks commence Course Lewis Gun	GR
		0900	Battalion attend Lecture on Gas + use of Gas Helmets. All Present on Parade entered Room filled with Gas.	GR
	16th	1030	Regimental Tour for Officers not on duty.	GR
	18th	1000	50 all Ranks attend demonstration in Flammenwerfer and effects of Lachrymatory Shells	GR
	20th		Indifferent shots + Snipers practiced in Musketry	GR
	23rd		New Course of Bombing + Lewis M. Gun Commence	GR
			Casualties week ending 23rd sick to Hospital Officers Nil. O. Ranks 23. From Hospital 3.	GR
			Capt J. R. MEIKLEJOHN proceeded to take Command of 1st Essex Regt 16th	GR
			Lt Col. A. E. St V. POLLARD rejoined from 4th Army Infantry School of Instruction	GR

[illegible] Lieut
a/Adj. 1st Border Regt

1577 Wt. W10791/1773 500,000 1/15 D. D. & L. A.D.S.S./Forms/C. 2118.

WAR DIARY
or
~~INTELLIGENCE SUMMARY.~~
(Erase heading not required.)

Army Form C. 2118.

Instructions regarding War Diaries and Intelligence Summaries are contained in F. S. Regs., Part II. and the Staff Manual respectively. Title pages will be prepared in manuscript.

1st Battn. The BORDER REGIMENT

Place	Date	Hour	Summary of Events and Information	Remarks and references to Appendices
ACHEUX			2nd Lieut ~~D~~ BREMNER + 48. O.Ranks detached for mining duties 21/4/16	GP
			Lieut (T.Capt) W. CLAGUE Struck off strength from 13th-4-16	GP
			~~T~~ Captain H. MILLARD 8th NORTHANTS Regt. Struck off Strength 21-4-16	GP
			1 O.Rank to ROUEN as Instructor 15th-4-16. 10 O.Ranks detached for Traffic Control duties	GP
			armourer S.Sgt. Watson A.O. Corps attached 20-4-16.	GP
			2nd Lieut H. PALMER + 2 O.Ranks to 4th Army Infantry School of Instruction	GP
			2nd Lt G.W.N. ROWSELL appointed Temp. Lieutenant whilst performing duties of adjutant 22nd	GP
	24th to 29th		Courses of Instruction continue:- Bombing & Lewis Gun.	GP
			36 O.Ranks received instruction in Wiring & making Obstacles	
	25th		all officers + 2 effective N.C.Os attend Lecture on Bayonet Fighting	GP
			Casualties week ending 29th:- ~~Killed 2. Died of Wounds 2. wounded 15.~~ GP 2nd Lt. G BADGER-CLARKE	GP
			whilst injured by Bomb 24th To Hospital 24th. sick to Hosp. O.Ranks 34 from Hosp. 2	
			2nd Lt (T.Capt) J. W. STREATER Struck off Strength 19-4-16. 6 O.Ranks detached for mining 26th-4-16	GP
			2nd Lt D. MACLEOD + 3 O.Ranks to CAMIERS for Lewis Gun Course	GP
			2nd Lt H BUNTING + 4 O.Ranks attend course of Instruction in Bayonet Fighting at 29th Divl School	GP
			1 O.Rank to Hosp Self Inflicted wound 29th	GP

G.W.N. Rowsell Lieut
A/adjutant 1st Border Regt

1577 Wt. W10791/1773 500,000 1/15 D. D. & L. A.D.S.S./Forms/C. 2118.

Army Form C. 2118.

Instructions regarding War Diaries and Intelligence Summaries are contained in F. S. Regs., Part II. and the Staff Manual respectively. Title pages will be prepared in manuscript.

WAR DIARY
or
~~INTELLIGENCE SUMMARY~~.

(Erase heading not required.) 1st Battn. The BORDER REGIMENT

Place	Date	Hour	Summary of Events and Information	Remarks and references to Appendices
ACHEUX	28th	1830	Battn Parade to Relieve 2nd Royal Fus in Fron Line	GR
		2225	Relief Complete	GR
	29th	2330	Bombardment by our artillery. Party of S.W. Borderers leave our trenches to Raid enemys line	GR
	31	2340	Enemy retaliate & Bombard our trenches heavily, all telephonic communication interrupted.	GR
	30th	0035	our Bombardment ceases.	GR
		0045	all quiet for the remainder of the day.	GR
			Great difficulty experienced in removing casualties from Firing Line	GR
			Casualties. 2 Killed 2 Died of Wounds 16 Wounded. 2 Self Inflicted wounds to Hospital. 1 shell shock to Hosp (other Ranks)	GR
			sick to Hospital 2 OR.	

G.W.N. Powsell Lieut
Adjt 1st Border Regt.

29th Division.

87th Infantry Brigade.

11

1st BATTALION

THE BORDER REGIMENT

M A Y 1916

Army Form C. 2118.

1 May 1916 21

Instructions regarding War Diaries and Intelligence Summaries are contained in F. S. Regs., Part II. and the Staff Manual respectively. Title Pages will be prepared in manuscript.

WAR DIARY
or
INTELLIGENCE ~~SUMMARY~~

(Erase heading not required.) 1st Bn THE BORDER REGIMENT.

Vol 2

Place	Date	Hour	Summary of Events and Information	Remarks and references to Appendices
Front line	1st to 3rd		Quiet Period and nothing to record	E.R.
	3rd		Battalion relieved by 1st ESSEX Regt, relief commenced at 2030.	E.R.
	4th	0100	Relief completed and Battn. proceed to Billets at ENGLEBELMER less 2 officers + 100 other Ranks which proceeded to occupy Forts PROWSE + MOULIN.	E.R.
ENGLEBELMER	5th & 6		Battalion engaged as working Parties in various Parts of the line	E.R.
	6th		2nd Lt. A. CAMBBELL 10th BORDER rejoined from Hospital	E.R.
			Extract from London Gazette:- To be Lieutenants 2nd Lt. W. F. H. CHAMBERS dated 14-9-15 — J. R. FARRELL — 1-10-15 — J. W. STREATER — 1-10-15	E.R.
			Casualties week ending 6th May:- officers - Nil other Ranks - Killed 1. Wounded 6. accidentally wounded 1. wounded (at duty) 5 wounded (Self Inflicted) 2. sick to Hosp. 11. Rejoined from Hosp. 9.	E.R.
ENGLEBELMER	7th to 12th		Battalion engaged as working Parties	E.R.
	13th		Battalion proceed to Relieve 1st S.W.Bs in the front line commencing at 2000, with the exception of the Garrisons at the Forts, which remained there	E.R.
—	9th		Captains J. G. HEYDER, T. H. BEVES } Joined from Base	E.R.

Gerald Cowsell Lieut
a/adjutant 1st Border Regt

H.K.

2449 Wt. W14957/M90 750,000 1/16 J.B.C. & A. Forms/C.2118/12.

II

Army Form C. 2118.

WAR DIARY ~~or INTELLIGENCE SUMMARY~~ May 1916

(Erase heading not required.)

1st Battalion The Border Regt

Instructions regarding War Diaries and Intelligence Summaries are contained in F. S. Regs., Part II. and the Staff Manual respectively. Title Pages will be prepared in manuscript.

Place	Date	Hour	Summary of Events and Information	Remarks and references to Appendices
ENGLEBELMER	11th		2nd Lt D. BREMNER rejoined from 252nd Tunnelling Coy R.E.	WP
	11th		Capt T H BEVES to Hospital. 2nd Lt A.W.H. BARNES – F.H. TALBOT – J.Y. BAXENDINE } Segregated for 10 days on account of Capt BEVES admitted to Hospital with German measles	WP
	8th		2nd Lt H BUNTING Rejoined from course of instruction in Bayonet fighting	WP
			— W.P. RETTIE proceeded for — do — do	WP
			Casualties week ending 13th – Wounded 2. Sick to Hospital 35. From Hosp 18	WP
			Honours and Awards	
			The undermentioned officer, N.C.Os & men are mentioned in Sir IAN HAMILTONS despatch dated 11-12-15 published in a Supplement to the LONDON Gazette dated 28-1-16 –	
			Capt. H.E. FESTING.	
			No. 6088 A/C.S.M. G.G. KEMPTON; 9318 L/C W FOX; 4173 Pte R FOWLER; 10083 Pte E GISBY, 10026 Pte G.H. RICHARDS; 8629 Pte. H. SELVEY; 10758 Pte. H SMITH; 9596 Pte H TURNER.	WP
			H M The KING has been graciously pleased to approve of the undermentioned award for distinguished Service in the Field.	
			The Distinguished Service Order: – Capt H.E. FESTING.	WP
FRONTLINE	14th	0010	Relief of 2nd S.W.B. completed. Quiet day & nothing to record	WP
	15th	2045	Nothing happened until 2045 when sounds of aircraft were heard.	WP

[signature] Lieut Adjt, 1st Border Regt

2449 Wt. W14957/M90 750,000 1/16 J.B.C. & A. Forms/C.2118/12.

Instructions regarding War Diaries and Intelligence Summaries are contained in F. S. Regs., Part II. and the Staff Manual respectively. Title Pages will be prepared in manuscript.

WAR DIARY MAY 1916
or
INTELLIGENCE SUMMARY
(Erase heading not required.)

Army Form C. 2118.

III

1st Battn THE BORDER REGIMENT

Place	Date	Hour	Summary of Events and Information	Remarks and references to Appendices
FRONT LINE	16th	0025	Enemy commence bombardment of our trenches	E.P.
		0027	A Coy report enemy shells appear to be falling behind the front line	E.P.
			Communication trenches not being shelled	E.P.
		0037	outburst of Machine Gun fire, apparently our own	E.P.
		0043	communication by telephone with B Coy interrupted	E.P.
		0055	—— do —— A – do	
		0058	another outburst of M. G. Fire.	E.P.
		0107	shelling now confined to the left and clear of Sector occupied by Battn	E.P.
		0115	message from B Coy report no shelling of front occupied by that Coy	E.P.
		0118	messenger from B Coy report our own artillerys' shells falling on our front line	E.P.
		0120	all quiet in front of our Sector	E.P.
		0137	A + B Coys report all quiet + telephone communication connected again	E.P.
		0220	shelling decreases	E.P.
		0230	all quiet	E.P.
	15th		2nd Lieut W. K. SANDERSON joined for duty	E.P.
	17th		—"— F S LAYARD — do — 2 Lieut PALMER sick from FLEXICOURT	E.P.
	18th		—"— D. CARGILL — do — Battn. Relieved from front line and marched to Billets in LOUVENCOURT	E.P.
LOUVENCOURT	19th		Lieut J. B. SINCLAIR and 2nd Lieut E.A. BARRY to Hospital (sick)	E.P.
	20th		Lt. Col A.E. St V POLLARD to England	E.P.

2449 Wt. W14957/M90 750,000 1/16 J.B.C. & A. Forms/C.2118/12.

G.W.N. Rowsell Lieut
Adjt 1st Border Regt

Army Form C. 2118.

Instructions regarding War Diaries and Intelligence Summaries are contained in F. S. Regs., Part II. and the Staff Manual respectively. Title Pages will be prepared in manuscript.

WAR DIARY
or
~~INTELLIGENCE SUMMARY~~

(*Erase heading not required.*) 1st Bn THE BORDER REGIMENT

Place	Date	Hour	Summary of Events and Information	Remarks and references to Appendices
LOUVENCOURT	20/5/16		Casualties week ending 20th - officers nil -	
			O Ranks wounded 2. (1 died of wounds). sick to Hospital 47. Rejoined from Hospital 18.	GB
			Major A J. ELLIS 1st Border Regt assumed command of battalion	TGH
	22		30 other ranks joined from BASE	TGH
	21st		Capt T.H. BEVES rejoined from Hospl	TGH
	22nd		MAJOR MEIKLEJOHN rejoined from Comm'g 1st ESSEX Regt.	TGH
	26th		116 Other ranks joined from Base	TGH
	27th		2 Lieut W.P. RETTIE rejoined from 29th Divisional Course	TGH
			Casualties week ending 27th. Killed NIL Wounded NIL Sick to Hosp 26 Rejoined from Hosp 16	TGH
	28th		Battalion moved to Brigade Reserve at ENGLEBELMER in relief of 4th WORCESTERSHIRE Regt.	TGH
ENGLEBELMER	28th		2 LIEUT M. DUFF } 2 LIEUT H.L. CHOLMELEY } 3rd BORDER Regt joined Battalion	TGH
			Capt J G HEYDER took over duties acting adjt.	TGH
			Capt J. W. EWBANK to 4th Army School FLEXICOURT	TGH
	29th		2nd LIEUT P. NEW 3rd Border Regt joined Battn	TGH
	30th		2 LIEUT D. CARGILL and 2nd Lieut F.S. LAYARD to 29th Div. School ACHEUX	TGH
	31st		Other ranks to Hospital 17 rejoined from hospital 4	TGH

T G Heyder Capt adjt
1/ Border Regt

2449 Wt. W14957/M90 750,000 1/16 J.B.C. & A. Forms/C.2118/12.

29th Division.

87th Infantry Brigade.

1st BATTALION

THE BORDER REGIMENT

JUNE 1916

Army Form C. 2118

29

1 Border Regt

Vol 3

WAR DIARY
or
INTELLIGENCE SUMMARY
(Erase heading not required.)

Instructions regarding War Diaries and Intelligence Summaries are contained in F. S. Regs., Part II. and the Staff Manual respectively. Title Pages will be prepared in manuscript.

Place	Date	Hour	Summary of Events and Information	Remarks and references to Appendices
[illegible]	1/6/16		2 Lt DCR. STUART joins battalion	[illegible]
			2 Lt E.A. BARRY on attached list. Struck off strength of battalion 29-5-16	[illegible]
			Casualties for week ending 3/6/16.	[illegible]
			Killed – nil; Wounded – 1; Missing – nil; Sick – 5; Rejoined fr. Hosp – 6 } other ranks	[illegible]
[illegible]	/6/16		15 men attached to Divisional Reserve Coy.	[illegible]
FRONT [illegible]	[illegible]/6/16		Relieved SWB in left subsector of right sector relief complete by 19.10.	[illegible]
	[illegible]/6/16		2 Lt [illegible] CAMPBELL to course at Division school.	[illegible]
			Casualties for week ending 10/6/16	
			Killed nil; Wounded 2 (accidentally at Demonstration of T. mortars); Missing nil; Sick 23; Rejoined Hosp 15 } other ranks	[illegible]
	12.6.16		2 Lt SAMPSON H.E. [illegible] 2 Lt CHEVERTON struck off strength of battalion 12.6.16	[illegible]
	13.6.16		Lt SINCLAIR J.B. rejoins fr. Hosp	
	[illegible]		2 Lt CAMPBELL rejoins from Div school [illegible]	
	15.6.16		Battalion relieved by 1 NFLD Regt and went into billets at LOUVENCOURT	[illegible]

[illegible] Capt & Adjt 1 Border Regt

15K

1875 Wt. W593/826 1,000,000 4/15 J.B.C. & A. A.D.S.S./Forms/C. 2118.

Army Form C. 2118

WAR DIARY
or
~~INTELLIGENCE~~ SUMMARY
(Erase heading not required.)

[Re]garding War Diaries and Intelligence [Sum]maries are contained in F. S. Regs., Part II. and the Staff Manual respectively. Title Pages will be prepared in manuscript.

Place	Date	Hour	Summary of Events and Information	Remarks and references to Appendices
FRONT LINE	15-6-16		During period 7-6-16 to 15-6-16 little activity shown by enemy, generally quiet. Heavy rain continuous.	
			Casualties week ending 17th	
			Other Ranks: Killed nil, Wounded 6, Missing nil, Sick 11, Rejoined fr Hosp 12 — To 87th MG Coy 1.	
LOUVENCOURT	16-6-16		40 other ranks joined from base.	
	19th		Capt J R FARRELL to Rouen as instructor 29th Div. base.	
	20th		2Lt DUFF - 2 Lt WHITEHOUSE - 2 LT MACLEOD to course at 29th Div. School.	
	22nd		2Lt H E WATKINS 13th R. Warwickshire Regt (attd 1/Border Regt) struck off strength. Sentence of G.C.M.	
	24th		2 Lt F H PRESCOTT 3rd Border joined from Base.	
			Casualties wk ending 25th Killed - nil. Wounded - nil. Missing nil. Sick to hosp 11 - Rejoined from hosp. - 10	
	23rd		21 OR joined from base.	
	23rd		Battn marched to camp ACHEUX	
ACHEUX	26th		2 Lt DUFF rejoined from Div. School ACHEUX.	
	25th		2Lt BADGER CLARK rejoined from sick leave.	
	29th		2 Lt K C HAMILTON (10th Border) joined from Base	
			Casualties during wk ending 30th Killed — 0, Wounded — 2, Missing — 0, Sick — 6, Rejoined fr Hosp — 2	

[signature] Capt.
Adjt 1/Border Regt

1875 Wt. W593/826 1,000,000 4/15 J.B.C. & A. A.D.S.S./Forms/C. 2118.

Army Form C. 2118.

Instructions regarding War Diaries and Intelligence Summaries are contained in F. S. Regs., Part II. and the Staff Manual respectively. Title Pages will be prepared in manuscript.

WAR DIARY
or
INTELLIGENCE SUMMARY
(Erase heading not required.)

Place	Date	Hour	Summary of Events and Information	Remarks and references to Appendices
ACHEUX.	27th		A raiding party (D coy) 50 men with Lieut BREMNER left ACHEUX in the afternoon proceeding to front line.	
			The raiding party moved off from KNIGHTSBRIDGE BKS at 10.45 pm & arrived at the top of SHAFTESBURY AV (point of exit) at 11.30 pm. with the exception of the two Bangalore torpedoes which were sent in charge of a guide provided by R.I.F. to move over the top of the trenches & form up at the point of exit.	
			This arrangement was made on account of the extreme difficulty of getting them along the trenches.	
			Apparently the guide lost his way & the torpedoes did not turn up till 12.5 am & it was then found that the fuse holes were choked with mud.	
			The hour fixed for the party to issue from our trenches was 11.50 pm but owing to the non arrival of the torpedoes this was delayed till 12 m.n.	
			At this hour the party started out & LT BREMNER succeeded in finding the cut in the wire at Q 17 A 8.85.	
			All the wire was cut with the exception of the last 8' which consisted of a thick mass of iron knife rest trestles.	
			Just as he got to the wire the NFLD Regts' raid on the German salient started & at once machine gun & rifle fire was opened by the enemy & a large number of very lights were sent up. LT BREMNER was trying all this time to cut through the wire with clippers but progress was too slow & at 1.5 am he gave the order for the party to return to our trenches, reaching our line at 1.20 am.	
			No casualties.	

[illegible signature]

1875 Wt. W593/826 1,000,000 4/15 J.B.C. & A. A.D.S.S./Forms/C. 2118.

29th Division.

87th Infantry Brigade.

1st BATTALION

THE BORDER REGIMENT

JULY 1916

87/29.

War Diary

of

1st Bn. Border Regiment

for

July 1916

Army Form C. 2118.

Instructions regarding War Diaries and Intelligence Summaries are contained in F. S. Regs., Part II. and the Staff Manual respectively. Title Pages will be prepared in manuscript.

WAR DIARY
or
~~INTELLIGENCE SUMMARY~~
(Erase heading not required.)

82/29 Vol 4 1

1st BTN. THE BORDER REGT.

Place	Date	Hour	Summary of Events and Information	Remarks and references to Appendices
FRONT LINE	1/7/16	7.30 a.m.	The Btn (less 10%) advanced just SOUTH of BEAUMONT HAMEL. their objective being BEAUCOURT REDOUBT. The 2nd S.W.Bs., whose objective was the first two GERMAN LINES, were wiped out by MACHINE GUN fire in our own wire. The 1st Btn. The BORDER REGT., then went over the top from our support line, and over our first line, the bridges over our front trench having been ranged by the GERMAN MACHINE GUNNERS the day previously, we met with heavy losses, while crossing these bridges + passing through the lanes cut in our wire. The men were absolutely magnificent, and formed up as ordered outside our wire, made a right incline, and advanced into "NO MAN'S LAND" at a slow walk, also as ordered. The advance was continued until only little groups of half a dozen men were left here and there, and these, finding that no reinforcements were in sight, took cover in shell holes or wherever they could.	
		8 a.m.	The advance was brought entirely to a standstill.	
		8.15 a.m.	Enemy re-opened his bombardment on our trenches, for which our guns retaliated.	
		9.15 a.m.	LIEUT-COL ELLIS having been wounded and brought in by No. 8409 PTE. NEWCOMBE, MAJOR MEIKLEJOHN (who had been in command of the 10%s) assumed command of the BTN., and collected all the men he could in the support line, as ordered by the BRIGADIER.	
		10.30 a.m.	The 10% ordered back to reserve line, where they stayed until next morning. Advance definitely given up on this sector. The BTN. strength of those who took part in advance was OFFICERS 23. OTHER RANKS. 809.	

CASUALTIES. KILLED. CAPT. F.R JESSUP.
" T.H. BEVES.

MISSING BLVD. KILLED 2LIEUT. W.K. SANDERSON.
" F.T. BAXENDINE.
" A.W. FRASER
" L. JACKSON.

WOUNDED + MISSING. " H.L. CHOLMELEY.
" W.P. RETTIE.

WOUNDED LT. COL. A.J. ELLIS.
CAPT. J.G. HEYDER.
LIEUT. BL.A. KENNETT.
" J.B. SINCLAIR.
2LIEUT. G.W.N. ROWSELL.
" F.H. TALBOT.
" A.W.H. BARNES.
" D. BREMNER.
LIEUT. H.F. SAMPSON.
2LIEUT. F.T. WILKINS.
" D.C.R. STUART.
" D. CARGILL.

OTHER RANKS.
KILLED 64
WOUNDED 411
MISSING. 144.

16 K

Army Form C. 2118.

2

Instructions regarding War Diaries and Intelligence Summaries are contained in F. S. Regs., Part II. and the Staff Manual respectively. Title Pages will be prepared in manuscript.

WAR DIARY
or
~~INTELLIGENCE SUMMARY~~

(Erase heading not required.) 1st BTN. THE BORDER REGT.

Place	Date	Hour	Summary of Events and Information	Remarks and references to Appendices
FRONT LINE	2/7/16	10 a.m.	The remnants of the BTN. relieved the 9TH R.I.R. just N. of R. ANCRE, and immediately set to work to repair the trenches, which had suffered severely by the bombardment.	[illegible]
		2.30 a.m.	At this time we sent out parties to bring in wounded and bury dead of the R.I.Rs. who were lying in front of our line. These continued intermittently all day and during the night, the enemy continually sniping our rescue parties. 2nd LIEUT. R.G. COLLIS promoted LIEUT. + ACTING ADJUTANT.	[illegible]
	5/7/16		CAPT. J.N. EWBANK rejoined from course of instruction at 4th ARMY SCHOOL.	[illegible]
			2 LIEUT. C.N. WHITEHOUSE and 2 LIEUT D. McLEOD rejoined from course at 29th DIV. SCHOOL.	[illegible]
	7.7.16.		2 LIEUT. CAMPBELL to course at 4th ARMY SCHOOL.	[illegible]
	8.7.16	6 p.m.	Relieved and back to REST CAMP at ACHEUX.	
ACHEUX.	9.7.16		Casualties week ending ~~2.7.16~~ 9.7.16:- OFFICERS WOUNDED. 2nd LIEUT. BROSER-CLARK. SICK " M. DUFF to F.A. OTHER RANKS. KILLED. 1. WOUNDED. 6. SICK TO HOSPITAL. 5.	[illegible]
	14.7.16		Rejoined from HOSPITAL. 4. FROM BASE. 32. (6.7.16).	[illegible]
	15.7.16		From BASE 74 other ranks.	
			Casualties week ending 15.7.16:- OFFICERS. SICK to HOSPITAL. 2 LIEUT. R.C. HAMILTON 11.7.16. OTHER RANKS SICK to HOSPITAL 7. Rejoined from HOSPITAL 4.	[illegible]

2449 Wt. W14957/M90 750,000 1/16 J.B.C. & A. Forms/C.2118/12.

Instructions regarding War Diaries and Intelligence Summaries are contained in F. S. Regs., Part II. and the Staff Manual respectively. Title Pages will be prepared in manuscript.

WAR DIARY
or
~~INTELLIGENCE~~ SUMMARY
(Erase heading not required.)

Army Form C. 2118.

3

1st BTN THE BORDER REGT.

Place	Date	Hour	Summary of Events and Information	Remarks and references to Appendices
MAILLY	7/7/16.		Relieved 4th WORCESTERS in BRIGADE RESERVE.	[illegible]
	16/7/16.		MAJOR F.H.S. LE MESURIER joined BTN. from D.L.I. LIEUT. W. de H. ROBINSON rejoined Btn. from TOWN. COMMDT. ENGLEBELMER.	[illegible]
	19/7/16.		The following Officers joined Btn. from BASE:– 2LIEUT. W.S.M. RUXTON, " F.G. LYALL, " O.C.H. COX, " C.F. SUTRO, " G.R. KEMP; 2LIEUT. D.M. BOWYER, " L.W. ARMSTRONG, " R.G. TELFER, " R.E.S. JOHNSON, " H.M. WOOLF.	[illegible]
* FRONT LINE.	22/7/16.		2L Btn relieved the 2nd S.W.B. in front line S. of BEAUMONT HAMEL.	[illegible]
			Casualties week ending 22.7.16:– OFFICERS. NIL. OTHER RANKS. WOUNDED. 2. SICK & HOSPITAL. 9. 8214 PTE. REED died of wounds received 1.7.16.	
			2 other ranks rejoined from a Refresher course of signalling, and 2 O.R. left for course of signalling 15.7.16.	
*	21/7/16		Joined Btn from BASE – CAPT. DURLACHER, R.B. 6th BTN. 2 LIEUT. MORRIS, J.W. 10th ". 2 LIEUT. BEATTIE, W.L. 10th BTN. " SPEAR-MORGAN, R.H. 10th ".	[illegible]
	22.7.16		2 LIEUT. DUFF, M., invalided Home struck off strength. " PALMER, H., rejoined Btn from Sickness.	[illegible]
BUS.	24.7.16		Left for BUS. No. 8589. A/C.S.M. CRAINE joined Btn. from BASE.	[illegible]
AMPLIER.	25.7.16.		Arrived at AMPLIER.	[illegible]
	27.7.16.	9.30p.m.	Entrained at DOULLENS.	[illegible]
	28.7.16	6.30am	Arrived at PROVEN, and encamped about 3 miles out on the PROVEN–POPERINGHE ROAD.	[illegible]
	29.7.16.		128 other ranks joined Btn from BASE. 10 other ranks left to join 177th TUNNELLING COMPANY.	[illegible]

2449 Wt. W14957/M90 750,000 1/16 J.B.C. & A. Forms/C.2118/12.

Army Form C. 2118.

Instructions regarding War Diaries and Intelligence Summaries are contained in F. S. Regs., Part II. and the Staff Manual respectively. Title Pages will be prepared in manuscript.

WAR DIARY
or
INTELLIGENCE SUMMARY
(Erase heading not required.)

4

Place	Date	Hour	Summary of Events and Information	Remarks and references to Appendices
BALVEN	30.7.16.		2 LIEUT. C. N. WHITEHOUSE (13th ROYAL WARWICKS) and 13 other ranks left Btn. to join 177th TUNNELLING COY.	
			Casualties week ending 30.7.16 :- Other ranks. KILLED. 1. WOUNDED. 3. SICK to HOSPITAL. 1.	
"	31.7.16.			

R. G. Lewellin Lieut.
a/Adjt. 1st Btn. The Border Regt.

29th Division.

87th Infantry Brigade.

1st BATTALION

THE BORDER REGIMENT

AUGUST 1 9 1 6

66. 17K.

12th Bn. Border Regiment

Confidential

War Diary

From August 1st 1916
To August 31st 1916

Volume 17

Vol 5

Army Form C. 2118

Instructions regarding War Diaries and Intelligence Summaries are contained in F. S. Regs., Part II. and the Staff Manual respectively. Title Pages will be prepared in manuscript.

WAR DIARY
or
~~INTELLIGENCE SUMMARY~~
(Erase heading not required.)

1st BTN THE BORDER REGT.

Place	Date	Hour	Summary of Events and Information	Remarks and references to Appendices
PROVEN ~~VLAMERTINGHE~~	1-8-16		Moved from N. CAMP on PROVEN – POPERINGHE ROAD. to YSER CANAL in BRIGADE RESERVE.	RGL
	5-8-16		" " CANAL BANK to firing line	RGL
			CASUALTIES – week-ending 5/8/16. To hospital 4 from hospital 4.	RGL
			CAPT. DURLACHER to course at 2nd ARMY SCHOOL.	RGL
			3 N.C.Os. to course of Instruction at Divl. School 4/8/16.	RGL
	6/8-16		Armourer Sergt. joined Btn.	RGL
	7-8-16		29 O.R. joined from Base.	RGL
	8-8-16		MAJOR F.H.S. LE MESURIER wounded by shell. Gas attack on Right & Left flanks, nothing on our front.	RGL
	9-8-16		2nd LIEUT. A. CAMPBELL joined from course of Instruction, and took over command of "D" Company.	RGL
	11-8-16		15 O.R. joined from Base. 8 O.R. rejoined from 177th TUNNELLING COMPANY.	RGL
	12-8-16		8 O.R. attached to 87th M.G. Coy.	RGL
			Casualties week-ending 12/8/16. KILLED 3. WOUNDED 9. SICK to HOSPITAL 11.	RGL
	13-8-16		7 O.R. joined from Base. MAJOR F.G.G. MORRIS joined Battalion.	RGL
	14-8-16		MAJOR F.G.G. MORRIS appointed Tempy. LT. COLONEL. CAPTAIN (Tempy. MAJOR) J.R. MEIKLEJOHN resumed the duties at the Headquarters of the Battalion on relinquishing command of the Battalion. 3 N.C.Os rejoined from Divl. School. 3 N.C.Os to course at Divl. School.	RGL
	15-8-16		20 O.R to course of Bombing. 2nd LIEUT BEATTIE to course of Bombing. 2nd LIEUT LYALL to course at Divl. School.	RGL
	16-8-16		8 O.R. to course of TRENCH MORTAR BATTERY.	RGL

1875 Wt. W593/826 1,000,000 4/15 J.B.C. & A. A.D.S.S./Forms/C. 2118.

Instructions regarding War Diaries and Intelligence Summaries are contained in F. S. Regs., Part II. and the Staff Manual respectively. Title Pages will be prepared in manuscript.

WAR DIARY
or
~~INTELLIGENCE SUMMARY~~
(Erase heading not required.)

Army Form C. 2118

1st BTN. THE BORDER REGT.

Place	Date	Hour	Summary of Events and Information	Remarks and references to Appendices
FLANDERS.	19-8-16		From 'A' CAMP, VLAMERTINGHE to CANAL. 1 O.R to course of Sniping.	[illegible]
			Casualties week-ending 19-8-16. SICK to hospital 11. REJOINED from " 2.	[illegible]
			HONOURS & AWARDS. No. 22711 SGT. DRURY, J. / " 7329 CPL. BOYCE, T. / " 9244 PTE CHILDS, R. / " 8408 " NEWCOMBE, J. / " 18803 L/SGT. MOYE, E. } Awarded MILITARY MEDAL. Auty. 29th Dvn. A/SB d/14-8-16.	[illegible]
	20-8-16		2nd LIEUT. BEATTIE rejoined from Bombing Course.	[illegible]
	21-8-16		20. O.R. rejoined from Bombing Course. 1. O.R transferred from D.L.I.	[illegible]
	23-8-16		2nd LIEUT. D.M. BOWYER, killed in action (shell).	[illegible]
			" F.H. PRESCOTT, 3rd attd 1st BTN. THE BORDER REGT., attached R.F.C.	[illegible]
			Casualties week ending 26-8-16. KILLED. Officer. 2nd LIEUT. D.M. BOWYER. O.R. 1. WOUNDED. 6. SICK to Hospital. 9. Rejoined from " 1.	[illegible]
			HONOURS & AWARDS. MAJOR A.J. ELLIS. 1st Bn. / 2nd LIEUT A.W. FRASER. 3rd Bn. } Awarded D.S.O.	[illegible]

1875 Wt. W593/826 1,000,000 4/15 J.B.C. & A. A.D.S.S./Forms/C. 2118.

Instructions regarding War Diaries and Intelligence Summaries are contained in F. S. Regs., Part II. and the Staff Manual respectively. Title Pages will be prepared in manuscript.

WAR DIARY
or
INTELLIGENCE SUMMARY
(Erase heading not required.)

Army Form C. 2118

Place	Date	Hour	Summary of Events and Information	Remarks and references to Appendices
CANAL.	29-8-16		Moved up to CANAL.	RGG
			8 O.R. joined from BASE	RGG.
			1 O.R. attached to Intelligence Branch, 2nd ARMY.	
			Casualties week ending 31st 8-16. KILLED. NIL. WOUNDED. 17. to Hospital 8. rejoined from hospital 3. Accidentally injured. 3.	
			Joined from Base. 27-8-16. 2nd LIEUT. BLOMFIELD. V. 1st Btn. } to "B" Company.	RGG
			" CLARK, A.M. "	
			" GAMON, J.L.P. " to "C" —	
			" THOMPSON, A.T. " to "D" —	
	28-8-16		EXTRACT from BTN. ORDERS:- The Commanding Officer wishes it to be made known to all ranks that he is greatly pleased with the conduct of the Officers, N.C.Os and men of the working party on the night of the 26/27th inst., who completed their task under very trying circumstances. This was in the new MONMOUTH TRENCH. He has had great pleasure in bringing their conduct to the notice of the G.O.C. BRIGADE.	RGG

R G Cullis Lieut.
A/Adjt. 11th Bn. The Border Regt.

1875 Wt. W593/826 1,000,000 4/15 J.B.C. & A. A.D.S.S./Forms/C. 2118.

" 29th Division
87th Infantry Brigade.

1st BATTALION

THE BORDER REGIMENT

SEPTEMBER 1 9 1 6

CONFIDENTIAL

WAR DIARY

Vol 6

1st Bn. BORDER. REGIMENT

From 1-9-16 To 30-9-16

Volume No 18

18 K
5 mub

Army Form C.

Instructions regarding War Diaries and Intelligence Summaries are contained in F. S. Regs., Part II. and the Staff Manual respectively. Title Pages will be prepared in manuscript.

WAR DIARY
or
~~INTELLIGENCE SUMMARY~~
(Erase heading not required.)

1st BTN. THE BORDER REGT.

SEPTEMBER 1916.

1

Place	Date	Hour	Summary of Events and Information	Remarks and references to Appendices
FIRING LINE YPRES SALIENT	1-9-16.		Very wet and conditions bad.	[illegible]
	2-9-16	11.30 pm.	Gas Alarm. None on our front, but well away to the S.	[illegible]
			Casualties week-ending 2-9-16. OFFICERS. NIL. OTHER RANKS. KILLED. 1. WOUNDED. 2. SICK to HOSPITAL. 5.	[illegible]
	5-9-16		HONOURS & AWARDS. CAPT. J. G. HEYDER, LIEUT. J. B. SINCLAIR. } THE MILITARY CROSS. (Authy. 29th Divisional Order No. 299)	[illegible]
			PROMOTION. LIEUT. G. G. D. CARGILL to be TEMPY. CAPTAIN whilst commanding a Company. Dated 16th JULY 1916. (Authy. 2nd Army No. 129/39).	[illegible]
	6-9-16	9pm/12pm	Machine Gun fire troublesome on the ST. JEAN RD., 7 casualties.	[illegible]
	7-9-16		More casualties from above but not in this Battalion.	[illegible]
	8-9-16		Arranged retaliation for above with 4th Divisional Artillery.	[illegible]
		9.15 pm.	Enemy M.G. opened. Our Guns retaliated with 96 rds. H.E. + Shrapnel on sap. heads, front line, support line and communication trenches. Nothing more heard from M.G.	[illegible]
	9-9-16		Relieved. Back to "A" Camp, BRANDHOEK.	[illegible]
	3.9.16		2 LIEUT. LYALL, F. G. rejoined from 29th Div. leave.	[illegible]
	4.9.16		" COX, G. C. A. and LIEUT. NEW, R. to 29th Div. leave.	[illegible]
	8.9.16.		" McDONALD, G. H. S., to Sniping Course, MONT DES CATS.	
			Casualties week-ending 9-9-16. OFFICERS. SICK to F.A. 2nd LIEUT. JOHNSON, R. E. S. OTHER RANKS. KILLED. 3. WOUNDED. 7. To HOSPITAL. 5. REJOINED from " 1. JOINED from BASE. 3 (3-9-16).	[illegible]

2449 Wt. W14957/M90 750,000 1/16 J.B.C. & A. Forms/C.2118/12.

Army Form C. 2118.

Instructions regarding War Diaries and Intelligence Summaries are contained in F. S. Regs., Part II. and the Staff Manual respectively. Title Pages will be prepared in manuscript.

WAR DIARY ~~or~~ ~~INTELLIGENCE SUMMARY~~

(Erase heading not required.)

1st BTN THE BORDER REGT.

2

SEPTEMBER 1916 (contd.)

Place	Date	Hour	Summary of Events and Information	Remarks and references to Appendices
"A" Camp	10-9-16		CAPT. H. BUNTING to course at 2nd Army School.	R.E.C.
BRANDHOEK.	11-9-16		LIEUT. W.F.H. CHAMBERS took over command of "D" Company from 2nd LIEUT. CAMPBELL with effect from forenoon. Shelled in camp. Very little damage done. 1 man wounded.	R.E.C.
			2nd LIEUTS. B.H. SPEAR-MORGAN, and H. PALMER took over command of "A" + "C" Companies respectively, during the absence of CAPT. H. BUNTING + CAPT. CARGILL on courses.	R.E.C.
			WIRING and REVETTING PARTIES to be under the command of 2nd LIEUT. CAMPBELL for training.	R.E.C.
			2nd LIEUT. R.G. TELFER to TRENCH MORTAR COURSE.	R.E.C.
			" J.L.P. GAMON " BOMBING COURSE.	R.E.C.
	12-9-16.		" A. CAMPBELL transferred to "D" Company.	R.E.C.
	15-9-16		" G.H.S. McDONALD rejoined from Sniping Course.	R.E.C.
			CAPT. C. RUSSELL, RAMC. attached temporarily as M.O.	R.E.C.
			Casualties week ending 16.9.16.	
			OFFICERS.	
			2nd LIEUT. C.N. WHITEHOUSE (13th ROYAL WARWICKS) transferred to 16th ROYAL WARWICKS.	R.E.C.
			CAPT. W.B. WAMSLEY, RAMC, to Hospital. (15.9.16).	R.E.C.
			OTHER RANKS. KILLED. NIL. WOUNDED. 1. SICK to HOSPITAL. 13. RETURNED from " 7.	
			1 other rank released for munitions. (14.9.16)	R.E.C.
			11 " " joined from Base. (15.9.16).	
	18.9.16.		CAPT. J.W. EWBANK to VIII Corps Training School as Officer Comdg. Composite Company	R.E.C.
			" G.B. CARGILL to VIII Corps Senior Officers' Course	R.E.C.
			2nd LIEUT. H.M. WOOLF to Trench Mortar Course, TREDEGHEM.	R.E.C.
1/6 CANAL BANK	19.9.16		Relieved 2nd S.W.B.s. ~~A. CAMPBELL~~ H. PALMER took over command of "B" Company while CAPTAIN EWBANK is absent.	R.E.C.
	22.9.16		2nd LIEUT. A. CAMPBELL granted leave to ENGLAND.	R.E.C.
			" M.H.E. ASHBY joined Btn. from Base.	R.E.C.

2449 Wt. W14957/M90 750,000 1/16 J.B.C. & A. Forms/C.2118/12.

Army Form C. 2118.

Instructions regarding War Diaries and Intelligence Summaries are contained in F. S. Regs., Part II. and the Staff Manual respectively. Title Pages will be prepared in manuscript.

WAR DIARY
or
~~INTELLIGENCE SUMMARY~~
(Erase heading not required.)

1st BTN. THE BORDER REGT.

SEPTEMBER 1916 (contd)

3

Place	Date	Hour	Summary of Events and Information	Remarks and references to Appendices
CANAL BANK (YPRES)	23.9.16.		2nd LIEUT. F. A. PRESCOTT struck off strength on being accepted as a probationer to R.F.C.	RLB
			Casualties week ending 23.9.16.	
			OFFICERS. CAPTAIN B.R. DURLACHER sick to ENGLAND 10.9.16. 2nd LIEUT. C.F. SUTRO sick to Hospital.	RLB
			OTHER RANKS. KILLED. NIL. SICK to Hospital 37. REJOINED from Hospital 11.	
			WOUNDED. 2. LEAVE to ENGLAND. 6. JOINED from BASE. 2.	
			Transferred to 87th M.G.C. 2.	
			Attached to VIII Corps. H.Q. for Composite Company. 18.	
FIRING LINE	24.9.16	8 p.m.	Relieved 2nd S.W.Bs. in left sub-sector.	RLB
			2nd LIEUT. H.M. WOOLF rejoined from TRENCH MORTAR COURSE.	RLB
			CAPT. W.B. WAMSLEY, R.A.M.C., rejoined from FIELD AMBULANCE.	RLB
			" C. RUSSELL ceased to be attached to BTN as M.O.	RLB
	26.9.16		2nd LIEUT. W.S.M. RUXTON wounded by shell.	RLB
	27.9.16		LIEUT. P. NEW and 2nd LIEUT G.C.H. COX rejoined from 29th Divl. School.	RLB
			CAPT. E.C. CLEGG joined BTN, and took over command of 'C' Coy.	RLB
	28.9.16		2nd LIEUTS. A.M. CLARKE & G.F. KEMP, to course at 29th Divl. School.	RLB
	29.9.16		LIEUT. & Q.Mr F. WHYBROW joined BTN.	RLB
			RELIEVED by 2nd S.W.Bs.	RLB
CANAL BANK	30.9.16	[illegible]	RAIDING PARTY under LIEUT. W. de H. ROBINSON, & 2nd LIEUTS. G.C.H. COX & V. BLOMFIELD, ~~[illegible]~~ and composed of 35 N.C.Os & men, entered the GERMAN trenches, killing about 8 and bringing back eight prisoners, 4 of whom were wounded. Our casualties were 2 slightly wounded. The whole raid was executed exactly as at the dress rehearsal, and the conduct of all concerned was absolutely great, and elicited a special wire of congratulation from the Corps Commander, LIEUT-GENERAL SIR AYLMER HUNTER-WESTON, K.C.B., D.S.O! This is the most successful raid yet accomplished by the VIII Corps.	RLB
		9.15 p.	Returned to our line.	RLB

2449 Wt. W14957/M90 750,000 1/16 J.B.C. & A. Forms/C.2118/12.

Instructions regarding War Diaries and Intelligence Summaries are contained in F. S. Regs., Part II. and the Staff Manual respectively. Title Pages will be prepared in manuscript.

WAR DIARY
or
~~INTELLIGENCE SUMMARY~~
(Erase heading not required.)

Army Form C. 2118

4

1st Bn. THE BORDER REGT.

Place	Date	Hour	Summary of Events and Information	Remarks and references to Appendices
			Casualties week-ending 30th Sept. 1916.	
			KILLED. NIL. SICK 17.	
			WOUNDED OFFICERS. 1. REJOINED. 6.	[initials]
			OTHER RANKS. 7.	
			1 man left to ENGLAND for Munition work. 28.9.16.	[initials]
			64 other ranks joined from BASE during week.	[initials]

1875 Wt. W593/826 1,000,000 4/15 J.B.C. & A. A.D.S.S./Forms/C. 2118.

GENERAL NOTES ON THE RECENT RAID CARRIED OUT IN THE SALIENT.

Raiding party consisted of approximately - 3 Officers and about 40 other ranks, and worked in co-operation with our Artillery and Trench Mortar Batteries. The section of the German line selected about 100 yards in length, was clearly understood. The Raiding Party was to enter in the centre of this length of trench, and search laterally to definite limits.

O.C. Raiding Party made the necessary arrangements, and obtained the material etc., which was, roughly - a tape about 400 yards long, wire-cutters, Bangalore Torpedoes, revolvers for the Blocking Party, a stretcher, Hand bells, Field Telephones, Lewis gun, supply of grenades, and Bludgeons.

O.C. had made a preliminary reconnaissance, and the Raiding party had been practised over the ground by means of patrols some days beforehand.

There were two good landmarks between our trench and the Germans', in the form of a line of trees about midway between the two lines, and a line of willow trees about 70 yards from the enemy's line.

8.15 p.m.	O.C. Party moved out followed by remainder in formation shown on the attached diagram.
8.30 p.m.	Our Artillery began bombardment of the enemy front line assisted by Trench Mortars.
8.45 p.m.	Raiding Party had crossed the first line of trees.
8.50 p.m.	Halted at Willows - last line of trees before enemy trenches.
8.55 p.m.	Bombardment lifted to second line of trenches, and the party started through the wire.

Previous to moving a COVERING PARTY had been told off, consisting of 2 N.C.Os. and 12 men with 1 Lewis Gun, and they had received instructions how to act in case of emergency.

O.C. remained in a central position.

BLOCKING PARTY, organised into Right and Left parties, moved along the parapets and established 'blocks' opposite communication trenches. These were BOMBERS, BAYONET MEN, THROWERS & CARRIERS.

SEARCH PARTY, organised into Right and Left parties, each under an Officer, began searching the dugouts and trenches. These were Infantry armed with Rifles, Bayonets, and Bludgeons.

STRETCHER BEARERS remained in a central position.

TELEPHONES were ready to open up communication with Battalion Headquarters

AFTER A PERIOD OF 8 MINUTES - BOTH BELLS RUNG - and the parties assembled on the O.C. Raiding party, and the prisoners, following in rear of a guide, were marched back to our lines.

There was no Machine gun fire from the German line, and movement was made impossible by the barrage put up, on the Right and Left flanks of the raid, on the support trenches in rear.

LESSONS FROM THE RAID

1. Forethought and careful preliminary arrangements - clearly explained to everyone by O.C. i/c Raid - was the chief factor of success.

2. Essential to rehearse the part EACH man has to play - many times beforehand - and ensure that he can explain every other man's job in the party.

3. Raiding parties must be familiar with the ground - this is ensured by sending them out on patrols a few days beforehand.

4. The Officer Commanding Party must confer with O.C. Artillery covering the raid area, and watches must be synchronised.

5. Fixing, priming, and detonating of Bangalore Torpedoes require very careful arranging, and on no account during the advance across 'No Man's Land' must the fuse be allowed to get wet. This is of great importance.

6. Raiding Party must be in such close proximity to the enemy's front line that they can, without any loss of time, rush straight into the trenches immediately after the barrage lifts - a few seconds delay would enable the Germans to man their defences and bring Machine guns into action.

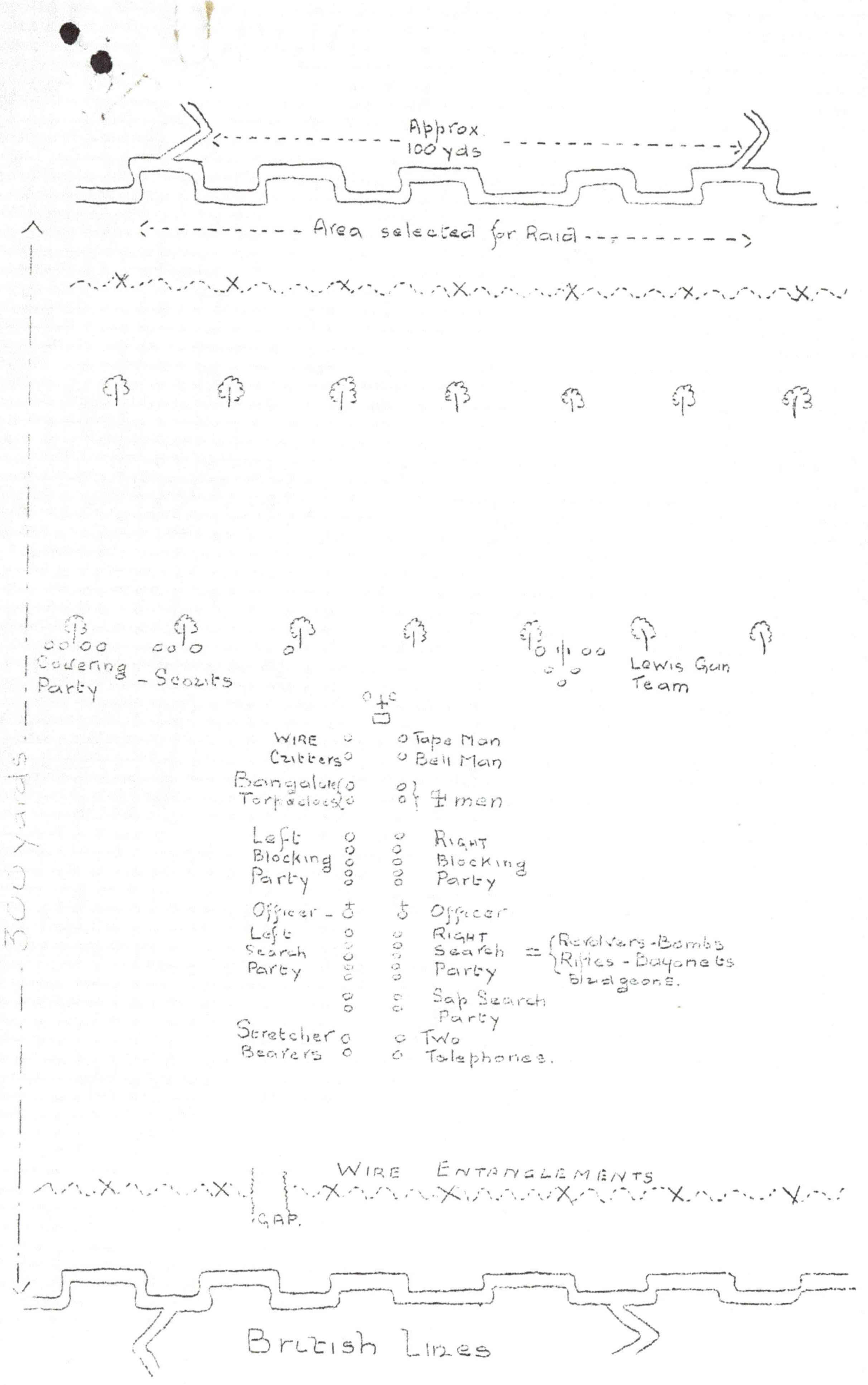

Approx 100 yds
Area selected for Raid
Covering Party
- Scouts
Lewis Gun Team
WIRE Cutters
Tape Man
Bell Man
Bangalore Torpedoes
4 men
Left Blocking Party
Right Blocking Party
Officer -
Officer
Left Search Party
Right Search Party
= Revolvers - Bombs Rifles - Bayonets bludgeons.
Sap Search Party
Stretcher Bearers
Two Telephones.
300 Yards
WIRE ENTANGLEMENTS
GAP.
British Lines

R.B. 116

Dear General,

I had a long talk the other day with the Officer who commanded the Raiding Party of the Border Regt. which carried out the recent successful raid in the Salient. From the conversation I made the attached notes, which I thought you would like to see.

Yours sincerely,

J. Kirby

5

Report on Raid made by 1st Border Regiment on night 30th Sept.1916.

The Covering Party consisting of a Sergeant and 6 riflemen to guard the left flank, a Sergeant and 7 men with Lewis Gun to guard the right flank, were posted at about 7.45 p.m. in the nearer line of trees opposite WIELTJE SALIENT. At 8.10 p.m. the raiding party began to leave our trench and were all in position in "NO MANS LAND" as arranged by 8.15 p.m.

During the first 15 minutes of the bombardment the party worked forward to the line of big trees without mishap, and crossed to the line of willows in front of enemy trench by 8.50 p.m. During this second stage of the advance one lance-corporal sustained a slight wound in the hand from a fragment of one of our shells.

At 8.50 p.m. the O.C. Raid left the head of the column by the willows and went forward to reconnoitre the wire. There were a great many enemy flare lights, but there was no firing from the enemy front line and it is probable that enemy were on the flanks or in the support trenches. The wire proved tom have been very successfully knocked about by Trench Mortar fire but some inner belts of wire remained too high for easy passage. Accordingly wire-cutters were tried, but this method seemed slow, and at 8.55 p.m. the O.C. returned to party to begin advance through wire prepared to use bangalore torpedoes for any considerable obstructions near parapet. On a roll of concertina wire which remained little damaged in the line of advance, 3 bangalore torpedoes were tried. The fitting of the torpedoes in concertina wire turned out to be quite simple and was well done. Each of the torpedoes failed, however, to detonate owing to the dampness of fuzes. They had evidently been injured in the journey across "NO MANS LAND", as the Very light cases used to protect them had come off.

The O.C. Raid then noticed an easy gap which had been blown in the wire to the right, and the party trampled down what was left of the wire, and made a rush for the parapet. All arrangements worked as they had been planned, the point

/ of

of entry being only a matter of yards away from that intended. The Right and Left Blocking Parties both experienced some bombing from enemy on flanks. The trench on right of point of entry had been rather badly blown in by our Artillery, and a group of men protected by the blockage sent up Very lights, and brought rifle fire and bombs to bear on right blocking party, from trench in rear of our right. Our bombers retaliated with evident effect, as the enemy party retreated and the sending up of Very lights ceased.

The right searching party found in the main communication trench for some 30 yards to right of the point of entry, 2 dugouts under the parapet. These were securely built, but small, and had merely wooden frames. They were carpeted with straw. In one of these a man was found who was made prisoner. The right communication trench was badly knocked about, and the large dugout shown in the aerial photo, was entirely demolished.

Several dead or unconscious bodies were found in the barbed wire in front of this sector, and several of the enemy who retreated down the communication trenches were fired on and chased, one at least was killed.

Left Blocking Party.

This party got into position opposite the left communication trench noticed in the aerial photo. The enemy threw a large number of bombs at them, but without effect. Our men replied vigorously throwing almost all the bombs they had and kept the enemy on the flank at bay, even if they did no further damage. Four dugouts were found in this section of trench and produced 6 prisoners. The dugouts were of the same pattern as those noted above and all under the parapet. Two of the enemy were killed, one shot and one bayonetted.

All prisoners (8) seemed unwilling to surrender themselves but were obviously frightened.

General.

The trenches were slightly deeper and wider than our

/ front

front line, they had no trench boards but a good wooden firestep. The revetting was for the most part, wooden trellis-work. The floor of the trench was covered with straw. A considerable quantity of bombs, equipment, clothing and papers were found. A large bell for Gas Alarm was found on the parapet at point of entry, and the trench seemed liberally supplied with long-handled bombs. About 25% of the men seen in the trench wore metal helmets. Uniforms and equipment were in a very good state of repair, and everything was noticeably clean and tidy.

The Sap search party.

A recent reconnaissance of the Boche front line by daylight had led us to suppose that this sap was now very little used, and would not produce anything of interest. This was confirmed in fact, and the junction of the sap and the trench had been so blown in by our shells as to be hardly recognizable. Accordingly the sap party which had been sent to search it returned to the main party for work in the front line trench.

29th Division

87th Infantry Brigade

1st BATTALION

THE BORDER REGIMENT

OCTOBER 1 9 1 6

C O N F I D E N T I A L.

WAR DIARY OF 1st Bn Border Regiment.

FROM-1st October 1916 to 31st October 1916.

VOLUME NO. ~~12~~.

=*=

Army Form C. 2118.

WAR DIARY
or
~~INTELLIGENCE SUMMARY~~

1st BTN. THE BORDER REGT.

OCTOBER 1916.

Instructions regarding War Diaries and Intelligence Summaries are contained in F. S. Regs., Part II. and the Staff Manual respectively. Title Pages will be prepared in manuscript.

(Erase heading not required.)

Place	Date	Hour	Summary of Events and Information	Remarks and references to Appendices
1-10-16 CANAL BANK YPRES.	1-10-16		32 Other Ranks joined from Base.	RKB.
	2.10.16		2nd LIEUT. CAMPBELL rejoined from leave to England.	RKB.
	3-10-16		Relieved by LIVERPOOL SCOTTISH, 55th BDE.	RKB.
"J" CAMP INTERNATIONAL CORNER.	4.10.16		Arrived J. CAMP. 2nd LIEUT. SUTRO rejoined from Field Ambulance	RKB.
	5.10.16		2nd LIEUTS. CLARK & KEMP rejoined from 29th Divl. School. CAPT. J.E. EWBANK rejoined from Command, VIII Corps.	RKB.
	7.10.16		Marched from J. CAMP to HOPOUTRE SIDING, POPERINGHE, and entrained for the SOMME and the "Push".	RKB.
	6.10.16		CAPT. H. EWBANK joined Battalion as Chaplain.	
			Casualties week ending 7.10.16. KILLED. NIL. — Rejoined from Hospital 12. — To Hospital 14. WOUNDED. 2 — " Kent R.E. 3. — Transferred to R.E. SIGNALS. 1. " Leave to England 3 — Leave to England 1. " Divl. Reserve Co. 14 " 177th Tunnelling Co. 12 " VIII Corps Camp. Co. 15 " 29th Divl. School. 2	RKB.
LONGEAU.	8.10.16		Arrived about 4.30 a.m. and marched to ALLONVILLE where the Btn. occupied Billets.	RKB.
BUIRE.	10.10.16		Marched to BUIRE via QUERRIEU and LA HOUSSOYE. (BILLETS).	RKB.
			CAPT. BUNTING rejoined from 2nd ARMY SCHOOL.	RKB.
	12.10.16		2nd LIEUT. BEATTIE to Brigade Pioneers.	RKB.

2449 Wt. W14957/M90 750,000 1/16 J.B.C. & A. Forms/C.2118/12.

Army Form C. 2118.

Contd 2.

WAR DIARY
~~or~~
INTELLIGENCE ~~SUMMARY~~ 1st BORDER REGT.

(*Erase heading not required.*)

Instructions regarding War Diaries and Intelligence Summaries are contained in F. S. Regs., Part II. and the Staff Manual respectively. Title Pages will be prepared in manuscript.

OCTOBER 1916.

Place	Date	Hour	Summary of Events and Information	Remarks and references to Appendices
FRICOURT. ~~[illegible]~~ CAMP	13.10.16		Left BUIRE and marched ~~there~~ to FRICOURT CAMP. Men in bivouacs and Officers in tents. very cold.	[illegible]
	14.10.16		Casualties week ending 14.10.16. From Hospital. 15. — To Hospital 13. " Courses 2 — Leave to England 3. " Leave to England 1. — To Base (under age) 1. To Bde. Pioneers 8. " Divl Reserve Co. 1.	[illegible]
	15.10.16.		2 Lieut. Morris to take command of Divl. Baths. 2nd Lieut. Palmer rejoined from leave to England. 2nd Lieut. Delfer to T.M.B.	[illegible] [illegible] [illegible]
BERNAFAY WOOD	19.10.16		Marched from FRICOURT to BERNAFAY WOOD. Within 10 minutes of arrival shell burst & killed & wounded 14 men. 2nd Lieut. Johnson from Field Ambulance.	[illegible] [illegible]
	20.10.16		Moved up to SWITCH TRENCH.	
FIRING LINE. GUEDECOURT.	21.10.16		Moved up to front line beyond GUEDECOURT. (GREASE + GAP TRENCHES, SUNKEN ROAD + PILGRIMS WAY.	[illegible]
			Casualties week ending 21-10-16. KILLED. 3. Accidentally wounded WOUNDED. 11. (premature Rifle Grenade) 4. MISSING. 1. " (detonator bursting) 1. To Hospital. 3. " Divl. Baths 18. " Courses 4. " Base (Munitions) 1. " T.M.B. 1. " Reserve Co. 4. " Bde employ 3. " D.A.D.O.S. 1. " Leave to England 1. Joined from Base 18.10.16 85. " " 21.10.16 64.	[illegible]

2449 Wt. W14957/M90 750,000 1/16 J.B.C. & A. Forms/C.2118/12.

Army Form C. 2118.

Cont'd. 3

Instructions regarding War Diaries and Intelligence Summaries are contained in F. S. Regs., Part II. and the Staff Manual respectively. Title Pages will be prepared in manuscript.

WAR DIARY
or
~~INTELLIGENCE SUMMARY~~

(Erase heading not required.)

1st BORDER REGT.

OCTOBER 1916.

Place	Date	Hour	Summary of Events and Information	Remarks and references to Appendices
FIRING LINE.	22.10.16.		2nd Lieut. Blomfield to Lewis Gun Course at ETAPLES.	RGG.
	23.10.16		2nd Lieut. Ashby wounded by shell.	RGG.
			CAPT. CARGILL rejoined from VIII Corps Senior Officers' Training School.	RGG.
	24.10.16		LIEUT NEW to Course (Telescopic Sight):	RGG.
	25.10.16		LIEUT ROBINSON, M.C., wounded.	RGG.
	27.10.16.		From firing line to SWITCH TRENCH.	RGG.
			To BERNAFAY WOOD.	
	28.10.16		Casualties week ending 28-10-16.	RGG.
			KILLED. 18. — To Hospital 25. — From Courses. 3.	
			WOUNDED. 50. — " Courses. 8. — " Leave to England 2.	
			Died of WOUNDS. 1. — " Hospital 8.	
			MISSING. 5. — " Base. 29.	
	29.10.16		To ALBERT via MAMETZ. LIEUT ROBINSON rejoined on recovery from wound.	RGG.
	30.10.16		2nd Lieut. Morris rejoined from Divl. Baths.	RGG.
	31.10.16		Casualties MISSING BELVD. KILLED attd. T.M.B. 1. — To Hospital 8. Rejoined from Hospital. 11. Joined " Base. 4. " " Leave to England 1.	RGG.

[signature] Lieut.
a/Adjt 1st Bn The Border Regt.

2449 Wt. W14957/M90 750,000 1/16 J.B.C. & A. Forms/C.2118/12.

29th Division.

87th Infantry Brigade.

1st BATTALION

THE BORDER REGIMENT

NOVEMBER 1 9 1 6

Confidential

War Diary of

1st Bn The Border Regiment

from 1st November 1916 to 30th November 1916

Volume No ~~IX~~

Vol 8

20 K
5 [illegible]

Army Form C. 2118.

WAR DIARY
~~or~~
~~INTELLIGENCE SUMMARY.~~
(Erase heading not required.)

Instructions regarding War Diaries and Intelligence Summaries are contained in F. S. Regs., Part II. and the Staff Manual respectively. Title pages will be prepared in manuscript.

1st BTN. THE BORDER REGT.

NOVEMBER 1916.

Place	Date	Hour	Summary of Events and Information	Remarks and references to Appendices
ALBERT.	1-11-16		Still resting at ALBERT. The town was shelled slightly.	RGG.
			2nd LIEUT. BLOMFIELD rejoined from Lewis Gun Course at ETAPLES.	RGG.
"	2-11-16		2nd LIEUT A. CAMPBELL to course of instruction (9th Flying Squadron).	RGG.
			2nd " H.T. THOMPSON " " " " " "	RGG.
"	3-11-16		Entrained at noon.	RGG.
			Arrived AIRAISNES about 7.30pm. and marched to ALLERY. Very nice billets for Officers and men.	
ALLERY	4-11-16		Casualties week-ending 4-11-16. From Base 59 O.R. To Courses of Instruction 4 O.R. " Hospital 7 " " " 87th Bde M.G. Co. 4 " " " Courses 3 " " " Base 3 " "	RGG.
"	6-11-16		LIEUT. W. de H. ROBINSON, M.C., granted leave to England.	RGG.
			2nd LIEUTS. CAMPBELL & THOMPSON from Course of Instruction.	RGG.
			" J.N. MORRIS attd 87th Bde Pioneers.	
"	7-11-16		" BEATTIE from " " " " " . 2nd LIEUT. P. NEW from Course of Instruction	RGG.
			" WISE to Field Ambulance	RGG.
"	8-11-16		LIEUT. W.F.H. CHAMBERS granted leave to England.	
"	11-11-16		Casualties week ending 11-11-16. To Hospital 1 Officer. From F.A. 6 O.R. To Base (under age) 1 O.R. 21 O.R. " Courses 6 " " " Bde M.G. Coy 1 " " Evacuated from F.A. 13 " " " leave 1 " " " Courses 7 " " " 87th Bde M.G. 3 " "	RGG.

A5834 Wt. W4973/M687 750,000 8/16 D. D. & L. Ltd. Forms/C.2118/13.

Instructions regarding War Diaries and Intelligence Summaries are contained in F. S. Regs., Part II. and the Staff Manual respectively. Title pages will be prepared in manuscript.

WAR DIARY

~~or~~

~~INTELLIGENCE SUMMARY.~~

(Erase heading not required.)

Army Form C. 2118.

No. 2

1st BTN THE BORDER REGT.

NOVEMBER 1916 (contd).

Place	Date	Hour	Summary of Events and Information	Remarks and references to Appendices
ALLERY	13-11-16		2nd LIEUT G.H.S. McDONALD granted leave to England. also LIEUT. J.G. ROWAN.	R.E.G.
"	14-11-16		CAPT. J.W. EWBANK granted leave to England. " WISE from FIELD AMBULANCE	R.E.G.
			Left in French Motor busses to BUIRE. Marched from BUIRE to CITADEL CAMP which was very muddy. 2nd LIEUT. WISE granted leave to England.	R.E.G.
			2nd LIEUTS, BLOMFIELD & CLARK to Course of Instruction at Divl. School.	R.E.G.
CARNOY.	15-11-16		Marched to CARNOY CAMP.	R.E.G.
			CAPT. BUNTING granted leave to England	R.E.G.
LES BOEUF	16-11-16		To firing line in front of LE TRANSLOY. practically no accommodation for Officers or men.	R.E.G.
	17-11-16		MAJOR MEIKLEJOHN granted leave to England. LIEUT. NEW to F.A. Snow.	R.E.G. R.E.G.
	18-11-16		1 German prisoner. The frost turned to rain.	R.E.G.
			Casualties week ending 18-11-16. WOUNDED shell 11 O.R. From Base 1 Other Rank. " Bayonet 1 " ". SICK. 4 " To Field Ambulance. 11 " To Base (underage) 1 " " England (leave) 1 " " Courses 10 " " T.M. Battery. 1 " " 183rd Tunnelling Co. (Transferred) 6 " " (attached) 8 " " Brigade Employ 7	R.E.G.

A5834 Wt. W4973/M687 750,000 8/16 D. D. & L. Ltd. Forms/C.2118/13.

Instructions regarding War Diaries and Intelligence Summaries are contained in F. S. Regs., Part II. and the Staff Manual respectively. Title pages will be prepared in manuscript.

Army Form C. 2118.

WAR DIARY
or
~~INTELLIGENCE SUMMARY.~~
(Erase heading not required.)

No. 3

NOVEMBER 1916.

1st BTN THE BORDER REGT.

Place	Date	Hour	Summary of Events and Information	Remarks and references to Appendices
FIRING LINE LESBOEUFS	19-11-16		1 Boche captured. Trenches are in a very bad state owing to rain.	[illegible]
			To support line. CAPT. CLEGG wounded (shell). LIEUT ROBINSON, M.C. rejoined from leave.	[illegible]
OX TRENCH	20-11-16			
MAMETZ	21-11-16		Back to MANSEL CAMP S. of MAMETZ. Men accommodated in tents, with a brazier to each tent. Officers in huts. Everybody quite comfortable.	[illegible]
			2nd LIEUTS BEATTIE + SPEAR-MORGAN to course at ARMY SCHOOL.	[illegible]
	23-11-16		LIEUT. CHAMBERS rejoined from leave. 2nd LIEUT. H.M. WOOLF to course of Transport.	[illegible]
	25-11-16		Casualties week ending 25-11-16 KILLED. 6 O.R. WOUNDED. 1 Officer. " 18 O.R. SICK F.F.A. 15 " To England Munitions. 1 " " Base. Medically unfit. 1 " Evacuated from F.A. (sick) 44 " To Brigade employ. 10 " " Courses. 2 " Leave to England. 4 " From courses. 11 O.R. rejoined from F.A. 5 " From Base 1 " " 9th Entrenching Btn 1 "	[illegible]
OX TRENCH	27-11-16		To support line. CAPT EWBANK rejoined from leave.	[illegible]
FIRING LINE	28-11-16		LIEUT. ROWAN rejoined from leave	[illegible]
			2nd LIEUT MCDONALD " " "	[illegible]
			THOMPSON sick to Field Ambulance.	[illegible]
	29-11-16		LIEUT. CHAMBERS wounded.	

A5834 Wt. W4973/M687 750,000 8/16 D. D. & L. Ltd. Forms/C.2118/13.

Instructions regarding War Diaries and Intelligence Summaries are contained in F. S. Regs., Part II. and the Staff Manual respectively. Title pages will be prepared in manuscript.

WAR DIARY
or
INTELLIGENCE SUMMARY.
(Erase heading not required.)

Army Form C. 2118.

No. 4

NOVEMBER 1916

1ST BTN THE BORDER REGT.

Place	Date	Hour	Summary of Events and Information	Remarks and references to Appendices
29-11 FIRING LINE	29-11-16		LIEUT. P. NEW rejoined from Field Ambulance.	RKb.
GUILLEMONT	30-11-16		In support. MAJOR MEIKLEJOHN rejoined from leave.	RKb.
		2 pm.	To MANSEL CAMP.	
			Casualties 25-11-16 to 30-11-16.	RKb.
			WOUNDED Officers 1. — From leave to England 1 O.R.	
			O.R. 7. — Rejoined from F.A. 18 "	
			Sick to F.A. 24 O.R. — From Base. 2 "	
			To Brigade employ 9 "	
			" Courses 5 "	
			" Divl. Reserve Coy. 4 "	
			" leave to England. 8 "	
			Transferred to XIV Corps Railway Coy. 2 "	

A5834 Wt. W4973/M687 750,000 8/16 D. D. & L. Ltd. Forms/C.2118/13.

29th Division.

87th Infantry Brigade.

1st BATTALION

THE BORDER REGIMENT

DECEMBER 1 9 1 6

Confidential

Vol 9

War Diary

of

1st Batt: The Border Regt

From 1st December 1916 to 31st December 1916

Volume 21.

21 K
Archive

EXTRACT FROM ARMY ROUTINE ORDERS.

1

Army Form C. 2118.

Instructions regarding War Diaries and Intelligence Summaries are contained in F. S. Regs., Part II. and the Staff Manual respectively. Title pages will be prepared in manuscript.

WAR DIARY
or
~~INTELLIGENCE SUMMARY.~~
(Erase heading not required.)

DECEMBER 1916

1st BORDER REGT.

Place	Date	Hour	Summary of Events and Information	Remarks and references to Appendices
MANSEL CAMP	2-12-16		Casualties week ending 2-12-16. OFFICERS nil OTHER RANKS KILLED NIL. WOUNDED NIL. SICK to F.A. 20. FROM " 5. Transferred to XIV Corps Rly Coy 2. " " 2nd Army Intelligence Corps 1 Detailed for duty with 16th Sanitary Section 2.	RGb.
			2nd LIEUT. H.M WOOLF rejoined from Transport Course	RGb.
"	3-12-16		2nd LIEUT. R.E.S JOHNSON proceeded to Lewis Gun Course	RGb.
			LIEUT. P. NEW to Brigade Pioneers	RGb.
GUILLEMONT	5-11 16		Marched from MANSEL CAMP to reserve at GUILLEMONT.	RGb.
FIRING LINE	8-12-16		From Guillemont to firing line at LES BOEUFS.	RGb.
"	9-12-16		Relieved by 10th Bn. Rifle Brigade	RGb.
			Casualties week ending 9-12-16 Other Ranks KILLED. NIL WOUNDED NIL SICK to HOSPITAL 34 REJOINED from — 12. To Course of Trench Mortar 4. " 256th Tunnelling Coy. 21. " Course Lewis Gun 4. " 86th Bde Pioneers 17. Rejoined from Bombing Course 4.	RGb.

A5834 Wt. W4973/M687 750,000 8/16 D. D. & L. Ltd. Forms/C.2118/13.

Instructions regarding War Diaries and Intelligence Summaries are contained in F. S. Regs., Part II. and the Staff Manual respectively. Title pages will be prepared in manuscript.

WAR DIARY or ~~INTELLIGENCE~~ SUMMARY.

(Erase heading not required.)

Army Form C. 2118.

2

DECEMBER 1916.

1st BTN. THE BORDER REGT

Place	Date	Hour	Summary of Events and Information	Remarks and references to Appendices
CARNOY CAMP	10-12-16		Entrained at Plateau for CORBIE	RGL
			1st LINE TRANSPORT by road	RGL
CORBIE	11-12-16		Entrained at CORBIE for LONGPRÉ	RGL
			Detrained at LONGPRÉ and marched to CONDÉ where billeted for night	RGL
CONDÉ	12-12-16		Marched by road from CONDÉ to PICQUIGNY 2nd LIEUTS L.W. ARMSTRONG + J.L. GAMON to Divl. School	RGL
PICQUIGNY	13-12-16		All billeted in the Town, but some of the men in bad billets.	RGL
"	14-12-16		Cleaning up.	RGL
"	15-12-16		Still cleaning the mud off clothing + equipment.	RGL
"	16-12-16		Casualties week-ending 16-12-16. OFFICERS KILLED. 2nd LIEUT. F.G. LYALL 9-12-16. SICK to F.A. " A. CAMPBELL 9-12-16. " C.F. SUTRO 9-12-16. REJOINED from Courses " A.M. CLARK. } from Divl. School V. BLOMFIELD } " R.E.S. JOHNSON " Lewis Gun from F.A. " THOMPSON.	RGL
			OTHER RANKS. KILLED. 4. To XIV Corps Labour Btn 37. WOUNDED. 7. Rejoined from Lewis Gun Course 4. SICK to F.A. 27. " " 86th Bde Pioneers 17. from F.A. 34 " " 256th Tunnelling Coy 21.	RGL

A5834 Wt. W4973/M687 750,000 8/16 D. D. & L. Ltd. Forms/C.2118/13.

Army Form C. 2118.

Instructions regarding War Diaries and Intelligence Summaries are contained in F. S. Regs., Part II. and the Staff Manual respectively. Title pages will be prepared in manuscript.

WAR DIARY
~~or~~
~~INTELLIGENCE SUMMARY.~~
(Erase heading not required.)

8

DECEMBER 1916

1st BTN. THE BORDER REGT.

Place	Date	Hour	Summary of Events and Information	Remarks and references to Appendices
PICQUIGNY ~~17-12-16~~	17-12-16		Marched to HANGEST.	R.E.L.
			2nd LIEUT. A. CAMPBELL rejoined from F.A.	R.E.L.
HANGEST.	18-12-16		The men much better off here	R.E.L.
"	19-12-16		Training started. Pioneers busy fitting up ovens, latrines + making good billets.	R.E.L.
"	21-12-16		2nd LIEUT G.C.A. COX to 86th Bde. Pioneers.	R.E.L.
			" J.N. MORRIS from " "	R.E.L.
"	23-12-16		" A CAMPBELL, J.N. MORRIS, + G.F. KEMP to Musketry Camp, PONT REMY.	
			Casualties week ending 23-12-16	
			OTHER RANKS	
			KILLED NIL. To Prisoner of War Coy (under age) 3.	R.E.L.
			WOUNDED NIL. " XIV Corps Composite Labour Btn 19.	
			SICK to F.A 15. " Musketry Camp, PONT REMY. 89.	
			Rejoined from F.A. 11.	
"	23-12-16		2nd LIEUTS. B.H. SPEAR-MORGAN + W.L. BEATTIE rejoined from 4th ARMY SCHOOL.	R.E.L.
	29-12-16		" A. CAMPBELL, J.N MORRIS, + G.F. KEMP rejoined from Musketry Camp	R.E.L.
	30-12-16		Casualties week ending 30-12-16.	
			OTHER RANKS. To England for Commissions. 3.	
			KILLED NIL. Course of Bombing 4.	R.E.L.
			WOUNDED NIL. " " Stokes Mortar 5.	
			SICK to F.A 4. " " Lewis Gun. 4.	
			Rejoined from F.A. 7. " M.G. Corps. 8.	
			Rejoined from Musketry Camp. 86.	
"	31-12-16		2nd LIEUT C.F. SUTRO rejoined from F.A.	R.E.L.

R. E. Lewthis Lieut
A/Adjt. 1st Bn. The Border Regt.

A5834 Wt. W4973/M687 750,000 8/16 D. D. & L. Ltd. Forms/C.2118/13.

29/87

87/29

C O N F I D E N T I A L

W A R   D I A R Y

- of -

1st Battalion BORDER REGIMENT.

From January 1st 1917 to January 31st 1917

V O L U M E No. 22.

=*=*=*=*=*=*=*=*=*=*=*=*=*=*=*=*=*=*=*

Instructions regarding War Diaries and Intelligence Summaries are contained in F. S. Regs., Part II. and the Staff Manual respectively. Title pages will be prepared in manuscript.

WAR DIARY
or
~~INTELLIGENCE SUMMARY.~~
(Erase heading not required.)

1st BTN THE BORDER REGT.

Army Form C. 2118.

JANUARY 1917

Place	Date	Hour	Summary of Events and Information	Remarks and references to Appendices
HANGEST.	1-1-17	9am-1pm	Practice in the attack, with dummy barrage. No. 8589 Cr. SGT CRAINE granted commission in this Btn.	R.E.B.
			2nd LIEUT. CAMPBELL employed as TOWN MAJOR.	R.E.B.
"	2-1-17.	7.30am to 2 p.m.	Inspection by MAJOR GENERAL B. de LISLE K.C.B., D.S.O., who afterwards watched a practice assault by ourselves + 1/R. Inniskilling Fusiliers. He expressed his gratification both with the appearance of the troops and with the way they manoeuvred.	R.E.B.
"	3-1-17		Bombing, Musketry + other parades. 2nd LIEUT H. T. THOMPSON rejoined from Stokes Mortar Course.	R.E.B.
			4 O.R. to Grenade Course 4 O.R rejoined from Stokes Mortar Course	R.E.B.
"	4-1-17		Company parades in morning. ~~Btn~~ paraded 3.30pm. marched to LE MESGE, and dug strong points in the dark. Returned to HANGEST 11p.m.	R.E.B.
			2nd LIEUTS. J. L. P. GAMON + W. L. ARMSTRONG rejoined from Divl. School	R.E.B.
			2nd LIEUT. A. M. CLARK + 42 O.R to course at IV Army Musketry School.	R.E.B.
			No. 18133 L/SGT LUCAS + No. 22957 L/CPL KEELING to England for Commissions.	R.E.B.
"	5-1-17	9-1	Ordinary parades.	R.E.B.
		2-3	Gas Lecture + demonstration by Divl. Gas ~~School~~ Officer.	R.E.B.
"	6-1-17	9-1	Route March. Football match in afternoon.	R.E.B.
			Casualties week-ending 6-1-17:—	R.E.B.
			To Field Ambulance. Other Ranks 11 2nd LIEUT C.F. SUTRO from F.A. 31/12/16	
			From " " " 3	R.E.B.

A5834 Wt. W4973/M687 750,000 8/16 D. D. & L. Ltd. Forms/C.2118/13.

Instructions regarding War Diaries and Intelligence Summaries are contained in F. S. Regs., Part II. and the Staff Manual respectively. Title pages will be prepared in manuscript.

2

Army Form C. 2118.

WAR DIARY
or
~~INTELLIGENCE SUMMARY.~~
(Erase heading not required.)

1st BTN. THE BORDER REGT.

JANUARY 1917.

Place	Date	Hour	Summary of Events and Information	Remarks and references to Appendices
HANGEST	7-1-17		CHURCH PARADE in MAIRIE.	[illegible]
"	8-1-17	8-2pm	Practice assault before BRIG. GEN BRAY, CMDG. 87th INF BDE. 2 O.R to Course of Signalling. 1 O.R. to England for Munitions.	[illegible] [illegible]
"	9-1-17	8-1pm	Marched to LE MESGES and did an assault before Divl. General, Major Gen. B. de LISLE	[illegible]
"	10-1-17	9-12noon	Bombing etc. 2nd LIEUT C F SUTRO accidentally wounded. 2nd LIEUT A.M. CLARK + 42 O.R. rejoined from IV Army Musketry School. 4 O.R. to course of Lewis Gun.	[illegible] [illegible]
"	11-1-17	9-12.30	Ordinary parades. Btn. Sports in afternoon	[illegible]
		10pm	210 O.R. joined from Base. All untrained.	
"	12-1-17	10am	Billet inspection. LIEUTS. S.C. CHEVERTON + G. LINDSAY joined from Base.	[illegible]
		11am	Btn paraded + entrained at 12.40 p.m. 2nd LIEUT. J.N. MORRIS to employ as TOWN MAJOR, HANGEST.	
MERICOURT	"	3pm	Arrived, de-trained and marched to BRESLE.	[illegible]
BRESLE	13-1-17		Commanding Officer inspected new draft	[illegible] [illegible]
			Casualties week ending 13-1-17.	
			To Field Ambulance 10 O.R.	
			From " " 6 "	[illegible]

A5834 Wt. W4973 M687 750,000 8/16 D. D. & L. Ltd. Forms/C.2118/13.

3.

Army Form C. 2118.

WAR DIARY
or
~~INTELLIGENCE SUMMARY.~~

(*Erase heading not required.*)

1st BTN. THE BORDER REGT

JANUARY 1917.

Instructions regarding War Diaries and Intelligence Summaries are contained in F. S. Regs., Part II. and the Staff Manual respectively. Title pages will be prepared in manuscript.

Place	Date	Hour	Summary of Events and Information	Remarks and references to Appendices
BRESLE	14-1-17	9.45am	Btn paraded and march to MEAULTE.	RGG.
MEAULTE		12.40pm	Arrived. 2LIEUTS. A.H. CRAINE + G.H.S. McDONALD to course Div. School + 2 O.R.	RGG.
"	15-1-17	10.30am	Btn paraded and marched to CARNOY.	RGG.
CARNOY	"	1pm	Arrived. 23 O.R to Labour Btn. 11 O.R. to Reserve Company	RGG.
			3 O.R employed with Road construction unit ABBEVILLE. 1 O.R transferred to Field Survey Co.	RGG.
"	16-1-17	2.45pm	Marched to GUILLEMONT.	RGG.
GUILLEMONT	17-1-17	4pm	Moved off to firing line.	RGG.
Firing line	18-1-17		Quiet.	RGG.
"	19-1-17		6 O.R joined from Base 7 O.R. to XIV Corps Rly Workshops.	RGG.
		11pm	Relieved by 1/NEWFOUNDLAND REGT.	RGG.
CARNOY.	20-1-17		Casualties week ending 20-1-17:–	RGG.
			To Field Ambulance O.R. 11	
			From " " " 1	RGG.

A5834 Wt. W4973 M687 750,000 8/16 D. D. & L. Ltd. Forms/C.2118/13.

4.

Instructions regarding War Diaries and Intelligence Summaries are contained in F. S. Regs., Part II. and the Staff Manual respectively. Title pages will be prepared in manuscript.

WAR DIARY

~~or~~

~~INTELLIGENCE SUMMARY.~~

(Erase heading not required.)

Army Form C. 2118.

1st BTN. THE BORDER REGT.

JANUARY 1917.

Place	Date	Hour	Summary of Events and Information	Remarks and references to Appendices
CARNOY	21-1-17	2pm	Moved off to firing line.	RLC
Firing line.	22-1-17		Our guns bombarded the Boche in the afternoon.	RLC
	"	8.30pm	Relieved by 2nd S.W.Bs.	RLC
CARNOY	23-1-17		Resting.	RLC
"	24-1-17	11am	Bn parade & practice assault.	RLC
"	25-1-17		" " "	RLC
"	26-1-17	5.30pm	Marched to firing line.	RLC
Firing line	27-1-17	5.30am	Zero hour. Ourselves + 1/R Inniskilling Fus. on right attacked portion of LANDWEHR TRENCH, S. of LE TRANSLOY.	RLC
"		7am	Prisoners starting to come through. Reports received that 1st + 2nd objectives gained.	RLC
			117 prisoners passed Bn. H.Q., ANTELOPE TRENCH.	RLC
"		7.16am	First written report from Right Coy received, confirming 1st objective taken, 45 prisoners sent back by this Coy alone. Very few casualties.	RLC
"		8.12am	Report received by O.C. "Moppers up" that 1st objective cleaned up, and prisoners sent back.	RLC
"		8.45am	2nd report from Right Coy saying sending back 75 prisoners. Consolidation very difficult owing to frozen ground. No shelling of captured position, but good bit of hostile sniping.	RLC
"		11.45am	3rd Report from Right Coy. No change, but enemy evidently aware of situation & shelling of captured position increasing.	RLC
"		12.45pm	Consolidation proceeding slowly, a certain amount of wire put down around strong point which we are digging. Lewis Gun emplacements being dug & entanglements put up across SUNKEN ROAD on right flank of strong point.	RLC RLC

A5834 Wt. W4973 M687 750,000 8/16 D. D. & L. Ltd. Forms/C.2118/13.

5.

WAR DIARY
or
~~INTELLIGENCE SUMMARY~~.
(Erase heading not required.)

Army Form C. 2118.

1st BTN. THE BORDER REGT.

JANUARY 1917.

Instructions regarding War Diaries and Intelligence Summaries are contained in F. S. Regs., Part II. and the Staff Manual respectively. Title pages will be prepared in manuscript.

Place	Date	Hour	Summary of Events and Information	Remarks and references to Appendices
Firing Line ~~27-1-17~~	27-1-17	2pm	All objectives gained + consolidation proceeding very slowly owing to hardness of ground.	RLC.
"	"	4pm	Following received from Commander-in-Chief "Congratulate the 29th Div warmly and in particular the 1st Border Regt + 1/R. Inniskilling Fusiliers on the success of their operations carried out this morning. In forwarding this message the Army Commander wishes to add his congratulations to the 29th Div in their most successful enterprise". In reply following message was sent to Army Commander "The 29th Div is most gratified by your kind message which will be communicated to all ranks. The message from the Commander-in-Chief has been conveyed to the 1st Border Regt. + 1/R. Inniskilling Fus. who wish to thank him for his kind message, which has given great pleasure to myself and all the Division." (Sd) General de Lisle. Congratulations were also received from the Corps Commander - Lieut. General The Earl of Cavan - + from LIEUT. GEN. SIR WILLIAM BIRDWOOD, 1st A + N. Z. A. Corps, the 20th Div., + the 4th + 5th Australian Divisions. The following telegram was received from G.O.C. 29th Div. "I send you warmest congratulations on the fine attack of your battalions" "Messages have also been received for you from the Corps C. in C. which will be given to you later." (Sd) Gen. de Lisle.	RLC.
"	27-1-17	11pm	~~Relieved by~~. Casualties week-ending 27-1-17. Officers. KILLED. LIEUT. W. de H. ROBINSON M.C. " S. C. CHEVERTON 2nd " A. M. CLARK. LIEUT. W. L. BEATTIE WOUNDED. 2nd LIEUT. H. T. THOMASON. Other Ranks. KILLED 12. WOUNDED. 87. MISSING. 33. SICK to Hospl 44. Do " 2.	RLC.

A5834 Wt. W4973/M687 750,000 8/16 D. D. & L. Ltd. Forms/C.2118/13.

Volume 23

6.

WAR DIARY
or
~~INTELLIGENCE SUMMARY~~.
(Erase heading not required.)

Army Form C. 2118.

Instructions regarding War Diaries and Intelligence Summaries are contained in F. S. Regs., Part II. and the Staff Manual respectively. Title pages will be prepared in manuscript.

1st BTN THE BORDER REGT

JANUARY 1917.

Place	Date	Hour	Summary of Events and Information	Remarks and references to Appendices
Firing line	27-1-17		The total prisoners for the day was 6 Officers + 355 O.R. unwounded, and about 25 wounded. 5 Machine Guns were captured, including 3 captured by this Btn. We also captured a very valuable map with all the enemy dumps, H.Q.s, railway tracks, + batteries marked on it. It also had most of ours marked pretty accurately. We captured 4 Officers + 200 prisoners.	R.G.G.
			1 O.R. to England under age	R.G.G.
"	28-1-17	11p.m.	Relieved by 1/K.O.S.Bs.	R.G.G.
CARNOY.	29-1-17	11a.m.	The Corps Commander, accompanied by the Divl. Cmdr paid a visit to the camp, and congratulated the Officer Cmdg. + all Officers on the splendid action achieved on the 27th inst, afterwards entering each hut and thanking the men.	R.G.G.
"	30-1-17	2.15pm	Commemoration service in Y.M.C.A. in memory of those Officers + men who fell on the 27th inst. was held, the Battalion turning out in full strength.	R.G.G.
"	31-1-17	3 p.	Paraded + marched to GUILLEMONT.	R.G.G.

R.G. Gullis Lieut.
Adjt. 1st Bn. The Border Regt

A5834 Wt. W4973/M687 750,000 8/16 D. D. & L. Ltd. Forms/C.2118/13.

Instructions regarding War Diaries and Intelligence Summaries are contained in F. S. Regs., Part II. and the Staff Manual respectively. Title pages will be prepared in manuscript.

8/79

WAR DIARY or INTELLIGENCE SUMMARY.

(Erase heading not required.)

1st Bn THE BORDER REGT Army Form C. 2118.

Feby 1917

Place	Date	Hour	Summary of Events and Information	Remarks and references to Appendices
			General	
			The following awards were made for gallantry on 27/1/17	
			Lieut Colonel F.G.G. MORRIS — D.S.O	
			Capt. H. BUNTING, " J.H. EMBANK, Lieut G LINDSAY, 2/Lieut C.R. WISE, " D. MACLEOD — Military Cross	
			No 9610 a/C.S.M. BURYLE, 22650 Sgt R. PEAD, 3334 " ALLBEURY, 22029 Cpl SMITH, 22855 " A ROBINS — D.C.M	
			No 9760 a/Cpl. CAIN, 5275 Pte TRAINER, 33753 " MOORE, 10420 Cpl WEBER, 22945 L/C VERGE, 33805 Pte WHITEHEAD, 17890 " KERFOOT, 22900 " BLACK, 9991 " COLYER — Military Medal	MB

A5834 Wt. W4973/M687 750,000 8/16 D. D. & L. Ltd. Forms/C.2118/13.

23 K

1st BTN THE BORDER RGT. Army Form C. 2118.

WAR DIARY
or
~~INTELLIGENCE SUMMARY.~~
(Erase heading not required.)

Instructions regarding War Diaries and Intelligence Summaries are contained in F. S. Regs., Part II. and the Staff Manual respectively. Title pages will be prepared in manuscript.

FEBRUARY 1917

Place	Date	Hour	Summary of Events and Information	Remarks and references to Appendices
GUILLEMONT	1-2-17	4.30pm	Moved off to firing line	JHB
Firing line	2-2-17		Bosche artillery fairly active) 2LIEUT. LINDSAY wounded.	JHB
"	3-2-17	9.30pm	Relieved by 2nd S.W.B.) Entrained at GUILLEMONT for CARNOY. Casualties for week ending 3/2/17: Killed 2, Wounded 17, Missing nil, Sick to Hosp 7, From Hosp 11	JHB
CARNOY	4-2-17		Resting + cleaning clothing	JHB
"	5-2-17		Resting	JHB
"	6-2-17	9.45am	Bn paraded + marched to MEAULTE. 2LIEUT. C.B. COLBOURNE-SMITH, " H GIBSON, " R.S. POOLEY, " R. RAE, " J. WHIGHAM, " T. MAXWELL } 3rd R. SCOTS. FUS. Joined from Base	JHB
MEAULTE	7-2-17	10 am	Coys paraded under O.C. Coys for ~~rifle~~ Bayonet fighting etc	JHB
	8-2-17	10 am – 12 md	Coys paraded as yesterday.	JHB
"	9-2-17		2LIEUT. McDONALD and 2LIEUT. CRAINE rejoined from Course	JHB
		10am – 12 md	Parades as usual.	
"	10-2-17	10-12	Parades as usual. 2LIEUT. C.R. WISE to Field amb. 2LIEUT. D. MACLEOD to IV Army School. 2LIEUT. F MAXWELL, " A GIBSON } to Course Lewis School. 24 other ranks joined from Base. Casualties for week ending 10/2/17: Killed 1, Wounded 2, Missing 3, Sick to Hosp 25, From do 11.	JHB

A5834 Wt. W4973/M687 750,000 8/16 D. D. & L. Ltd. Forms/C.2118/13.

Instructions regarding War Diaries and Intelligence Summaries are contained in F. S. Regs., Part II. and the Staff Manual respectively. Title pages will be prepared in manuscript.

WAR DIARY
or
~~INTELLIGENCE SUMMARY.~~
(Erase heading not required.)

1st BN THE BORDER REGT.

Army Form C. 2118.

Place	Date	Hour	Summary of Events and Information	Remarks and references to Appendices
MEAULTE	11/2/17	11am	Church parade.	H.B.
"	12/2/17	9-1pm	Parades under O.C. Coys. General training	H.B.
"	13/2/17	9-1pm	Parades as yesterday LIEUT. R.G. COLLIS to 87th Bde. 2LIEUT. WHIGHAM to Stokes Mortar Course	H.B.
			LIEUT. THORBURN-BROWN, 2LIEUT. THOMPSON } 3rd K.O.S.B. joined from Base.	H.B.
"	14/2/17	9-1pm	Parades under O.C. Coys	H.B.
"	15/2/17	9-1pm	Parades under O.C. Coys	H.B.
"	15/2/17		65 Other Ranks joined from Base. 2LIEUT. F.S. LAYARD rejoined from 87th Bde H.Q. SEC LIEUT. COLBOURNE SMITH retransferred to 6/7 R.S.F.	
		9-1pm	Parades as usual.	H.B.
	16/2/17	9-1pm	Parades as usual.	H.B.
"	17/2/17	11am	Batn paraded & practiced ceremonial parade for distribution of medals	H.B.
			Casualties week ending 17/2/17. Killed Nil, Wounded Nil, Missing Nil, Sick to Hospl 11, From do 1	H.B.

A5834 Wt. W4973/M687 750,000 8/16 D. D. & L. Ltd. Forms/C.2118/13.

Instructions regarding War Diaries and Intelligence Summaries are contained in F. S. Regs., Part II. and the Staff Manual respectively. Title pages will be prepared in manuscript.

Army Form C. 2118.

WAR DIARY 1ST BN THE BORDER. REGT.
or
~~INTELLIGENCE SUMMARY.~~
(Erase heading not required.)

Place	Date	Hour	Summary of Events and Information	Remarks and references to Appendices
MEAULTE	18/2/17	1030 am	Parade 10.30 am & march to MONTAUBAN where Bn had dinners then on to COMBLES. Billeted in trenches & dugouts. 2LT. KEMP to course. MAJOR MEIKLEJOHN to 86 Bde as Brigade Major. 2LIEUT. RAE rejoined from course	HB
COMBLES	19/2/17	4.30 pm	Move up to firing line. Relieved 6th Dorsets. 2LIEUT. ARMSTRONG to L.G. Course	HB
Firing line	20/2/17		Nothing unusual. Fairly quiet. 2LIEUT. THOMPSON to England for Indian army	HB
"	21/2/17		Bosche artillery active. Very wet. Relieved very late this night by 2 ROYAL FUSILIERS who were kept back by Bosche barrage on duck boards. March to COMBLES.	HB
COMBLES.	22/2/17	11 am	March to TRONES. WOOD & entrain for BRONFAY CAMP at 1.30 pm	HB
BRONFAY	23/2/17		Resting. 22 other ranks joined from Base	HB
"	24/2/17	1.45 am	Paraded ~~[illegible]~~ & marched to COMBLES	HB
"	~~25/2/17~~	~~5 pm~~	~~Move to firing line & relieved 2 Hants~~	
"	~~26/2/17~~		~~Firing~~	
			Casualties for week ending 24/2/17 – Killed 2 Wounded 4 Missing Nil Sick to Hospital 19 From Hospital 2	HB

Instructions regarding War Diaries and Intelligence Summaries are contained in F. S. Regs., Part II. and the Staff Manual respectively. Title pages will be prepared in manuscript.

WAR DIARY
or
INTELLIGENCE SUMMARY.
(Erase heading not required.)

Army Form C. 2118.

1 Border Regt

Vol XI

Place	Date	Hour	Summary of Events and Information	Remarks and references to Appendices
COMBLES.	25/2/17	5 pm	Moved to firing line & relieved 2/Hants. 2Lt DANNIELLI joined from base.	H.B.
Firing line	26/2/17		Firing line. Enemy artillery very active.	H.B.
"	27/2/17		Firing line Enemy artillery very active. We bombard his front line heavily. LIEUT. C. MILLS 2LIEUT. W.S.M. ROXTON } joined from base.	H.B.
		12 mn	Relieved by 1/INNESKILLINGS on right and by 2 RF on left March back to FREGICOURT to trenches.	H.B.
FREGICOURT	28/2/17	3 pm	March to TRONES WOOD & entrain for BRONFAY CAMP	H.B.
			2LIEUT. L.W. ARMSTRONG rejoined from Course.	H.B.
			Casualties 25th to 28/Feby 1917:–	
			Killed Nil	H.B.
			Wounded 6	
			Missing Nil	
			Sick to Hospl 8	
			From " 1	

1/3/17

H Bruling Capt
a/adjutant
1/Border Regt

A5834 Wt. W4973/M687 750,000 8/16 D. D. & L. Ltd. Forms/C.2118/13.

23 K
5 mile

Instructions regarding War Diaries and Intelligence Summaries are contained in F. S. Regs., Part II. and the Staff Manual respectively. Title Pages will be prepared in manuscript.

WAR DIARY
or
~~INTELLIGENCE SUMMARY~~
(Erase heading not required.)

Army Form C. 2118.

1st Bn the BORDER RGT.

March 1917

Place	Date	Hour	Summary of Events and Information	Remarks and references to Appendices
BRONFAY	1/3/17	2pm	Bn marched to VILLE. 2Lt. CRAINE rejoined from 3.A.	HB
VILLE	2/3/17	2pm	Bn marched to BOSSY. 2Lt. FOOLEY rejoined from 3.A	HB
BOSSY	3/3/17		Resting	HB
			Casualties week ending 3/March 1917:-	
			Killed Nil	
			Wounded Nil	HB
			Missing Nil	
			Sick to Hosp 16	
			From " 5	

23/3/17

[illegible] Capt
& Adjutant
1/Border Rgt.

2449 Wt. W14957/M90 750,000 1/16 J.B.C. & A. Forms/C.2118/12.

Army Form C. 2118.

WAR DIARY
or
~~INTELLIGENCE~~ SUMMARY 1st Bn. THE BORDER Rgt.
(Erase heading not required.)

~~February~~ March 1917

Instructions regarding War Diaries and Intelligence Summaries are contained in F. S. Regs., Part II. and the Staff Manual respectively. Title Pages will be prepared in manuscript.

Place	Date	Hour	Summary of Events and Information	Remarks and references to Appendices
BOSSY	4/3/17	10.30	Church parade.	H.B.
"	5/3/17	9.am	Bathing of Companies	H.B.
"	6/3/17	7.am	Training under O.C. Coys. No. 6540 C.S.M. C.W. SMITH appointed to permanent commission as 2/LIEUT in 1/Border Rgt	H.B.
			2/Lt. C.W. SMITH posted to C. Coy	H.B.
	7/3/17	7.am	Training under O.C. Coys. 2Lt. G.C.A. COX rejoined from Brigade pioneers. 2/Lt. A. GIBSON to F.A.	H.B. H.B.
"	8/3/17	7.am	Training under O.C. Coys. CAPT. A.W. SUTCLIFFE joined from Base + posted to D. Coy	H.B. H.B.
"	9/3/17	9.am	Coy route marches under O.C. Coys.	H.B.
"	10/3/17	9am	Under Coy Cdrs. for intensive training	H.B. H.B.
			CAPT. R.P.M. ~~...~~ NIKOLS joined from Base.	H.B.
			Casualties for w/e. 10/3/17. Sick to Hospl 25 Drown " 11	H.B.

23/3/17

H. Bunting Capt
a/adjutant 1/Border Rgt

2449 Wt. W14957/M90 750,000 1/16 J.B.C. & A. Forms/C.2118/12.

Army Form C. 2118.

WAR DIARY
or
~~INTELLIGENCE SUMMARY~~
(Erase heading not required.)

Instructions regarding War Diaries and Intelligence Summaries are contained in F. S. Regs., Part II. and the Staff Manual respectively. Title Pages will be prepared in manuscript.

1st Bn THE BORDER RGT.
MARCH 1917

Place	Date	Hour	Summary of Events and Information	Remarks and references to Appendices
BUSSY	11/3/17	10 am	Church parade	HB
			2LIEUT. WHIGHAM attached to 84th T.M.B.	HB
			2LIEUT. CRAINE to F.A.	HB
"	12/3/17	9.15am	~~Bn route march~~. Training under Coy Cmdrs	HB
"	13/3/17	9.15am	Bn route march.	HB
"	14/3/17	9.15am	Outpost scheme by platoons.	HB
			Information received of award of V.C. to 9887 Sgt. E. MOTT.	HB
"	15/3/17	9.15	Parades same 14/3/17.	HB
"	16/3/17	9.15	Practice in attack by Platoons. 2LT CRAINE to F.A.	HB
"	17/3/17	9.15	Intensive training under O.C. Coys.	HB
			Casualties week ending 17/3/17	
			Sick to Hospl 16	
			From " 15	HB

23/3/17

H Bunting Capt
a/adjt 1/Border Rgt

2449 Wt. W14957/M90 750,000 1/16 J.B.C. & A. Forms/C.2118/12.

Army Form C. 2118.

Instructions regarding War Diaries and Intelligence Summaries are contained in F. S. Regs., Part II. and the Staff Manual respectively. Title Pages will be prepared in manuscript.

WAR DIARY

or

~~INTELLIGENCE SUMMARY~~

(Erase heading not required.)

1st Bn THE BORDER RGT.
March 1917

Place	Date	Hour	Summary of Events and Information	Remarks and references to Appendices
BOSSY.	18/3/17	10am	Church parade.	1HB
"	19/3/17	8am	Bn marched to EDGEHILL & entrained for HAGEST.	1HB.
HANCEST	20/3/17		Resting. Interior economy under O.C. Coys	1HB
"	21/3/17	9am	Intensive training under O.C. Coys	1HB
"	22/3/17	8.am	Practice of the attack by Coys as a manoeuvre	1HB
"	23/3/17	8am	Practice of attack as a Battn.	1HB
			LIEUT. G.B.D. CARGILL to E.A. 23/3/17	1HB
"	24/3/17	8 am	Bn practicing the attack as a manoeuvre.	1HB
			Casualties to/ E. 24/3/17.	
			Sick to Hpl 19	1HB
			From " 7	

2/8/3/17

H Bunting Capt
a/adjutant
1/Border Rgt

2449 Wt. W14957/M90 750,000 1/16 J.B.C. & A. Forms/C.2118/12.

Army Form C. 2118.

5

WAR DIARY
~~or~~
~~INTELLIGENCE~~ SUMMARY

(*Erase heading not required.*) 1st BN THE BORDER REGT.

Instructions regarding War Diaries and Intelligence Summaries are contained in F. S. Regs., Part II. and the Staff Manual respectively. Title Pages will be prepared in manuscript.

Place	Date	Hour	Summary of Events and Information	Remarks and references to Appendices
[illegible]	25-3-17		Bn practising attack, open warfare. LIEUT R G CULLIS rejoined from Staff duties and resumed duties of acting Adjutant 24-3-17	RGC
"	26-3-17	9-4	88 + 87th Bdes attacked a position held by 86th Bde under supervision of G.O.C. Div.	RGC
"	27-3-17	9-4	Bde attacks as a manoeuvre	RGC
"	28-3-17		Interior Economy under Coy Commdrs. 2nd LIEUT L MACHELL joined from Base	RGC
"	29-3-17		Bn moved to VIGNACOURT.	RGC
"	30-3-17		FIEFFS. 2nd LIEUT. H. COWARD joined from Base	RGC
"	31-3-17		Resting.	RGC
			Casualties week ending 31-3-17.–	
			66 other ranks joined from Base 24-3-17	
			16 " " 28-3-17.	RGC
			Sick to Hospital 19	
			From " 8.	

R G Cullis Lieut
A/Adjt 1st Bn The Border Regt

2449 Wt. W14957/M90 750,000 1/16 J.B.C. & A. Forms/C.2118/12.

1

Vol 13

Army Form C. 2118.

Instructions regarding War Diaries and Intelligence Summaries are contained in F. S. Regs., Part II. and the Staff Manual respectively. Title pages will be prepared in manuscript.

WAR DIARY
or
~~INTELLIGENCE SUMMARY.~~
(Erase heading not required.)

1ST BTN. THE BORDER REGT.
APRIL 1917.

Place	Date	Hour	Summary of Events and Information	Remarks and references to Appendices
FIEFFS	1-4-17		Btn marched to BOISBERGUE.	RLb.
BOISBERGUE	2-4-17		Marched to LUCHEUX	RLb.
LUCHEUX.	3-4-17		Training. Wood fighting. Attack on Strong point. Open war-fare.	RLb.
"	4.4.17.		Training as above. All kits cut down to 35lbs. & dumped here.	RLb.
"	5.4.17.		Marched to LIENCOURT.	RLb.
LIENCOURT.	6.4.17		Training in morning. ~~and afterwards marched to GRAND RULLECOURT.~~ RLb	RLb.
~~GRAND RULLECOURT.~~ LIENCOURT.	7.4.17.	*	Training in morning, and afterwards marched to GRAND RULLECOURT. LIEUT. P. NEW, 2LTS. A. CAMPBELL A.J.F. DANIELLI, T.L.P. GAMON + T.N. MORRIS to Corps Depot, ST. POL.	RLb.
GRAND RULLECOURT.	8.4.17		Marched to BAVINCOURT.	RLb.
BAVINCOURT.	9.4.17.		Hail snow rain and wind. Men allowed to stay in huts. Offensive started at ARRAS.	RLb.
"	10.4.17.		As above. Good news, 10,000 prisoners and about 10 guns. 2LT. J WHIGHAM rejoined from T.M.B. LT COL MORRIS D.S.O. sick to F.A.	RLb.
"	11.4.17.		About the same weather. Nothing done except, issued with battle stores. MAJOR A.J. ELLIS, D.S.O. joined from ENGLAND.	RLb.
"	12.4.17.	9.30 a.m.	Marched to DAINVILLE where we had dinner on the roadside. Then on to ARRAS, two hours rest then on to MAISON ROUGE near FEUCHY CHAPEL (leaving 10 per cent. officers + O.Rs. behind) where we relieved 7th NORFOLKS, 9th Bde. Captured country and no accommodation except shell holes. Very muddy + cold. 2 LIEUT. A.H. CRAINE to F.A.	RLb.
		*	Casualties week ending 7th inst. SICK to HOSP. 7. FROM – 3. 66 O.Rs joined from BASE.	RLb

A5834 Wt. W4973/M687 750,000 8/16 D. D. & L. Ltd. Forms/C.2118/13.

Instructions regarding War Diaries and Intelligence Summaries are contained in F. S. Regs., Part II. and the Staff Manual respectively. Title pages will be prepared in manuscript.

2.

WAR DIARY ~~or~~ INTELLIGENCE SUMMARY.

(Erase heading not required.)

Army Form C. 2118.

1st BTN. THE BORDER REGT.

APRIL 1917

Place	Date	Hour	Summary of Events and Information	Remarks and references to Appendices
MAISON ROUGE.	13.4.17		Relieved 7th K.S.L.I. in BROWN LINE. (old BOSCHE TRENCHES) Fairly comfortable Near ORANGE HILL, about 2 miles E. of MONCHY and between latter place and GUEMAPPE.	[illegible]
"BROWN LINE"	14.4.17		Saw where Cavalry had taken it in the neck.	[illegible]
			Our Right about 400 yds S. of main ARRAS-CAMBRAI RD. A/C.S.M. CRONE + A/C.Q.M.S. killed in their dug-out by shell during night. A great loss	[illegible]
		3 p.m.	Ordered to "stand to" + be ready to reinforce 86th BDE or our own firing line 2nd S.W.Bs. Bosche put tremendously heavy barrage on and behind MONCHY and drove the 1st ESSEX and NEWFOUNDLANDS back to the WOOD E. of MONCHY. Barrage stopped about 400 yds from our trenches.	[illegible]
*		6 p.m.	All quiet again. Stood down. Were not wanted.	
		8-4 a.m.	Digging Comm: Trench	
"	15.4.17	8 p.m. to 4 a.m.	Whole Bn. digging Comm: Trench N side of ARRAS-CAMBRAI RD from BROWN LINE to skirting LA FOSSE and LA BERGERE FARMS.	[illegible]
	16.4.17	"	As above.	[illegible]
" *	14-4-17		* Casualties week ending 14th inst KILLED. NIL. WOUNDED. NIL. MISSING. NIL. SICK to F.A. 16. FROM – 1. 40 O.Rs to Corps Depot.	[illegible]
"	17.4.17		To firing line, relieved 2nd S.W.Bs.	[illegible]
"	18.4.17		Improving firing line. One platoon of 'B' Coy under 2Lt G.C.H. COX attempted to take a Bosche strong point about 250 yds from our line. Unsuccessful owing to the fact that it was not known exactly the position and on arrival was found to be held strongly with M.Gs. 2 Lieut Cox wounded + 5 O.Rs.	[illegible] [illegible]

A5834 Wt. W4973 M687 750,000 8/16 D. D. & L. Ltd. Forms/C.2118/13.

Instructions regarding War Diaries and Intelligence Summaries are contained in F. S. Regs., Part II. and the Staff Manual respectively. Title pages will be prepared in manuscript.

3

WAR DIARY
~~or~~
~~INTELLIGENCE SUMMARY.~~
(Erase heading not required.)

Army Form C. 2118.

1st BTN THE BORDER REGT.

APRIL 1917.

Place	Date	Hour	Summary of Events and Information	Remarks and references to Appendices
FIRING LINE ~~ARRA~~	19.4.17.		Relieved by 2nd HANTS, 88th Bde on left, 6/7th R. SCOTS FUS. 45th BDE in centre + 6th CAMERON H. 44th BDE. on right. to ARRAS cellars. 2nd LIEUTS COWARD + LIEUT MILLS wounded in ARRAS by shell. (4 a.m. 20th). Casualties week-ending 19th inst. WOUNDED. 2nd LIEUTS. G.C.A COX (severe) " H.M WOOLF. (slight) " H. COWARD (seriously) LIEUT. C. MILLS. (slight) O.Rs. KILLED 7. WOUNDED 18. Died of WOUNDS 2. MISSING 1. SICK to HOSP. 16. SHELL SHOCK 1. from HOSP. NIL.	Rkb. Rkb. Rkb.
ARRAS	20.4.17		Battalion moved into SCHRAMM BARRACKS as billets. The 10% details moving out to 87 Brigade Details Camp to the WEST of ARRAS. Reorganisation to replace casualties sustained in the previous tour of trench duty was carried out.	[illegible]
ARRAS	21.4.17		The Battalion completed all arrangements for moving out to the attack. Rifle grenadiers were ordered to dispense with their rifle grenades, chiefly the W.N. PITTIN variety as many of these had 'weathered' badly during the few days they had been carried – rods had become bent & the grenades generally unserviceable.	[illegible]
ARRAS	22.4.17		The Battalion was ordered to stand by ready to move out & take up a position in the line preparatory to an assault tomorrow morning.	[illegible]

A5834 Wt. W4973/M687 750,000 8/16 D. D. & L. Ltd. Forms/C.2118/13.

Instructions regarding War Diaries and Intelligence Summaries are contained in F. S. Regs., Part II. and the Staff Manual respectively. Title pages will be prepared in manuscript.

WAR DIARY

or

~~INTELLIGENCE SUMMARY.~~

(*Erase heading not required.*)

Army Form C. 2118.

Place	Date	Hour	Summary of Events and Information	Remarks and references to Appendices
ARRAS	22/4/17	21.00	The 1st Battalion The Border Regiment, under command of Lt Col A.J. ELLIS D.S.O. paraded in ARRAS and marched to a point on the ARRAS - CAMBRAI road 600 yards WEST of FEUCHY CHAPEL cross roads. At this point companies were met by guides & conducted at 10 minute intervals to the crucifix at N.6.b.93 (N.W. entrance to village of MONCHY-LE-PREUX). At this point platoon guides were met and platoons proceeded at 2 minutes intervals to their jumping off place. The jumping off place was the line O.1.d.57 to O.1.b.55, that is, a line about 30 yards WEST of our front line fire trench up to the sunken road.	
			Companies were formed up in the following order D.A.B.C. in practically a continuous line, and Battalion Headquarters was originally established in the shallow trench at O.1.a.3.5.	
	23/4/17	2.30	All companies reported that they were in position.	
			The task of getting the battalion through MONCHY-LE PREUX village & into position was a difficult and dangerous one as the village was being pretty heavily shelled. The whole	

2

Instructions regarding War Diaries and Intelligence Summaries are contained in F. S. Regs., Part II. and the Staff Manual respectively. Title pages will be prepared in manuscript.

WAR DIARY
or
~~INTELLIGENCE~~ SUMMARY.
(*Erase heading not required.*)

Army Form C. 2118.

Place	Date	Hour	Summary of Events and Information	Remarks and references to Appendices
			time and, owing to the relief of other battalions proceeding at the same time MONCHY LE PREUX was very much congested with troops, pack animals, etc, and the arrangements for preserving intervals between companies & platoons consequently broke down. Casualties were, however, small, only one officer (2Lieut V. BLOMFIELD) and about a dozen men being wounded. Meanwhile the Adjutant (Lt. R.G. CULLIS) had been sent to look for a more suitable place	
		03.00	for Battalion Headquarters, and reported about 3AM. that he had discovered a deep hollow in the CHATEAU wood about O.1.b.2.5. where the Regimental Aid Post had already been established, the EAST slope of the hollow affording pretty good cover from direct shell-fire.	
		03.00	Battalion Headquarters were accordingly moved to this place.	
Trenches	23/4/17	04.45	C and D companies moved forward following the South Wales Borderers attack in accordance with orders, and A & B companies occupied the old firing line. In going forward, these companies lost very heavily from our own barrage which was	

T2134. Wt. W703–776. 500000. 4/15. Sir J. C. & S.

3.

Instructions regarding War Diaries and Intelligence Summaries are contained in F. S. Regs., Part II. and the Staff Manual respectively. Title pages will be prepared in manuscript.

WAR DIARY
~~or~~
~~INTELLIGENCE SUMMARY.~~
(*Erase heading not required.*)

Army Form C. 2118.

Place	Date	Hour	Summary of Events and Information	Remarks and references to Appendices
			terribly short. Immediately the attack was launched the enemy put down a barrage on a line just WEST of ARROW-HEAD COPSE and another following the line of the EAST edge of MONCHY LE PREUX village.	
		0630	A report was received from Lt. Col. RAIKES commanding the 2nd South Wales Borderers to the effect that his centre and reserve companies were digging in, and that he could see our men in ARROW HEAD COPSE. Owing to the heavy smoke from the barrage the situation could not be clearly ascertained.	
		0645	A report was received from o/c B company (Capt. J. W. EWBANK M.C.) to the effect that from information obtained from wounded men, orderlies and observers, the South Wales Borderers had ~~gained~~ gained their objective and were making strong points on it, and that our losses from our own and the enemy's barrage reported severe.	

T2134. Wt. W708—776. 500000. 4/15. Sir J. C. & S.

Instructions regarding War Diaries and Intelligence Summaries are contained in F. S. Regs., Part II. and the Staff Manual respectively. Title pages will be prepared in manuscript.

WAR DIARY

~~or~~

~~INTELLIGENCE SUMMARY.~~

(*Erase heading not required.*)

Army Form C. 2118.

Place	Date	Hour	Summary of Events and Information	Remarks and references to Appendices
		07.15	CAPT. EWBANK reported that C and D companies had established themselves in the German front line. S.O.S. flares had been sent up on our left at 06.15 ~~[illegible]~~ and considerable machine gun fire was coming from that flank and he had accordingly pushed out a Lewis gun section to O.1.b.5.4 to protect the left flank.	
		07.35	Lt Col RAIKES reported a gap in his line on his left occupied by Germans from about I.32.c.1.2. to O.2.a.3.9. from which line our men were being rather heavily sniped.	
		07.30	Instructions from 87th Brigade received to place one company at the disposal of Lt. Col. RAIKES in the event of the enemy endeavouring to turn his left flank. An order was consequently sent to CAPT. EWBANK to send a Bombing party to ARROW HEAD COPSE to work up the German trench to the sunken road and to clear it	

5

Instructions regarding War Diaries and Intelligence Summaries are contained in F. S. Regs., Part II. and the Staff Manual respectively. Title pages will be prepared in manuscript.

WAR DIARY ~~or INTELLIGENCE~~ SUMMARY.

(*Erase heading not required.*)

Army Form C. 2118.

Place	Date	Hour	Summary of Events and Information	Remarks and references to Appendices
			of the enemy.	
		08.20	LIEUT:COL. RAIKES reported ~~[illegible]~~ German trench still strongly held from I.32.C.3.0. to I.31. central. with a strong point about I.31.d.4.7. the garrison being estimated at about sixty or seventy, and also that he had sent off his left company to clear up the situation. This information was communicated to 87th Brigade immediately by telephone.	
		09.00	Message from the 87th Brigade was received stating that the 17th Division had been unable to advance and that therefore the South Wales Borderers left flank was in the air. In the event of the second phase taking place the Border Regiment was not to attempt to enter the BOIS DU SART, but to dig in on the WEST SIDE of it.	
		11.20	Report received from B company that the bombing party sent out to ARROW HEAD COPSE under command of 2 LIEUT. F.S. LAYARD. had returned with the following information	

T2131. Wt. W703–776. 500000. 4/15. Sir J. C. & S.

6.

Instructions regarding War Diaries and Intelligence Summaries are contained in F. S. Regs., Part II. and the Staff Manual respectively. Title pages will be prepared in manuscript.

WAR DIARY
or
~~INTELLIGENCE~~ SUMMARY.
(*Erase heading not required.*)

Army Form C. 2118.

Place	Date	Hour	Summary of Events and Information	Remarks and references to Appendices
			The enemy trench from about I.32.C. 4.0. up to the sunken road was non-existent. The patrol, however, made its way over the open up to the sunken road, and there discovered the enemy about eighty strong, entrenched from I.32.C.2.3 to I.31.d.5.8. On discovering this 2LIEUT LAYARD returned to ARROWHEAD COPSE and obtained a Lewis gun which he took up towards the sunken road and got it into a position from which he could enfilade the enemy trench. In this he was successful and inflicted several casualties upon the enemy. His whereabouts by this time were located by the enemy & he came under heavy machine gun fire, suffering four casualties. He thereupon withdrew his party & submitted the above report to his Company Commander.	
		11.25	Message received from 87th Brigade saying "You will not advance for second phase". According to programme	

Instructions regarding War Diaries and Intelligence Summaries are contained in F. S. Regs., Part II. and the Staff Manual respectively. Title pages will be prepared in manuscript.

WAR DIARY
or
INTELLIGENCE SUMMARY.
(Erase heading not required.)

Army Form C. 2118.

Place	Date	Hour	Summary of Events and Information	Remarks and references to Appendices
			companies were due to move at 11.33 to get up under the barrage by Zero + 7 hours and the only means of communication was by runner. Luckily the messenger got through in safety to B company at 11.30 and CAPT EWBANK was able to get the order through to the remaining companies in time to stop them.	
		11.40	Report was received from LIEUT. JOHNSON - O/C D company saying that he was dug in on the right rear of the South Wales Borderers at about O.2.a.7.5 and for a distance of 200 yards SOUTH of this point, with C company prolonging his left in a northerly direction towards the sunken road and with the Kings Own Scottish Borderers and Royal Inniskilling Fusiliers on his right flank. He also reported that 2 LIEUT. R.S. POOLEY (attached from 3rd Royal Scots Fusiliers) had been killed by shell fire about 02.00.	

T2134. Wt. W708–776. 500000. 4/15. Sir J. C. & S.

8.

Instructions regarding War Diaries and Intelligence Summaries are contained in F. S. Regs., Part II. and the Staff Manual respectively. Title pages will be prepared in manuscript.

WAR DIARY
or
~~INTELLIGENCE SUMMARY.~~
(Erase heading not required.)

Army Form C. 2118.

Place	Date	Hour	Summary of Events and Information	Remarks and references to Appendices
			From shortly after zero till about 10.00 the enemy kept his barrage down almost continually on the ARROW HEAD copse line and on the edge of MONCHY LE PREUX though it continually varied in intensity.	
		08.00	About 08.00 it became evident that Battalion Headquarters was taken in enfilade by a battery firing apparently from somewhere in the PELVES valley.	
		09.00	About 09.00 a big shell landed within a few yards of the telephone and did a lot of damage. The Regimental Sergeant-Major, the Scout Sergeant, a Signaller and two Scouts were killed outright. The adjutant (L^t. CULLIS) and several other ranks of the headquarter company wounded.	
		11.30	At about 11.30 another shell pitched bang on top of the funk hole in which the Commanding Officer and other headquarter officers were sitting, completely burying them, and wounding a runner.	

T2134. Wt. W708–776. 500000. 4/15. Sir J. C. & S.

9

Instructions regarding War Diaries and Intelligence Summaries are contained in F. S. Regs., Part II. and the Staff Manual respectively. Title pages will be prepared in manuscript.

WAR DIARY
or
~~INTELLIGENCE SUMMARY.~~
(Erase heading not required.)

Army Form C. 2118.

Place	Date	Hour	Summary of Events and Information	Remarks and references to Appendices
			Headquarters were then moved into a machine gun trench just on the EAST edge of the hollow, and CAPT EWBANK sent for from the firing line to take over the command of the Battalion as the Commanding Officer was temporarily knocked out.	
		12.00 to 20.00	During this period there was no appreciable change in the situation, and the intensity of the enemy's barrage slackened off somewhat.	
		13.00	About 13.00 Headquarters were moved back to the CHATEAU Dugout at O.1.c.7.8 and after dusk to the big dug out at O.1.c.3.8. As the situation on the left flank was by no means satisfactory orders were sent to CAPT EWBANK to move forward at Dusk and establish a defensive flank parallel to the sunken road. This he did with two platoons of his company leaving the remaining platoon in the old front line as reserve.	

T2134. Wt. W708—776. 500000. 4/15. Sir J. C. & S.

10

Instructions regarding War Diaries and Intelligence Summaries are contained in F. S. Regs., Part II. and the Staff Manual respectively. Title pages will be prepared in manuscript.

WAR DIARY

~~or~~

~~INTELLIGENCE~~ SUMMARY.

(*Erase heading not required.*)

Army Form C. 2118.

Place	Date	Hour	Summary of Events and Information	Remarks and references to Appendices
	24/4/17		As soon as this was accomplished CAPT EWBANK submitted a rough report of his disposition & followed it with a detailed report & sketch which was received at Battalion Headquarters about midday. From this report the Commanding Officer was able to put in the position of the various companies in a situation report map and forward it to Brigade Headquarters. A similar map is attached hereto shewing the positions of adjacent regiment.	
Night of 23/24	~~23~~/~~24~~ 24/4/17		An attempt was made to relieve the Regiment this night but as the Commanding Officer of the relieving Battalion only reached Brigade Headquarters at about 03.30. 24.4.17 it was out of the question and was postponed till the following night. The night was fairly quiet and only intermittent shelling went on and there was no change in the situation on the	

11.

Instructions regarding War Diaries and Intelligence Summaries are contained in F. S. Regs., Part II. and the Staff Manual respectively. Title pages will be prepared in manuscript.

WAR DIARY

~~or~~

~~INTELLIGENCE SUMMARY.~~

(*Erase heading not required.*)

Army Form C. 2118.

Place	Date	Hour	Summary of Events and Information	Remarks and references to Appendices
			Battalion front.	
	24/6/17	04.30 to 24.00	Both sides remained very quiet and there was very little shelling indeed and no infantry activity reported. The ground between the firing line and MONCHY LE PREUX was thoroughly well sniped the whole day and the movement of more than a couple men at once drew machine gun fire from the Northern side of the sunken road.	
		19.40	A message was received from the Officer Commanding 9th Northumberland Fusiliers fixing the line held by him as from O.1.b.8.10 across HARNESS LANE about I.31.c.7.5 to I.31.c.3.4. locating the enemy in position from I.32.c.2.3. to I.31.d.4.10.	
		20.00	Orders for relief received from 87th Brigade. A Company in the old firing line to be relieved by the 7th Kings Shropshire Light Infantry and B.C. and D companies by the 8th Kings Own (Royal Lancasters.)	

T2134. Wt. W708—776. 500000. 4/15. Sir J. C. & S.

12

Instructions regarding War Diaries and Intelligence Summaries are contained in F. S. Regs., Part II. and the Staff Manual respectively. Title pages will be prepared in manuscript.

WAR DIARY
or
INTELLIGENCE SUMMARY.
(Erase heading not required.)

Army Form C. 2118.

Place	Date	Hour	Summary of Events and Information	Remarks and references to Appendices
			There was considerable difficulty & delay in carrying out this relief owing to guides being ordered to go first to LES FOSSES FARM and then to H 34 central, at neither of which places were they required.	
	25/4/17.	02.00	The relief of A company was completed by 02:00 and of	
		03.00	B and C companies by 03:00 but owing to operations recommencing on the left flank at 03.30 it was found impossible to carry out the relief of D Company as the enemy at once put down his barrages. Orders were therefore sent to O.C. "D" Company to remain in the trenches till the following night, when the company was duly relieved and rejoined the Battalion at	
	26/4/17	04:00	DUISANS at 04:00 on the 26th inst. The total casualties for the action were 2 officers killed (2LIEUT. G.F. KEMP. and 2LIEUT. R.S. POOLEY.) 4 wounded (CAPT. W.B. WAMSLEY. RAMC. CAPT. B.H. SPEAR-MORGAN. 2LIEUT. V. BLOMFIELD and LIEUT and ADJUTANT. R. G. CULLIS.)	

T2134. Wt. W708–776. 500000. 4/15. Sir J. C. & S.

13

Instructions regarding War Diaries and Intelligence Summaries are contained in F. S. Regs., Part II. and the Staff Manual respectively. Title pages will be prepared in manuscript.

WAR DIARY
or
INTELLIGENCE SUMMARY.
(Erase heading not required.)

Army Form C. 2118.

Place	Date	Hour	Summary of Events and Information	Remarks and references to Appendices
			Other Ranks. Killed. 22. Wounded. 107. Missing 21. Total 150. Throughout the action intercommunication which was carried out almost entirely by runners (telephone to Brigade, although repaired 3 times only lasted about ten minutes each time) was distinctly good. The devotion to duty displayed by the men carrying messages was magnificent, and though casualties amongst them were heavy there was never the slightest delay or hesitation on the part of the survivors to go out again repeatedly with fresh messages.	

T2134. Wt. W708—776. 500000. 4/15. Sir J. C. & S.

Instructions regarding War Diaries and Intelligence Summaries are contained in F. S. Regs., Part II. and the Staff Manual respectively. Title pages will be prepared in manuscript.

WAR DIARY
or
INTELLIGENCE SUMMARY.
(Erase heading not required.)

Army Form C. 2118.

Place	Date	Hour	Summary of Events and Information	Remarks and references to Appendices
ARRAS	25/4/17	3-6AM	A.B.C coys and Battalion Headquarters were relieved, and moved back into ARRAS from the trenches where they had consolidated their positions at the end of their advance of the 23/24th. arriving at hours between 3 & 6 A.M. & were billetted in the SCHRAM BARRACKS. D Coy were unable to be relieved & remained in trenches.	
			Capt. A.W. Sutcliffe. M.C. was appointed acting Adjutant vice Lieut R.G. Cullis (wounded)	[initials]
DUISANS.			The Battalion moved by motor busses to DUISANS, going to No 4 camp. (Nissen huts) arriving about 5.30 P.M. – R.S.M. WINDLER reported late tonight, from England.	[initials]
DUISANS	26.4.17		DUISANS. D company rejoined the Battalion having been relieved the previous night (25/26th) about 11 P.m. arriving ARRAS about 1 AM. & being sent on	
"			immediately by motor busses. – The Battalion paraded about midday	
NOYELLETTE			marched to NOYELLETTE. – into Nissen huts again.	[initials]
"	27.4.17	10.45AM	Paraded at 10.45 AM & marched to SAULTY. Here the men were fairly	
SAULTY			comfortably billetted in barns, many having wire beds but the officers	[initials]

T2134. Wt. W708–776. 500000. 4/15. Sir J. C. & S.

Instructions regarding War Diaries and Intelligence Summaries are contained in F. S. Regs., Part II. and the Staff Manual respectively. Title pages will be prepared in manuscript.

WAR DIARY
or
INTELLIGENCE SUMMARY.
(Erase heading not required.)

Army Form C. 2118.

Place	Date	Hour	Summary of Events and Information	Remarks and references to Appendices
SAILTY	27/4/17		accommodation was nil in most cases, and what was given was disgusting practically the whole village being occupied by British civilian railway workmen & engineers. Labour battalions and other noncombatants. A little coercion however ameliorated the situation slightly.	
	27/4/17		2Lt [illegible] to hospital with sprained ankle (Field ambulance).	
SAILTY	28/4/17		The day was devoted to cleaning up & refitting as far as possible after the recent action.	
"		3PM	The details left behind at ST POL rejoined about 3PM including 2Lt CAMPBELL 2Lt P.NEW. Lt DANIELL. Lt MORRIS 2Lt GAMON and 77 other ranks. 2Lt OXLEY and 2Lt ~~Dunlop~~ DUNLOP reported for duty from England. Casualties week ending 28/4/17 Other Ranks. to Field Ambulance 24. from Field Ambulance 3.	
"	29/4/17	11.30AM	Church parade in the Chateau wood. Royal Inniskilling Fusiliers also being present. The Brigadier & Brigade Major also attended.	
"	30/4/17	8.30–12.45	Training was carried out, specialist classes in bombing, rifle grenadiering, Lewis Gunning, signalling & scouting, while companies did musketry & platoon drill.	
"		2–4PM	The C.O. inspected the kits of the Battalion in the afternoon.	
"		6.30PM	The Medical Officer inspected the feet of the entire battalion.	
"	1/5/17	8.30AM	The Battalion marched to WANQUETIN into billets.	

Instructions regarding War Diaries and Intelligence Summaries are contained in F. S. Regs., Part II. and the Staff Manual respectively. Title pages will be prepared in manuscript.

WAR DIARY
or
INTELLIGENCE SUMMARY.
(Erase heading not required.)

Army Form C. 2118.

Place	Date	Hour	Summary of Events and Information	Remarks and references to Appendices
WANQUETIN.	1.5.17		The battalion devoted the day to completing fighting kit, drawing up extra SAA. bombs etc, & reorganising platoons for action in the near future.	
	2.5.17	5.30PM.	Battalion paraded & marched to ARRAS.	[illegible initials]

T2134. Wt. W708—776. 500000. 4/15. Sir J. C. & S.

SCALE $\frac{1}{10.000}$. MONCHY LE PREUX.

SHEWING FINAL SITUATION OF
1ST BATT. THE BORDER REGT.
2ND " SOUTH WALES BORDERERS.
AFTER THE ACTION OF APRIL 23RD/24TH 1917.

WAR DIARY.
1ST BATT.
THE BORDER REGT.

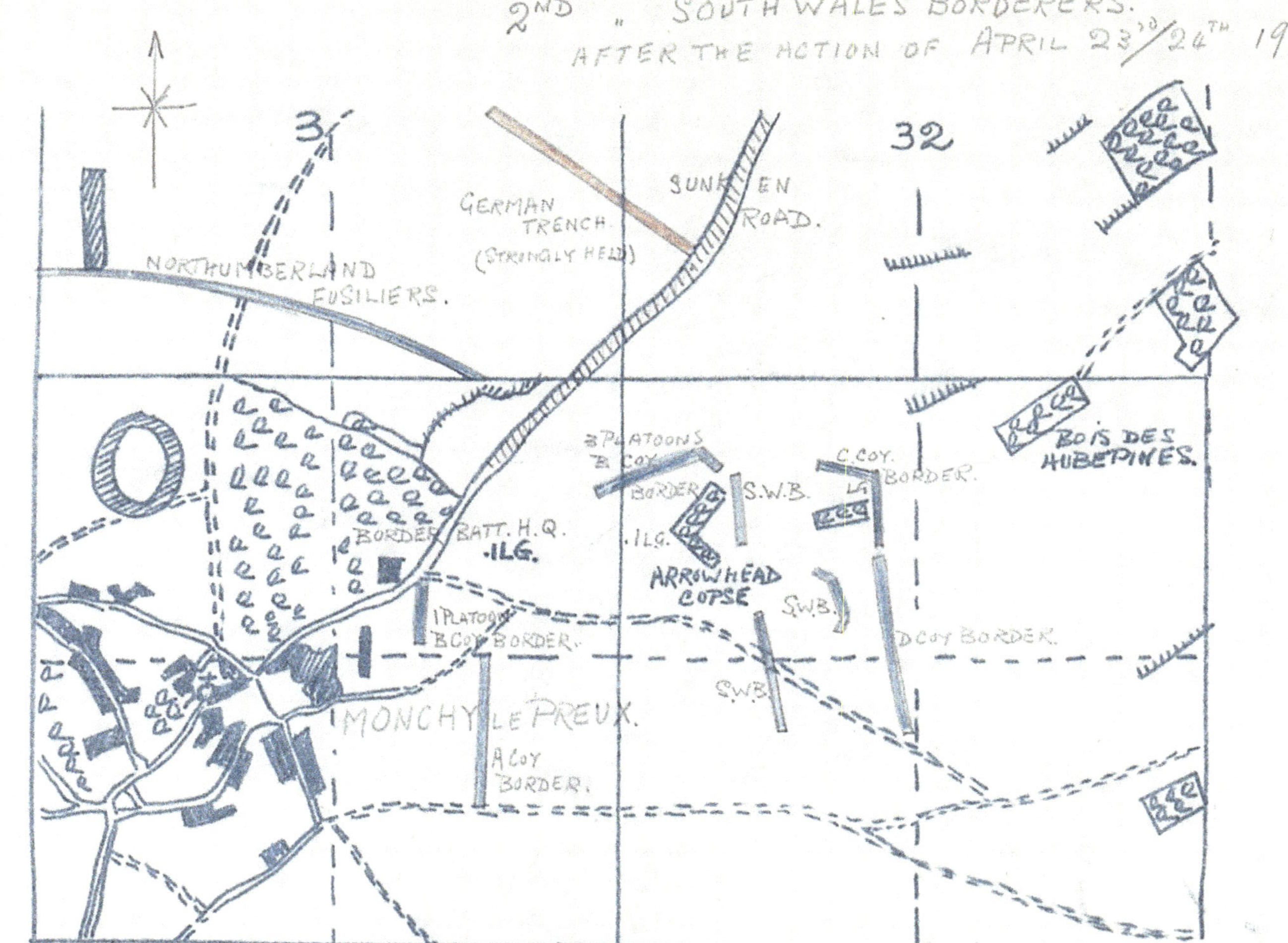

Confidential.

87/29

Vol 14

War Diary

of

1st Battalion The Border Regiment.

From 1st May 1917 To. 31st May 1917

Volume 27.

26. K.
22 sheets

Instructions regarding War Diaries and Intelligence Summaries are contained in F. S. Regs., Part II. and the Staff Manual respectively. Title pages will be prepared in manuscript.

WAR DIARY
or
~~INTELLIGENCE SUMMARY.~~
(Erase heading not required.)

MAY. 1

1st Batt. The Gordon Regt.

Army Form C. 2118.

Place	Date	Hour	Summary of Events and Information	Remarks and references to Appendices
LANQUETIN	1.5.17		Completing kit & drawing up battle stores.	[illegible]
ARRAS	2/5/17	5 PM	Battalion paraded & marched to ARRAS into comfortable billets.	[illegible]
ARRAS	3/5/17	6 AM	Stunt today by 1st 3rd & 5th Armies. VI Corps in the central area - i.e.	
TRENCHES			MONCHY LE PREUX - commenced at 3.45 AM. Heavy barrage. 29th Div. were in G.H.Q. reserve. 87th Brigade moving up at 9.45 AM (i.e. leaving ARRAS at this time) moving into the old Boche support line opposite TILLOY on the N. side of the road, on OBSERVATION Hill - sat down & waited for orders, gleaned little news, saw small parties (25?) of Huns coming down as prisoners, very comfy. Beautiful day & everybody happy. Spent night in Boche dugouts.	[illegible]
TRENCHES.	4/5/17		Moved back to ARRAS to billets about noon today. Draft of 1 officer 2/Lieut T. S. MIDDLETON & 5 other ranks joined the battalion having joined the 10% 3/5/17 from base via ~~St Pol~~ St Pol.	[illegible]
ARRAS	5/5/17		~~Arrangements made for cleaning up today~~ Cleaning up today, warned to be ready to go back to line if required.	[illegible]
	6/5/17		Arrangements made for training - but cancelled & whole day devoted to cleaning all billets streets etc. which were filthy.	[illegible]

T2134. Wt. W708-776. 500000. 4/15. Sir J. C. & S.

Instructions regarding War Diaries and Intelligence Summaries are contained in F. S. Regs., Part II. and the Staff Manual respectively. Title pages will be prepared in manuscript.

WAR DIARY
or
INTELLIGENCE SUMMARY.
(*Erase heading not required.*)

MAY 2

1st Bn The Border Regt

Army Form C. 2118.

Place	Date	Hour	Summary of Events and Information	Remarks and references to Appendices
ARRAS.	7/5/17	10.15 PM	Moved from ARRAS to DUISANS into B camp in Nissen huts. LIEUT. D. ELLIOT joined with draft of 23 other ranks joined today.	
DUISANS		1 PM	from St POL. Congratulatory message from G.O.C. 29th Div. for excellent work of 23/4/17.	
	8/5/17		Training was hampered by wet weather but specialists did training & huts & companies held inspections. Battalion parade 3 PM. – Bathing in DUISANS.	
"	9/5/17	9 AM	2/Lieut R.E.S. JOHNSON proceeded to general course at XVIII Corps school at AUXI LE CHATEAU this morning. Battalion training – all specialists under specialist officers remainder did physical training, musketry, bayonet fighting.	
"	10/5/17		Lieut Col A J Ellis DSO commanding, Lieut Cargill, Capt H Bunbury MC and Lieut D McCleod MC went to BEAUMONT HAMEL to see the positions ~~captured~~ attacked on 1st July 1916. LIEUT HALL R.A. RAMC joined the battalion for duty as M.O.	
"	10/5/17		Training during morning. Hockey match in the afternoon BORDER & INNISKILLEN Officers v. M.G. and RAMC.	
	11/5/17		Training today.	

T2134. Wt. W708–776. 500000. 4/15. Sir J. C. & S.

Instructions regarding War Diaries and Intelligence Summaries are contained in F. S. Regs., Part II. and the Staff Manual respectively. Title pages will be prepared in manuscript.

May 3

WAR DIARY
or
~~INTELLIGENCE SUMMARY.~~ 1st Battalion The Border Regt.

(*Erase heading not required.*)

France

Army Form C. 2118.

Place	Date	Hour	Summary of Events and Information	Remarks and references to Appendices
[illegible]	12/5/17		Brigade sports today under ideal weather conditions, Lieut Gen Haldane commanding VI Corps, Major General Sir Beauvoir De Lisle commanding 29th Division & Brig Gen Lucas, 87th Brigade being present. The guard mounting parade competition being easily won by the Border Regiment.	[initials]
~~ARRAS~~	~~13/5/17~~	~~4.30pm~~	~~moved to ARRAS today arriving at 6PM & going into billets. Preliminary preparations for attack being made.~~	
			Weekly strength variation. Offrs. Other Ranks	
			Draft from St Pol. 2 11	
			Evacuated sick 7	
[illegible]	13/5/17	[illegible]	Preparing to move. Moved off at 4.30 for ARRAS arriving 6PM & going into billets. Preliminary arrangements for an attack were made.	[initials]
[illegible]	14/5/17		Quiet restful day, moved off at 10PM & moved into the BROWN LINE near FEUCHY cross Roads (part of the German line captured on April 9th & part of the [illegible] Switch) relieving the 1st Suffolk Regiment getting into position about 3.30AM.	
[illegible]	15/5/17		Spent the day improving the trenches & making latrines which were non-existent	[initials]

2353 Wt. W2541/1454 700,000 5/15 D. D. & L. A.D.S.S./Forms/C. 2118.

May 4

Instructions regarding War Diaries and Intelligence Summaries are contained in F. S. Regs., Part II. and the Staff Manual respectively. Title Pages will be prepared in manuscript.

WAR DIARY
~~or~~
~~INTELLIGENCE SUMMARY~~
(Erase heading not required.)

1st Bn The Border Regt.
France.

Army Form C. 2118

Place	Date	Hour	Summary of Events and Information	Remarks and references to Appendices
Trenches	15-16/5/17		A patrol of 1 offr. LIEUT CRANE & 6 other ranks went up the line, attached to the 1st K.O.S.B. tonight to patrol DEVILS TRENCH, which will be one of our objectives in a few days, returning early the following morning with good information.	
TRENCHES.	16/5/17	8 P.M.	The trenches were fairly heavily shelled about 4 P.M. resulting in 7 casualties (wounded). Two platoons of A coy & two of B coy moved into strong points (N & S. of MONCHY LE PREUX) D.E. F & G. The remainder of the battalion remained in the BROWN LINE.	
TRENCHES. at MONCHY LE PREUX.	17/5/17	9.30-2.30 AM	The Battalion relieved the 1st K.O.S.B. in front line & Support from BIT LANE (the MONCHY – PELVES road) to TWIN COPSES inclusive, order N to South. D coy S.W.B. (attached) – B coy BORDER. C coy BORDER in SNAFFLE TRENCH A coy BORDER TWIN TRENCH. D coy BORDER in support in SHRAPNEL TRENCH. Battalion Headquarters were in the red house ("THE GOLF HOUSE") MONCHY LE PREUX. The battalion just got in as dawn was breaking. about 3.30 AM.	
TRENCHES	18/5/17		Preparations were made tonight, digging an assembly trench for A coy. through twin copse behind the front line, which latter was to be evacuated prior to the barrage falling. Jumping off steps were cut in the rest of the line & generally all final preparations made. D Coy established a battalion dump just behind the firing line at the junction of ARROW TRENCH and the front line	

Arthur W. Sutcliffe Capt. a/Adjutant.

1875 Wt. W593/826 1,000,000 4/15 J.B.C. & A. A.D.S.S./Forms/C. 2118.

Instructions regarding War Diaries and Intelligence Summaries are contained in F. S. Regs., Part II. and the Staff Manual respectively. Title pages will be prepared in manuscript.

WAR DIARY May 5 1st Bn The Border Regt.

or

~~INTELLIGENCE SUMMARY.~~

(Erase heading not required.)

The Second Battle of MONCHY LE PREUX. May 19/20. 1917.

Army Form C. 2118.

1

Place	Date	Hour	Summary of Events and Information	Remarks and references to Appendices
Trenches.	19/5/17.		The conditions under which the 1st Battalion The Border Regiment were called upon to go into action EAST of MONCHY LE PREUX in the evening of May 19/ 1917 were briefly these. After the 29th Division had fought itself to a standstill on the night of April 23rd the date of the first Battle of MONCHY. The remnants of the 87th Brigade dug in where they finally stopped advancing. From these positions they had been relieved, & this line more or less consolidated. These positions were however, distinctly bad from the point of view of observation. The enemy's in front were very good, it was patent that by means of a short advance, if these positions could be wrested from the enemy, the position would be greatly improved.	
			The British line from which the assault was to take place is shown in the attached sketch map. It will be seen that it presented no systematic or organised trench system for either defensive or offensive action, it was merely extensions of the digging in of the advanced troops where they were finally held up on 23/4/17. The front line was disjointed, there being no connection at all	

A5834 Wt. W4973/M687 750,000 8/16 D. D. & L. Ltd. Forms/C.2118/13.

Sheet VI.

Instructions regarding War Diaries and Intelligence Summaries are contained in F. S. Regs., Part II. and the Staff Manual respectively. Title pages will be prepared in manuscript.

May 6

WAR DIARY
or
~~INTELLIGENCE SUMMARY.~~
(Erase heading not required.)

1st Batt. The Border Regt.

Army Form C. 2118.

Place	Date	Hour	Summary of Events and Information	Remarks and references to Appendices
			EYW.	
			from North to South across the line running between the two TWIN COPSES. Also, the trenches being cut chiefly through clay or clay and chalk at all points where they passed through depressions they were wet and muddy, while in many parts they were shallow, in others deep and very narrow so that passage was difficult. Also there was no communication through to the front line by day, under cover, to SNAFFLE & TWIN TRENCHES. The nearest point to SNAFFLE accessible by day was where CHAIN trench cuts BIT LANE. from here it was a case of duck & run. and to reach this point from MONCHY village meant going via ORANGE TRENCH GRAPE TRENCH, RIFLE TRENCH, CHAIN TRENCH, to BIT. LANE. while to get to D company's line the route was via VINE LANE. Battalion headquarters had to be established at "THE RED HOUSE" (or THE GOLF HOUSE) MONCHY as there was no other possible place for it there being no dug outs of any sort in the trenches for officers or men.	
			The objectives of the 87th Brigade were in conjunction with an attack on their right, to attack on the evening of 19/20th May and capture (1). INFANTRY HILL.	
			(2). THE BOIS ~~du SART~~ des AUBEPINES	
			and establish a line of strong points running along a line DEVILS TRENCH. E edge of CIGAR COPSE & BOIS DES AUBEPINES. MAY TRENCH LONG TRENCH, TOOL TRENCH.	

A5834 Wt. W4973/M687 750,000 8/16 D. D. & L. Ltd. Forms/C.2118/13.

Sheet 3

2nd Battle of MONCHY LE PREUX. May 1917

Instructions regarding War Diaries and Intelligence Summaries are contained in F. S. Regs., Part II. and the Staff Manual respectively. Title pages will be prepared in manuscript.

WAR DIARY
or
INTELLIGENCE SUMMARY.

(Erase heading not required.)

1st Batt The Border Regt.

Army Form C. 2118.

Place	Date	Hour	Summary of Events and Information	Remarks and references to Appendices
EAST of MONCHY LE PREUX.	May 19/20 1917.		6 Platoons R. Inniskillings, 8 platoons 1 Border Regt & 1 Coy 2/SWB ~~the 87th Infantry Brigade~~ were given objectives between HOOK TRENCH and BIT LANE and the 1st Battalion The Border Regiment (under command of LIEUT COLONEL A. J. ELLIS D.S.O.) was allotted the line MAY TRENCH NORTH to 150x north of BIT LANE, in DEVILS TRENCH. No attack would take place on the Regiment's left flank. Consequently objectives were allotted as follows. A Company under command of CAPT. H. BUNTING M.C. would attack & capture the positions infront, push through, and establish (1) a platoon strong point about the enemy positions in map square O.2.b.6.5. This platoon was under the command of LIEUT. P. NEW. (2) a 2 platoon strong point in the EAST side of the BOIS des AUBEPINES. These two platoons were under the command of 2/LT. ARMSTRONG L.W. and 2LT. W.E.S. DIXLOP. B Company under the command of 2/LIEUT F.S. LAYARD M.C. were to capture the enemy positions infront and establish strong points. (1). a platoon strongpoint in the vicinity of the EASTERN edge of the CIGAR COPSE. This platoon was under the command of 2/LIEUT. L.S. MIDDLETON. (2) a platoon strong point near the SOUTHERN end of DEVILS TRENCH.	9

A5834 Wt. W4973/M687 750,000 8/16 D. D. & L. Ltd. Forms/C.2118/13.

Sheet 4

Instructions regarding War Diaries and Intelligence Summaries are contained in F. S. Regs., Part II. and the Staff Manual respectively. Title pages will be prepared in manuscript.

May 8

WAR DIARY or INTELLIGENCE SUMMARY.

(Erase heading not required.)

1st The Border Regt

2nd Battle of MONCHY

Army Form C. 2118.

Place	Date	Hour	Summary of Events and Information	Remarks and references to Appendices
			C company, under the command of LIEUT. T.E. THORBURN BROWN. (K.O.S.B. attached BORDER) less one platoon were to extend to their left on the assault taking place to occupy the line vacated by B Coy. and "D" Coy under command of ~~Capt.~~ CAPT. H. PALMER. were to advance over the open from SHRAPNEL TRENCH into the line vacated by A Company.	
			One platoon of C company was lent to "A" company as a carrying party. This platoon was under the command of 2Lt. B. CAMPBELL. A party of 10 REs of the 2nd West Riding Field Company R.E. under 2Lt BALL were also attached as wiring party to A company.	
			D Company South Wales Borderers were attached under command of CAPT DAVIES. and were set objectives in DEVILS TRENCH, with orders to dig strong points ~~on either side of B.I.T. LANE~~ in this trench about 50x N & S respectively of B.I.T. LANE.	
			It will be seen that "A" company was allotted ~~[illegible]~~ the most difficult task and that the most minute details had to be considered with regard to THE BOIS des AUBEPINES. which was known to be strong. As the front edge of the wood was only about 50x from our front line trench running round the N.E. corner of TWIN COPSE, and this front edge was discovered by patrols, to be fortified a new jumping off trench was required for A Coy. behind the original	

A5834 Wt. W4973/M687 750,000 8/16 D. D. & L. Ltd. Forms/C.2118/13.

Sheet 5.

Instructions regarding War Diaries and Intelligence Summaries are contained in F. S. Regs., Part II. and the Staff Manual respectively. Title pages will be prepared in manuscript.

Day 9

WAR DIARY
or
INTELLIGENCE SUMMARY.
(Erase heading not required.)

2nd Battle of MONCHY.

1st Bn The Border Regt. France.

Army Form C. 2118.

Place	Date	Hour	Summary of Events and Information	Remarks and references to Appendices
MONCHY-LE-PREUX. 19/20 May 1917			front line so as to allow a safety margin for our barrage & artillery fire. This trench was therefore dug about 60x inside the copse from the E. edge. also the short piece of open ground between CHAIN TRENCH and SNAFFLE TRENCH was to be dug through by a communication trench giving a makeshift communication which was as much as could be hoped for in the limited time. This latter was dug through on the night of the 17th/18th by the S.W.B. but the assembly trench through TWIN COPSE was found on taking over the line on the 17th to be very "scratchy" so that A company & 3 platoons of C Coy. had to dig all night on the 18/19th to make it tenable by day during the preliminary bombardment. The relief of the K.O.S.B. on the night 17/18 was only just completed by dawn so that no patrolling or work could be done that night but on the night of 18/19th in addition to work already noted, the Coy. established a battalion dump at the junction of ARROW TRENCH and the front line containing 80 coils barbed concertina wire, 10 boxes SAA, 10 boxes mills (No 5) hand grenades, screw pickets etc. The whole front was also patrolled & positions of the enemy generally reconnoitred, resulting in this being found to be fairly strongly held with numerous machine guns but not wired with the exception of ~~RIT LANE~~ DEVILS TRENCH where it cuts RIT LANE	

A5834 Wt. W4973/M687 750,000 8/16 D. D. & L. Ltd. Forms/C.2118/13.

Sheet 6.

Instructions regarding War Diaries and Intelligence Summaries are contained in F. S. Regs., Part II. and the Staff Manual respectively. Title pages will be prepared in manuscript.

May 19 **WAR DIARY** ~~or~~ ~~INTELLIGENCE SUMMARY.~~

(Erase heading not required.)

1st The Border Regt

2nd Battle of Monchy

Army Form C. 2118.

Place	Date	Hour	Summary of Events and Information	Remarks and references to Appendices
MONCHY LE PREUX	2nd 18/19 May 1917		here the S.W.B. found wire running Northwards, and reported it with a request that it should be specially treated before the advance. This was accordingly reported to Brigade H.Q. Afternoon both on the 18th and 19th parties of the enemy had been seen going into CIGAR COPSE and the BOIS des AUBEPINES from shell holes between these two woods. This was also reported and as a result of these two pieces of information the Commanding Officer sent the Adjutant (CAPT. A.W. SUTCLIFFE. M.C.) to Brigade Headquarters with a special message to request that the Barrage might be arranged to deal with these two matters, and this was arranged. During the night 18/19th barbed wire, no knife rests had been placed in front of our lines, with gaps through which the attacking troops could pass, and these were to be picked up by the wiring wave & carrying parties carried across to the objectives & arranged in front of the positions being consolidated, concertina barbed wire being put out between the knife rests completing the wiring. Jumping off steps were also [illegible].	
			At dawn of the 19th May then, saw all the preparations, so far as the infantry were concerned, completed, men in position & all required stores to hand. The day was perfect: a clear bright cloudless sky, hot and dry with scarcely a breath of wind, & so it continued throughout the day and night. The assault was not to take place till 9 P.m. so final orders etc were issued.	

A5834 Wt. W4973/M687 750,000 8/16 D. D. & L. Ltd. Forms/C.2118/13.

Sheet 4

Instructions regarding War Diaries and Intelligence Summaries are contained in F. S. Regs., Part II. and the Staff Manual respectively. Title pages will be prepared in manuscript.

May 11

WAR DIARY
or
INTELLIGENCE SUMMARY.
(Erase heading not required.)

1st Battn The Border Regt.
France.

2nd Battle of MONCHY

Army Form C. 2118.

Place	Date	Hour	Summary of Events and Information	Remarks and references to Appendices
MONCHY LE PREUX			Operation Orders were issued as follows Operation Orders by Lieut Col. A. J. Ellis D.S.O. Cmdg 1st The Border Regt. May 19th 1917. 1. The operations already outlined will take place on the 19th inst. 2. The hour of Zero will be 9 P.M. 3. Artillery barrage will be in accordance with artillery barrage programme map already issued. Two trench mortars from O.2.b.0.0. will go forward when the barrage has ceased to the strongpoint in the N.E. corner of BOIS des AUBEPINES. 4. At Zero, if the wind is favourable gas will be discharged into the BOIS du VERT and another gas[?] north of it in O.3.C. If gas is to be released the code word FOLKESTONE will be sent. If not, code word BOULOGNE will be sent. 5. A contact aeroplane will be up shortly after dawn on the 20th inst. Advanced troops will light GREEN flares when the plane calls for them by CLAXTON HORN or by firing white lights. 6. If for any reason the barrage does not fall, the attack will not take place, but unless something very unforeseen does take place the barrage will fall. 7. O/C A & B Companies RASHER (code name for 1st Border Regt) will communicate these orders to the platoons of C Company that are working with them. (Signed) A. W. Sutcliffe Capt. a/Adjutant.	

A5834 Wt. W4973/M687 750,000 8/16 D. D. & L. Ltd. Forms/C.2118/13.

Sheet 8

Instructions regarding War Diaries and Intelligence Summaries are contained in F. S. Regs., Part II. and the Staff Manual respectively. Title pages will be prepared in manuscript.

May 17

WAR DIARY
or
INTELLIGENCE SUMMARY.
(Erase heading not required.)

2nd Battle of Monchy

1st Battn The Border Regt.

Army Form C. 2118.

Place	Date	Hour	Summary of Events and Information	Remarks and references to Appendices
Field MONCHY LE PREUX	19/20 May 1917		Arrangement for Barrage had been made as follows. An intense barrage would fall along the enemy's front line at zero. This was the signal for the assaulting troops to get out of their trenches & close up to the barrage. At zero plus 5 this barrage would lift to the second line, i.e. final objectives in the case of heavy guns, while a drifting barrage would creep at the rate of 100x in 2 minutes back to the final objectives, then heavy & shrapnel barrages would lift to a new S.O.S. line running across all suspected points of danger at a safe distance from our final objectives. As a result of the patrol report from Capt. Davies commanding the attached company of S.W.B. to the effect that there was wire in front of DEVILS TRENCH N. of BIT LANE special request was made by the C.O. that this should be blown to bits before the attack. For this purpose, and also for registration there was intermittent fire from 18 pounders, of shrapnel & H.E. during the morning of the 19th. ~~[illegible]~~ At 11.45 am a message was received from CAPT BUNTING O/C A company that one or possibly two 18 pounders were firing short & on enfilade of Twin Trench at O.2.a.7.4 0.2.a.8.7. He enclosed a fragment of shell marked 18.	

A5834 Wt. W4973 M687 750,000 8/16 D. D. & L. Ltd. Forms/C.2118/13.

Sheet 9

Instructions regarding War Diaries and Intelligence Summaries are contained in F. S. Regs., Part II. and the Staff Manual respectively. Title pages will be prepared in manuscript.

May B

WAR DIARY
~~or~~
~~INTELLIGENCE SUMMARY.~~
(Erase heading not required.)

1st Bn The Border Regt

2nd Battle of MONCHY

Army Form C. 2118.

Place	Date	Hour	Summary of Events and Information	Remarks and references to Appendices
MONCHY LE PREUX	19/5/17	11.47	a message was immediately sent to Brigade reporting this & sending on fragment of shell. A code message was also sent over the phone.	
		13.47	At 13.47 Capt Davies o/c D Coy 1st B. reported the wire in front of DEVILS trench still uncut and that the nearest rounds had been about 70x short, & suggesting that he should alter his plan of attack by bringing up on his left & attacking with his left on BIT LANE & then on taking DEVILS TRENCH bomb up the requisite distance to establish his post. This was ordered, in the event of the wire not being cut by further efforts, to do this.	
		14.45	Capt L MACHELL was sent up to the front line as Battalion Liaison officer with the telephone there and at 15.10 he reported that as	
		15.10	a result of the short shooting of our 18 pdrs. we had had several casualties in A Coy. 3 in C Coy & one R.E. including 2 stretcher cases. Major DOLPHIN o/c 26th Battery R.F.A. who was doing F.O.O. in SHAFFLE TRENCH at the time corroborated this. This again was communicated by code over telephone to Brigade.	
			From this hour till several hours later nothing of marked importance occurred. The utmost concern was felt for the troops suffering from the erratic shooting of our artillery, & every effort was made to stop it, but as no F.O.O. or Liaison officer was present little or nothing could be done ~~strictly~~ beyond reporting each occurrence immediately to Bde HQrs.	

A5834 Wt. W4973/M687 750,000 8/16 D. D. & L. Ltd. Forms/C.2118/13.

Sheet 10

Instructions regarding War Diaries and Intelligence Summaries are contained in F. S. Regs., Part II. and the Staff Manual respectively. Title pages will be prepared in manuscript.

May '17

WAR DIARY
or
~~INTELLIGENCE SUMMARY.~~

(Erase heading not required.)

2nd Battle of MONCHY.

1st Batt. The Border Regt.

Army Form C. 2118.

Place	Date	Hour	Summary of Events and Information	Remarks and references to Appendices
MONCHY LE PREUX.	19/5/17.	20.55	The climax came at ~~8.55~~ 20.55 when a messenger arrived from the front line with two messages one in code & one in clear from O.C. A Coy. stating that at about 8 PM. (20.00) a battery of heavies or howitzers had opened fire, & the shells had all fallen short mainly into the new assembly trench dug in rear of our front line & in which our troops were massed for the assault. - through TWIN COPSE. As only 5 minutes remained to zero, the Commanding Officer spoke to the Brigade major in clear as follows. "Heavy battery is firing 100x short of W. edge of BOIS DES AUBEPINES AAA Why not lengthen at once."	
		21.00	This message had scarcely been sent, when the barrage, punctual to a second fell, and then gave the signal for the attack to commence. Naturally nothing was known for some time. Fire of all kinds was heard. Maxim gun, Lewis gun & German machine gun could be heard.	
		21.30	The Brigade major informed the Commanding Officer by phone that a yellow rocket had been sent up by the enemy. (a S.O.S. signal for barrage) apparently in the vicinity of BOIS DES AUBEPINES.	
		22.5	Pte Cook, an orderly who had been sent up to S.W.B. (D Coy.) arrived back at headquarters & stated that he had arrived at the front line just in time to see the attack start & the men go over. They went over splendidly officers leading & the rear parties picked up the wire trestles & carried them forward.	[initials]

A5834 Wt. W4973/M687 750,000 8/16 D. D. & L. Ltd. Forms/C.2118/13.

Army Form C. 2118.

Sheet 11.

Instructions regarding War Diaries and Intelligence Summaries are contained in F. S. Regs., Part II. and the Staff Manual respectively. Title pages will be prepared in manuscript.

May 15

WAR DIARY ~~or~~ INTELLIGENCE SUMMARY. 1st Battn The Border Regt

2nd Battle of MONCHY.

(Erase heading not required.)

Place	Date	Hour	Summary of Events and Information	Remarks and references to Appendices
MONCHY LE PREUX.	19/5/17	22.30	The Brigade major reported that he had had a report passed from the gunners that our attack was held up between CIGAR COPSE & the BOIS DES AUBEPINES — the very spot that the C.O. had requested should be particularly treated by the barrage, & the barrage altered to accomplish this.	
		23.12	The G.O.C. Brigade telephoned for any news we had. None was to hand however. The C.O. therefore decided to send the Adjutant - CAPT. A.W. SUTCLIFFE M.C. round the front of the battle to ascertain the situation & report. He accordingly moved off with two orderlies at 23.18.	
	20/5/17	00.15	Capt H. BUNTING M.C. reported at Battalion Headquarters, wounded in the eye by a bomb. He reported that our attack was completely spoiled by our barrage. It absolutely failed to do any damage to the hostile defences, knock out machine guns, or keep the enemy's heads down & by shelling our own men, disorganised the attack. The companies had however led on & reached close to their objectives when in A company's case they were met by a line of enemy bombers who rained bombs on them. Capt BUNTING therefore started to organise flanking attacks when he was hit by an enemy bomb cutting his eye which temporarily blinded him. Just before he was hit, however, he saw LIEUT E.B. DUNLOP standing up close to the enemy trench with a rifle picking off the enemy who were throwing the bombs, [illegible]	

A5834 Wt. W4973/M687 750,000 8/16 D. D. & L. Ltd. Forms/C.2118/13.

Sheet 12

May 16

Instructions regarding War Diaries and Intelligence Summaries are contained in F. S. Regs., Part II. and the Staff Manual respectively. Title pages will be prepared in manuscript.

WAR DIARY
or
INTELLIGENCE SUMMARY.
(Erase heading not required.)

Army Form C. 2118.

1st Bn The Border Regt.

2nd Battle of Monchy

Place	Date	Hour	Summary of Events and Information	Remarks and references to Appendices
MONCHY LE PREUX.	20/5/17		~~doing~~ Whilst doing so this gallant officer was killed. The R.E. officer Lt BALL had been killed by our barrage before he left our front line. CAPT DAVIES Capt H.PALMER 2Lt DURHAM were also known to be casualties. Lt DANIELLI reported that he was carrying on as O/C D Company. – his company being in position & in touch with C coy on left but no touch with right front or rear.	
		1.30	As the general situation by this time clearly indicated that the attack had not succeeded the Commanding Officer sent a message to the senior officer in the firing line Lt T.E THORBURN BROWN, who, tho' wounded in the early ~~afternoon~~ morning of the 19th was still carrying on as O/C C company, to make every effort before dawn to get everyone back to our original front line & reorganise for defence in case of a counter attack.	
			Reports came in to the effect that B company's attack had also been held up. 2Lt MIDDLETON killed 2Lt CRAINE wounded, & 2Lt LAYARD M.C. O/c company wounded & missing, also the S.W.B. attack had failed Capt Davies being wounded & missing.	
		3.10	Capt A.W SUTCLIFFE M.C. returned from front line & amplified his message of 00.50 AM stating A Company had been held up at the edge of BOIS DU AUBEPINES by strong bombing party in the	

A5834 Wt. W4973/M687 750,000 8/16 D. D. & L. Ltd. Forms/C.2118/13.

Sub B.

Instructions regarding War Diaries and Intelligence Summaries are contained in F. S. Regs., Part II. and the Staff Manual respectively. Title pages will be prepared in manuscript.

May 17

WAR DIARY
-or-
INTELLIGENCE SUMMARY.
(Erase heading not required.)

1st Bn The Border Regt

2nd Battle of MONCHY.

Army Form C. 2118.

Place	Date	Hour	Summary of Events and Information	Remarks and references to Appendices
MONCHY LE PREUX	23/4/17		strong point there. CAPT BUNTING M.C. wounded no news of Lt. ARMSTRONG. B Coy's attack had failed, having met with very heavy machine gun fire from between CIGAR COPSE and BOIS DES AUBEPINES. Lt LAYARD had been wounded & was missing. 2Lt MIDDLETON killed. 2Lt CRAINE wounded. 2Lt RAE was safe, & had rallied all available men to the original front line & was reorganising. With regard to the right of A Company very little was known. Lt [illegible] was known to be killed, most of his men casualties. Lt PIVEN [illegible] leading on his platoon but as they too came under very [illegible] machine gun fire it was feared that he too had been killed & most of his platoon become casualties. Company had intended to fill up the vacated line as far as possible [illegible] platoon supporting the advance of A Coy. has been badly cut up. D Company. CAPT H. PALMER had been wounded, also Lieut DURHAM. They had been under heavy fire while in trenches & came under a [illegible] in moving over the open to occupy the vacated front line. [illegible] DANELLI was in charge of the company what was left of it, in front line & reorganising for defence. The whole line was being put [illegible] defence, Vickers guns put in the line where weakly held. [illegible] Company [illegible] had lost CAPT DAVIES, wounded & missing	

A5834 Wt. W4973/M687 750,000 8/16 D. D. & L. Ltd Forms/C.2118/13.

Sheet 14

Instructions regarding War Diaries and Intelligence Summaries are contained in F. S. Regs., Part II. and the Staff Manual respectively. Title pages will be prepared in manuscript.

May 18

WAR DIARY
or
INTELLIGENCE SUMMARY.

(Erase heading not required.)

1st Bn The Border Regt.

Army Form C. 2118.

2nd Battle of MONCHY

Place	Date	Hour	Summary of Events and Information	Remarks and references to Appendices
MONCHY	20/5/17.		having come under very heavy machine gun fire from DEVILS TRENCH and THE CART. on BIT LANE. The attack had been broken up & a few men had gained ARROW TRENCH and were holding out, but a general retirement to our original line was ordered. The line which the SWB had vacated had been occupied by another company of SWB. but these had not got touch with either flank and on receiving the line, they were ordered to shake out about 50x to their right to gain touch with C Coy. BORDERS. & also to their left. Thus by about 4 AM the line was established as strongly as the number of troops would allow, and with two Vickers guns in the front line.	
			Patrols worked from the time the retirement to our original line was ordered & stretcher bearers worked unceasingly to clear casualties, with the result that by dawn the majority of our wounded were brought back to our line, & throughout the day the evacuation of stretcher cases though necessarily slow, was continued. It was reported that at dawn the enemy were seen taking in our wounded who had fallen near their line.	
			Owing to the heavy casualties arrangements were made during the day for us to be relieved	

A5834 Wt. W4973/M687 750,000 8/16 D. D. & L. Ltd. Forms/C.2118/13.

Sheet 15.

Instructions regarding War Diaries and Intelligence Summaries are contained in F. S. Regs., Part II. and the Staff Manual respectively. Title pages will be prepared in manuscript. 2nd Battle of MONCHY LE PREUX

May 19

WAR DIARY
or
~~INTELLIGENCE SUMMARY.~~ 1st Bn The Border Regt.
(Erase heading not required.)

Army Form C. 2118.

Place	Date	Hour	Summary of Events and Information	Remarks and references to Appendices
MONCHY LE PREUX.	30/5/17		by the Lancashire Fusiliers. These troops arrived about 11 P.M. & relief was reported complete by 3.15 AM. – The Battalion moving back to ARRAS to billets. The determined and unconquerable spirit of the Battalion was exemplified in the behaviour of CAPT. H. BUNTING. M.C. and LIEUT. T. E. THORBURN BROWN both of whom were wounded, but refused to leave the regiment, tho' their wounds were such that they might reasonably have done so. Casualties eventually proved to be as under:–	

Officers.

KILLED.	WOUNDED.	WOUNDED & MISSING.
2Lt. E. B. DUNLOP.	CAPT. H. PALMER.	2Lt. F. S. LAYARD M.C.
2Lt. T. S. MIDDLETON.	2Lt. A H CRANE	
LIEUT. P NEW.	CAPT. H. BUNTING. M.C.	
LIEUT. L. W. ARMSTRONG.	Lt. T E. THORBURN. BROWN.	
	2Lt. DURHAM.	

Men.

KILLED	WOUNDED	MISSING.
19.	116.	49.

TOTAL 10 officers & 184 other ranks.

Arthur W. Sutcliffe Capt. Adjt.
1st The Border Regt.

2353 Wt. W2544/1454 700,000 5/15 D. D. & L. A.D.S.S./Forms/C. 2118.

Army Form C. 2118.

May 17.

WAR DIARY ~~or~~ ~~INTELLIGENCE~~ SUMMARY

(Erase heading not required.)

1st Battn The Border Regt.

Instructions regarding War Diaries and Intelligence Summaries are contained in F. S. Regs., Part II. and the Staff Manual respectively. Title Pages will be prepared in manuscript.

Place	Date	Hour	Summary of Events and Information	Remarks and references to Appendices
ARRAS	21/5/17		The Battalion arrived back into ARRAS to billets this morning about 6 AM. & rested all day cleaning up in the evening.	[illegible]
"	22/5/17		Reorganising the remaining men of the battalion into platoons with complements of specialists.	[illegible]
"	23/5/17		Still at ARRAS reorganising & training. Requiem Mass for RC's and Special service for the men who had fallen on the 19th.	[illegible]
"	24/5/17		ARRAS in billets - Training.	[illegible]
"	25/5/17		Party of 15 men & CAPT H [illegible] MC went to Rest Camp BOULOGNE.	[illegible]
"	26/5/17		ARRAS in billets.	[illegible]
"	27/5/17		Lt.COL. WORRALL BORDER Regt. and CAPT E.R CHETHAM-STRODE visited the Battalion from 2nd Battalion - Church parade.	[illegible]
"	28/5/17		Training at ARRAS	[illegible]
"	29/5/17		— do —	[illegible]
"	30/5/17		Warned to stand by to go into the line. Subsequently cancelled & carried on training.	[illegible]
"	31/5/17		Moved up to trenches tonight - battalion relieving SWB in MONCHY defences. - very quiet.	[illegible]

[illegible] Capt.
Adjutant
1st The Border Regt.

2449 Wt. W14957/M90 750,000 1/16 J.B.C. & A. Forms/C.2118/12.

SKETCH MAP BATTLEFIELD. NEAR. MONCHY LE PREUX. MAY 19/20TH 1917.

SCALE 1/10,000. 36

Instructions regarding War Diaries and Intelligence Summaries are contained in F. S. Regs., Part II. and the Staff Manual respectively. Title Pages will be prepared in manuscript.

WAR DIARY
or
INTELLIGENCE SUMMARY
(Erase heading not required.)

Army Form C. 2118

Place	Date	Hour	Summary of Events and Information	Remarks and references to Appendices

1875 Wt. W593/826 1,000,000 4/15 J.B.C. & A. A.D.S.S./Forms/C. 2118.

Volume No 27.

Instructions regarding War Diaries and Intelligence Summaries are contained in F. S. Regs., Part II. and the Staff Manual respectively. Title Pages will be prepared in manuscript.

WAR DIARY
~~or INTELLIGENCE SUMMARY~~

(Erase heading not required.)

1st Bn. The Border Regt.
88
France

Vol 15

Army Form C. 2118.

Place	Date	Hour	Summary of Events and Information	Remarks and references to Appendices
MONCHY LE PREUX	1/6/17		Battalion holding Monchy defences. HQ in German General's dugout. Two men wounded today. Relieved tonight by 3rd Bn The Royal Scots & moved back to ARRAS. Rather heavy barrage put down by Boche during relief but as officers knew his barrage lines these were avoided & casualties saved. Arrived Arras 6 AM.	
ARRAS	2/6/17		Resting in Arras in billets during day, evening [illegible] from a Boche long range H.V. gun (Quick Dick).	
"	3/6/17		Training today on musketry ranges at citadel ARRAS.	
	4/6/17		Training continued. Leave for ones is allotted daily giving great satisfaction.	
CANDAS.	5/6/17		Battalion entrained at ARRAS station 11 AM arriving CANDAS 6 PM. Comfortable clean little village, beautifully situated.	
	6/6/17		Training at Candas.	
	7/6/17		Do interrupted by violent thunderstorm.	
	8/6/17		Field day for battalion at AUTHEUX from 8 AM to 6 PM with picnic lunch - very much enjoyed by all ranks.	
	9/6/17		Interior economy this morning - afternoon holiday.	
			Weekly strength variations.	
			Increase { Draft from base — Offrs 4 — Other ranks 136 { 2/Lt Park, 2/Lt Helm, 2/Lt [illegible], 2/Lt Gibson	
			Rejoined from Hospital — 1	
			Decrease } Wounded — 2 { Lt [illegible] Brown, 2/Lt [illegible] S.A.	

2449 Wt. W14957/M90 750,000 1/16 J.B.C. & A. Forms/C.2118/12.

Army Form C. 2118.

Instructions regarding War Diaries and Intelligence Summaries are contained in F. S. Regs., Part II. and the Staff Manual respectively. Title Pages will be prepared in manuscript.

WAR DIARY
or
INTELLIGENCE SUMMARY
(Erase heading not required.)

1st Batt The Border Regt
B. G. Frames.

Place	Date	Hour	Summary of Events and Information	Remarks and references to Appendices
CANDAS.	10/6/17		Divisional band played in CANDAS this afternoon.	[illegible]
"	11/6/17		Training at AUTHEUX. Field day from 8.30 AM – 4.30 P.M.	[illegible]
"	12/6/17		" " CANDAS.	[illegible]
"	13/6/17		" " CANDAS	[illegible]
"	14/6/17		" " AUTHEUX Field day from 8.30 AM to 4.30 P.M.	[illegible]
"	15/6/17		" " CANDAS.	[illegible]
"	16/6/17		" " CANDAS. Interior Economy	[illegible]
"	17/6/17		Church parade in orchard.	[illegible]
"	18/6/17		Field day at AUTHEUX. Major General Sir Beauvoir De Lisle came round training today.	[illegible]
"	19/6/17		Training at CANDAS.	[illegible]
"	20/6/17		Brigade field day at AUTHEUX. Sir De Lisle & B. General Lucas present.	[illegible]
"	21/6/17		Training at CANDAS	[illegible]
"	22/6/17		Another Brigade field day at AUTHEUX	[illegible]
"	23/6/17		Interior economy this morning – afternoon rest.	[illegible]
"	24/6/17		Day of rest – much appreciated by all ranks.	[illegible]
"	25/6/17		Training again	[illegible]
"	26/6/17		~~Bn. training~~ Entrained at DOULLENS 9.30 P.M. & trained to PROVEN (Belgium) arriving	[illegible]

2449 Wt. W14957/M90 750,000 1/16 J.B.C. & A. Forms/C.2118/12.

Instructions regarding War Diaries and Intelligence Summaries are contained in F. S. Regs., Part II. and the Staff Manual respectively. Title pages will be prepared in manuscript.

WAR DIARY
or
~~INTELLIGENCE SUMMARY.~~

(Erase heading not required.)

Army Form C. 2118.

1st Bn The Border Regt.
87th Bde
France.

Place	Date	Hour	Summary of Events and Information	Remarks and references to Appendices
PROVEN & CANAL BANK	27/6/17		Arrived PROVEN about 10 AM. Detrained & marched to "W" Camp - rested till 5 PM then marched to International Corner entrained for ~~[illegible]~~ ELVERDINGHE detrained & marched, with guides, to CANAL BANK (YSER CANAL.) into support trenches in relief of 15th Royal Welsh Fusiliers. 2/Lt R.S. Wynne injured his finger ~~[illegible]~~ on entraining & was evacuated to Field Ambulance.	
"	28/6/17		Moved into front line in relief of 14th Royal Welsh Fusiliers in line almost due S. of PILKEM. Bn H.Q. still canal bank. Sent out patrol, a stray shell fell among them killing ~~Sgt &~~ Pte Rotheray, wounding 4, including Sgt FIELDS who died of wounds.	
"	29/6/17		Another patrol went ~~out~~ out tonight 2 officers & 14 other ranks. Encountered a Boche patrol & had a running fight, resulting in our having one man wounded.	
"	30/6/17		Two patrols out tonight - nothing encountered.	
			Variations in ~~Strength~~. Weekly.	
			Week ending 13/6/17 Draft from Base 5 off. 131 O.R. Rejoined from Hospital 1. — 2/Lt Butler L.B., 2/Lt Nicholson, 2/Lt Thompson W.C., 2/Lt Johnston J.W., 2/Lt Clucas.	

2353 Wt. W2544/1454 700,000 5/15 D. D. & L. / A.D.S.S./Forms/C. 2118.

Instructions regarding War Diaries and Intelligence Summaries are contained in F. S. Regs., Part II. and the Staff Manual respectively. Title pages will be prepared in manuscript.

WAR DIARY

or

~~INTELLIGENCE SUMMARY.~~

(Erase heading not required.)

1st Bn The Border Regt
B.E.F.
France.

Army Form C. 2118.

Place	Date	Hour	Summary of Events and Information	Remarks and references to Appendices
			Off OR	
Trenches			Evacuated Sick . 1.	
			Decrease To Transportation Dept.	
			Boulogne 1	
			School Instructor [?] .2.	
			Week Ending 22/6/17. Off OR.	
			Increase from Base 2 . {2Lt Buttle [?] / 2Lt Beech [?]	
			Rejoined from Hospital 21.	
			Decrease. Evacuated Sick	
			Transportation Dept. 1.	
			Transfer to 776 Inf Coy. [?] .5.	
			Week ending 29/6/17	
			Increase. Draft from Base 2 - . {Lt Hatton [?] / 2Lt Wayne [?]	
			Rejoined from Hospital 1.	
			Decrease Death by misadventure 1.	
			Killed 1.	
			Wounded 5.	

Arthur [illegible] Capt
a/adjutant
1st The Border Regt.

2353 Wt W2544/1454 700,000 5/15 D. D. & L. A.D.S.S./Forms/C. 2118.

28 K.

Confidential

War Diary

of

1st Battalion, The Border Regiment

From 1st July, 1917 to 31st July, 1917

Volume 28.

Serial No. 28. July

Instructions regarding War Diaries and Intelligence Summaries are contained in F. S. Regs., Part II. and the Staff Manual respectively. Title pages will be prepared in manuscript.

Sheet I

WAR DIARY
or
~~INTELLIGENCE SUMMARY.~~
(Erase heading not required.)

1st Battn The Border Regt.

Army Form C. 2118.

Place	Date	Hour	Summary of Events and Information	Remarks and references to Appendices
CANAL BANK Nr BOESINGHE	1/7/17		Patrol out tonight, 2Lt D. MACLEOD MC and four other ranks. to reconnoitre CAESARS NOSE fired on from this point with M.G and rifle grenades. 2Lt MACLEOD MC. killed & 3 wounded.	[illegible]
	2/7/17		2 Patrols out tonight - but too light for close work. Lt D. MACLEOD'S body searched for but not found. 1st KOSB ~~relief~~ relieved us, & we moved back to CANAL BANK in Reserve. supplied working parties night	
	3/7/17		& day. on new front line	[illegible]
	4/7/17		Working parties as yesterday. No. 9215 PTE. WILLIAMSON. E volunteered to go out in search of Lt MACLEOD'S body & located it but could not get it in as it was too light & snipers were busy. ~~1st Newfoundland Regt relieved us tonight~~	[illegible]
	5/7/17		No 9215 PTE. WILLIAMSON brought in 2Lt MACLEOD'S body. Battalion relieved by 1st NEWFOUNDLAND Regt tonight & moved back.	[illegible]
SUEZ CAMP Nr CROMBEKE	6/7/17		Arrived SUEZ CAMP near CROMBEKE about 3AM. in tents & bivouacs. rested today.	[illegible]
	7/7/17		TRAINING - bayonet fighting & digging strong points. The King & Prince of Wales motored through Camp & were cheered by the troops	[illegible]

2353 Wt W2544/1454 700,000 5/15 D. D. & L. A.D.S.S./Forms/C. 2118.

Serial No 28 July

Sheet 2

WAR DIARY
or
~~INTELLIGENCE SUMMARY.~~
(Erase heading not required.)

Army Form C. 2118.

1st The Border Regt.
BEF Belgium

Instructions regarding War Diaries and Intelligence Summaries are contained in F. S. Regs., Part II, and the Staff Manual respectively. ~~Title pages~~ will be prepared in manuscript.

Place	Date	Hour	Summary of Events and Information	Remarks and references to Appendices
CROMBEKE SUEZ CAMP			Casualties week ending 6.7.17.	
			Increase.	
			Draft from Base. 1 Off. O.R. 64. [Lt CHAMBERS W.F.H.]	
			Rejoined from Hosp. 1 " CAPT AVH WOOD.	
			Decrease	
			Killed 1 Off. O.R. 3. {2Lt D MACLEOD M.C.}	
			Wounded 1 " " 15. [Capt AVH WOOD.]	
			Evacuated. 8.	[initials]
"	8/7/17		Training. Leave going strong. 2 or 1 per day.	[initials]
"	9/7/17		Training.	[initials]
"	10/7/17		Training. C.O. went to Divisional Scheme. - Coy Commanders Scheme this afternoon	[initials]
"	11/7/17		C.O. & 2nd in Command to Brigade Tactical Scheme. Officers compass marching by night	[initials]
"	12/7/17		Draft of 20 today. chiefly A.S.C. transfers - & looked it.	[initials]
	13/7/17		Moved to HOUNSLOW CAMP (near WOESTEN) arriving about 10 p.m.	[initials]
			C & D coys went to RIVOLI FARM near CANAL BANK relieving 2 coys	[initials]

2353 Wt. W2514/1454 700,000 5/15 D. D. & L. A.D.S.S./Forms/C. 2118.

Serial No. 28. July

Army Form C. 2118.

Instructions regarding War Diaries and Intelligence Summaries are contained in F. S. Regs., Part II. and the Staff Manual respectively. Title pages will be prepared in manuscript. Sheet 3.

WAR DIARY
or
~~INTELLIGENCE SUMMARY.~~
(Erase heading not required.)

1st The Border Regt.
BEF Belgium

Place	Date	Hour	Summary of Events and Information	Remarks and references to Appendices
RIVOLI FARM near WIESTEN	13/7/17		R/1st LANCS. Fifty details took over LANCASHIRE CAMP near PROVEN.	
HOUNSLOW CAMP.	14/7/17		Provided working parties from HOUNSLOW CAMP TRIVOLI FARM. to work on CANAL BANK.	
"	15/7/17		Similar working parties as above provided.	
	16/7/17		— DO — — —	
			Casualties week ending 13/7/17.	
			Increase. Draft from Base. O.R. 69.	
			from Hospital 1.	
			Decrease. Classified P.B. Off. 1 2Lt. IRESON.	
			Evacuated 3.	
			Transferred 3.	
	17/7/17		Working parties as for 16th	
	18/7/17		DO.	
PROVEN	19/7/17		Moved to LANCASHIRE CAMP. arriving 3P.M. 1 Off & 50 OR left behind as working party [illegible] R.F.A.	

2353 Wt. W2544/1454 700,000 5/15 D. D. & L. A.D.S.S./Forms/C. 2118.

Serial No 28. July 1917 Sheet 4

WAR DIARY or ~~INTELLIGENCE SUMMARY~~

(Erase heading not required.)

Army Form C. 2118.

1st The Border Regt. B.E.F. Belgium

Instructions regarding War Diaries and Intelligence Summaries are contained in F. S. Regs., Part II. and the Staff Manual respectively. Title Pages will be prepared in manuscript.

Place	Date	Hour	Summary of Events and Information	Remarks and references to Appendices
LANCASHIRE CAMP.	20/7/17		Interior Economy + resting.	
			Casualties. week ending 20th	
			Increase. Draft from Base. Offrs. 1. O.R. 14. [2Lt. H.T. THOMPSON]	[illegible]
			Decrease. To England Sick. 1. 4 [2Lt. E.S. WYNNE]	
			~~Killed.~~ Killed 1. Wounded. 8. ~~Sick~~ Transfer. 1.	
	21/7/17.		Training.	[illegible]
	22/7/17		~~Training~~ Church Parade.	[illegible]
	23/7/17		Training. – Officers reconnoitred routes to be used in the stunt	[illegible]
	24/7/17		Lt.Col. A.J. ELLIS D.S.O. returned from leave + took over command. MAJ. R.P.M. NICKOLLS having commanded during his absence.	[illegible]
	25/7/17		Bathing. + practice in gas mask marching by night.	[illegible]
	26/7/17		Preparing for coming ~~stunt~~, completing kit etc.	[illegible]
	27/7/17		Marched to HERZEELE + bivouaced for scheme tomorrow	[illegible]
	28/7/17		Practice attack scheme. Field day commencing 7.30 Am.	[illegible]

2449 Wt. W14957/M90 750,000 1/16 J.B.C. & A. Forms/C.2118/12.

Army Form C. 2118.

Serial No. 28. July 1917 | 1st Bn Border Regt.

Sheet 5.

Instructions regarding War Diaries and Intelligence Summaries are contained in F. S. Regs., Part II. and the Staff Manual respectively. Title Pages will be prepared in manuscript.

WAR DIARY
or
INTELLIGENCE SUMMARY

(Erase heading not required.)

Place	Date	Hour	Summary of Events and Information	Remarks and references to Appendices
PROVEN.	28/7/17		This area represented the area over which it was expected the battalion would attack, a stream representing the STEENBEEK etc. – Field day finished about 12.30 P.M. and the battalion moved back arriving in camp about 5 P.M.	
	29/7/17		Church parade at Proven.	
	30		Casualties week ending 27.7.17.	
			Increase. Draft from Base. O.R. 9.	
			Decrease. Killed O.R. 1	
			Wounded. 9.	
			Transferred 1.	
			Evacuated. 3.	
	31/7/17		Training. Moved to [illegible] Camp No. [illegible] at DE WIPPE CABARET CORNER arriving [illegible] 30 A.M.	
	31/7/17		Moved 3.30 to Moton Farm. Whole battalion on working party for Guards Division. 8 platoons & parties of 2 companies each worked making CLARGES ST to the CANAL from BOESINGHE & then across canal making roads as far as ARTILLERY WOOD (700x). CAPT. AVITWOOD wounded. C.S.M. Randolph killed. 8 other Ranks killed. 3 wounded. 3 missing.	

[illegible] Capt. a/Adjutant.

2449 Wt. W14957/M90 750,000 1/16 J.B.C. & A. Forms/C.2118/12.

87/29

29 K.
17 sheet + maps

War Diary

of

1st Battalion The Border Regiment

From 1 - 8 - 17 To 31 - 8 - 17

Volume

No. 29

Aug 17

Serial No. 29. August 1917 / Sheet No. 1.

Instructions regarding War Diaries and Intelligence Summaries are contained in F. S. Regs., Part II. and the Staff Manual respectively. Title Pages will be prepared in manuscript.

WAR DIARY
or
~~INTELLIGENCE SUMMARY~~
(Erase heading not required.)

1st THE BORDER REGT.
B.E.F. Belgium.

Army Form C. 2118.

Place	Date	Hour	Summary of Events and Information	Remarks and references to Appendices
[illegible] WIPPE CABARET	1/8/17		Companies were employed on laying duckboard tracks up over the captured ground. Weather appalling - pouring with rain incessantly. In spite of this however a few field guns were got across the canal today to continue the advance.	[illegible]
[illegible]	2/8/17		Another fearfully wet day today. Fighting practically impossible. St Julien [illegible] during the night & retaken before the morning. Battalion rested today.	[illegible]
[illegible]	3/8/17		Battalion employed making duck walks again up to the front line. Still fearful wet weather. Battalion moved back this evening to PROVEN [illegible] area & PENTON CAMP.	[illegible]
PENTON CAMP	4/8/17		Another wet day - little training. Several [illegible] visited the Battalion.	[illegible]
	5/8/17		[illegible] Training continued.	
			Casualties for week ending 3/8/17.	
			Increase	
			Quartermaster appointed from 10th East Yorks. — 1	
			[illegible] H. [illegible] — 1	
			of Lt Col. [illegible] Morris [illegible] Detail Depot [illegible]	
			Draft — 29. Total 2 + 21.	
			Decrease Killed — 1 — 3 (Capt. A.H. Wood)	
			Wounded — 3	
			Missing — 5	
			[illegible] — 2	
			Transferred — 12 — 1 + [illegible]	
			[illegible] — 1 — 44	

2449 Wt. W14957/M90 750,000 1/16 J.B.C. & A. Forms/C.2118/12.

Serial No. 29 Sheet 2.

Instructions regarding War Diaries and Intelligence Summaries are contained in F. S. Regs., Part II. and the Staff Manual respectively. Title Pages will be prepared in manuscript.

WAR DIARY
or
INTELLIGENCE SUMMARY

(Erase heading not required.)

1st Bn The Border Regt.
B.E.F. BELGIUM.

Army Form C. 2118.

Place	Date	Hour	Summary of Events and Information	Remarks and references to Appendices
6/8/17	6/8/17		Training again at PENTON CAMP, tho' the heavy ground made it difficult	[illegible]
PROVEN.	7/8/17		Moved this morning to DE WIPPE CABARET Camp 29 again. Previous to the move, all NCO's & men who had not had leave for 15 months or over were sent to BOLLEZEELE, the Divisional Depot Battalion & were replaced by an equal number from the Depot Bn. This party, replacing the leave party joined us on the march - 24 other ranks.	[illegible]
Nr. ELVERDINGHE	8/8/17		Resting at Camp 20.	[illegible]
BALLANTINE WOOD.	9/8/17		Moved to Bivouacs in the wood near DE WIPPE CABARET. - FOREST CAMP AREA. & practised forming up on a tape this evening in the dark & moving as was arranged for in the action to take place soon.	[illegible]
	10/8/17		Continued as yesterday. Training for Stunt.	
			Casualties for week ending 10/8/17. Off. O.R.	
			Increase	
			Draft from Base to 29th Div'l Depot Bn 2 17. 2+17	
			Decrease	
			Transferred to Employment Coy. 3.	
			Classified PB by ADMS. 1.	
			Evacuated from Div'l Area 11. 15	
	11/8/17		Battalion moved into the line tonight. Bath'n HQ at SADLES FM.	

2449 Wt. W14957/M90 750,000 1/16 J.B.C. & A. Forms/C.2118/12.

Serial Number 29

Instructions regarding War Diaries and Intelligence Summaries are contained in F. S. Regs., Part II. and the Staff Manual respectively. Title Pages will be prepared in manuscript.

Sheet 3.

WAR DIARY
or
INTELLIGENCE SUMMARY

(Erase heading not required.)

1st Bn The Border Regt
BELGIUM

Army Form C. 2118.

Place	Date	Hour	Summary of Events and Information	Remarks and references to Appendices
Trenches [illegible] STEENBEEK Sector	1/8/17		B C D Coys were in Wood 15. B Coy at SAULES FM. Battalion HQ. and A Coy moved into ARRI WOOD. The whole unit being attached to the 86th Brigade temporarily. No sooner had the battalion got into position [illegible] guides who were at least doubtful – than orders were received that a company was to be moved forward to "a line parallel to FOURCHES FM." When a map had been carefully studied & an idea formed as to what was probably meant orders were issued to O/C A Coy to occupy a portion of the GREEN LINE from FOURCHES FM. to the S.W. for about 300x. In moving to excellent judgment & skilful handling of his company 2/Lt A FULTON O/C A Coy got his men there just at dawn with few casualties. 2/Lt J.B. TROTTER was wounded.	
TRENCHES	12/8/17		Fairly quiet time for all coys. except A. who had a few casualties from fairly heavy shelling round the Green Line. Battn. moved up to front line. 3 coys. & Coy remained in Green line. Bn HQ. at FOURCHES FM.	
	[illegible]		The battalion struck the enemy barrage round FOURCHES FM. [illegible] the battalion had about 40 casualties.	
	[illegible]/8/17		Heavy shelling at stand to this morning. 2/Lt G.F.H. MALLETT killed. A/CAPT A FULTON (just promoted that day) wounded and about ten casualties to other ranks.	

2449 Wt. W14957/M90 750,000 1/16 J.B.C. & A. Forms/C.2118/12.

Serial No. 29

Instructions regarding War Diaries and Intelligence Summaries are contained in F. S. Regs., Part II. and the Staff Manual respectively. Title Pages will be prepared in manuscript.

Sheet H.

WAR DIARY
or
INTELLIGENCE SUMMARY
(Erase heading not required.)

1st Bn The Border Regt
B.E.F. Belgium.

Army Form C. 2118.

Place	Date	Hour	Summary of Events and Information	Remarks and references to Appendices
FRONT LINE TRENCHES	13/8/17		Again heavy shelling, principally in the early morning between 2.30 & 3.30 AM. an absolute barrage was put down on the line FOURCHES FARM – CAPTAINS FARM. getting 3 or 4 direct hits on FOURCHES FM. – Bn. H.Q. causing about 15 casualties in the green line & around.	
"	14/8/17		Another lively day at FOURCHES FARM from shell fire. The Company commander of the French company on our left paid us a visit & also the machine gun officer & a considerable entente resulted. Another barrage was put down by the BOCHE tonight about dusk.	
	15/8/17		Relieved early this morning & moved down to bivouacs at BLEUET FARM & slept till noon. Then cleaned up, issued battle stores & issued final orders for the battle. About 9 P.M. the companies began to move off, at intervals to the place of assembly EAST of the STEENBEEK in preparation for the second phase of the 3rd Battle of YPRES.	

Serial No 29. Sheet 5.

Instructions regarding War Diaries and Intelligence Summaries are contained in F. S. Regs., Part II. and the Staff Manual respectively. Title Pages will be prepared in manuscript.

WAR DIARY
or
~~INTELLIGENCE SUMMARY~~

(Erase heading not required.)

Army Form C. 2118.

1st Bn The Border Regt.
B.E.F. Belgium.

Place	Date	Hour	Summary of Events and Information	Remarks and references to Appendices
			Second Phase of the 3rd Battle of YPRES.	
	15/8/17.	9 P.M.	The Battalion marched from bivouacs at BLEUET FARM and proceeded via BRIDGE ST. – SAULES FARM. CAPTAINS FARM. SIGNAL FARM to the place of assembly EAST of the STEENBEEK.	
		10.30 P.M.	Battalion Headquarters with Regimental aid post were established at SIGNAL FARM. Battalion Headquarters party comprised.	
			Lt Col A. J. ELLIS D.S.O. commanding.	
			CAPT. and A/ADJt. A.W. SUTCLIFFE M.C.	
			Lt G.H.S. McDONALD. Signalling officer.	
			Lt MAYSTON R.A.M.C. medical officer.	
			[illegible] mortar & personnel, under 2Lt J. WHIGHAM accompanied Battalion H.Q. at SIGNAL FARM.	
			A Section of machine guns of the 87th M.G.C. under Lt PAGE were attached to C Co. – the support company – and proceeded direct with them to the place of assembly.	
EAST of STEENBEEK.	16/8/17.	2 A.M.	The battalion was formed up EAST of the STEENBEEK in rear of the 1st K.O.S.B. on a two company frontage D and B companies in the front line (forming the 1st 2 waves and A & C coys in support (forming the second two waves. A company was under the command of Capt W. J. H. Chambers with 2Lt M.C. NICHOLSON as the only other officer	

2449 Wt. W14957/M90 750,000 1/16 J.B.C. & A. Forms/C.2118/12.

Serial No 29. Sheet 8.

Instructions regarding War Diaries and Intelligence Summaries are contained in F. S. Regs., Part II. and the Staff Manual respectively. Title Pages will be prepared in manuscript.

WAR DIARY
or
~~INTELLIGENCE SUMMARY~~
(Erase heading not required.)

Army Form C. 2118

1st The Border Regt.
B.E.F. Belgium

Place	Date	Hour	Summary of Events and Information	Remarks and references to Appendices
	16/8/17	9.30	After battalion headquarters had been established at Wijdendrift situation reports were received from all companies which made it possible to write up a full situation report for the battalion which was then sent to the Brigade, with a map showing the exact positions taken up, similar to those shown on attached map. The work of consolidation went forward quite smoothly all morning and the casualties were light though considerable sniping from the enemy on the EAST side of the BROEMBEEK was kept up. A heavy howitzer, at first thought to be our own 9"2, but afterwards proved to be a French 8" caused no losses by dropping shells in PANTHER TRENCH WEST of the swamp and it took some considerable time to get it stopped though the F.O.O. Lt NAPIER R.A. at WIJDENDRIFT got his messages through with great promptitude.	
			During the consolidation the enemy artillery was fairly active between the green line and the Steenbeek and at times concentrated heavily on Wijdendrift itself, but they seemed unable to locate our front line, or at any rate made no attempt to shell it.	
			Enemy aeroplanes were very active all morning and continually flew up and down our line at very low altitude firing Machine guns at the garrison and also firing single red very lights.	
			None of our battle planes came over, to interfere with them and one gallant contact plane of ours which came over	

1875 Wt. W593/826 1,000,000 4/15 J.B.C. & A. A.D.S.S./Forms/C. 2118.

Serial No 29. Sheet 9.

Instructions regarding War Diaries and Intelligence Summaries are contained in F. S. Regs., Part II. and the Staff Manual respectively. Title Pages will be prepared in manuscript.

WAR DIARY

or

~~INTELLIGENCE SUMMARY~~

(Erase heading not required.)

1st The Border Regt. 87th Bde. Belgium

Army Form C. 2118

Place	Date	Hour	Summary of Events and Information	Remarks and references to Appendices
	11/9/17		unescorted was promptly brought down by them, so that they had matters pretty much their own way. Our contacts had been very busy & did splendid and gallant work earlier on in the morning.	
		1 P.M.	A report came from O/C B Company that the enemy could be seen 3 or 4 hundred strong massing in NEY WOOD. The guns were promptly turned on, chiefly owing to Lt. Col. A.J. ELLIS D.S.O. taking the matter personally in hand, and with excellent effect scattering the enemy. Still heavy casualties were further inflicted by the front line garrisons by rifle fire, many of the men whose rifles were clogged with mud using captured enemy rifles and ammunition. At various times through the afternoon the firing line companies reported enemy activity beyond the BROEMBEEK and this culminated in a definite report about	
		7.20	7.20 PM that the enemy were massing from NEY WOOD to a point opposite the right boundary of the Brigade sector, and were already pushing forward in small parties by short rushes.	
		7.40	A barrage was again asked for on the line of the BROEMBEEK from U.16.d.1.8. to U.16.c.1.9. (see map attached 1/10000 LANGEMARCK) and this barrage was put down with great accuracy.	

1875 Wt. W593/826 1,000,000 4/15 J.B.C. & A. A.D.S.S./Forms/C. 2118.

Serial No 39. Sheet 10

Instructions regarding War Diaries and Intelligence Summaries are contained in F. S. Regs., Part II. and the Staff Manual respectively. Title Pages will be prepared in manuscript.

WAR DIARY
or
INTELLIGENCE SUMMARY
(Erase heading not required.)

Army Form C. 2118

Place	Date	Hour	Summary of Events and Information	Remarks and references to Appendices
			at precisely the right moment, again due to Lt COL. A.J. ELLIS D.S.O. personal efforts + instructions.	
		7.45PM	CAPT. and ADJt A.W. SUTCLIFFE. M.C., who was observing from WINDENDRIFT. spotted the enemy advancing in large numbers clear of our barrage NW of NEYWOOD up to a point about U.15.b.2.6. After some little delay Lt COL ELLIS who was still at the telephone, was able to get the artillery group commander on the other end and personally instruct him exactly where to put down his barrage & to what point to extend it, with the result that all available guns heavy and light, were turned on ~~and an annihilating fire~~ The result of this fire was annihilating. It came down just at the right time and in the right place completely broke up the enemy's attack - he could be seen scattering in all directions, while parties could be seen being blown up all over by the heavier shells. - causing enormous casualties.	
			All this time a heavy rifle, machine gun and Lewis gun fire was kept up by our firing line troops, who had never had such a "picnic" opportunity since Gallipoli and as the enemy had practically no trenches to get into	

1875 Wt. W593/826 1,000,000 4/15 J.B.C. & A. A.D.S.S./Forms/C. 2118.

Special No 29. Sheet 11.

Instructions regarding War Diaries and Intelligence Summaries are contained in F. S. Regs., Part II. and the Staff Manual respectively. Title Pages will be prepared in manuscript.

WAR DIARY
or
~~INTELLIGENCE SUMMARY~~
(Erase heading not required.)

Army Form C. 2118

1st The Border Regt.
B.E.F. Belgium

Place	Date	Hour	Summary of Events and Information	Remarks and references to Appendices
			The losses inflicted by this fire were also very heavy.	
			Previous to and during this counter attack the enemy put down a fairly heavy barrage on the WINDENDRIFT and STEENBEEK lines but only a light and inaccurate one on the front line.	
		8.45	about 8.45 P.M. The 18 pounders withdrew their barrage from the BROEMBEEK line onto PANTHER TRENCH from the right brigade ~~sector~~ boundary up to the swamp causing some few casualties in the firing line. The barrage was never asked to be withdrawn from the Broembeek line, and consequently this contretemps cannot be explained, and certainly not a single BOCHE ever got to the WEST of the stream alive.	
			During the late afternoon patrols were sent out & reconnoitred the BROEMBEEK & exploited its crossings. They encountered no enemy West of the stream, but were sniped at ~~from~~ by the enemy who appeared to be holding a shell hole line about 200x East of the stream.	
			The failure of the counter attack finished the enemy activity and the Battalion was relieved by the Inniskillen Fusiliers during the	

Serial No. 29.

Instructions regarding War Diaries and Intelligence Summaries are contained in F. S. Regs., Part II. and the Staff Manual respectively. Title Pages will be prepared in manuscript.

Sheet 12

WAR DIARY
or
~~INTELLIGENCE SUMMARY~~

(Erase heading not required.)

1/The Border Regt.
BEF Belgium

Army Form C. 2118.

Place	Date	Hour	Summary of Events and Information	Remarks and references to Appendices
			night and early morning of the 17th. The operation as far as this battalion was concerned being a complete success and carried out with remarkably light casualties. The advance was a difficult one owing to the swamp running diagonally across our front from CANNES FARM to the BROEMBEEK and its success reflects the greatest credit upon the company commanders & their subordinates in keeping direction etc. Touch & direction were kept throughout and they arrived at their allotted objectives to time. The endurance displayed by all ranks ~~reflected~~ was beyond all praise as the going throughout was in an appalling state. and during the previous three days the battalion had held the firing line for 48 hours and carried out two difficult reliefs under most adverse conditions and suffered considerable from shellfire. Notwithstanding their morale was unimpaired. and worthy of the highest traditions of the regiment.	
			Casualties for the action were as follows.	

2449 Wt. W14957/M90 750,000 1/16 J.B.C. & A. Forms/C.2118/12.

Serial No. 29 Sheet 6

Army Form C. 2118.

WAR DIARY

or

INTELLIGENCE ~~SUMMARY~~

(Erase heading not required.)

1st Bn The Border Regt. 88th Bde Belgium.

Instructions regarding War Diaries and Intelligence Summaries are contained in F. S. Regs., Part II. and the Staff Manual respectively. Title Pages will be prepared in manuscript.

Place	Date	Hour	Summary of Events and Information	Remarks and references to Appendices
E of STEENBEEK. NE of LANGEMARCK	16/8/17		B Coy was under command of A/CAPT J.W. ENBANK M.C. with platoon commanders 2Lt H.R. CLUCAS. 2Lt W.D.C. THOMPSON	
			C . . . . A/CAPT. R.E.S. JOHNSTON. with platoon commanders. 2Lt J.L.P. GAMON. 2Lt W.S.M. RUXTON. 2Lt WATSON.	
			D . . . . A/CAPT. W.B. BUTLER with platoon commanders 2Lt A.J.F. DANIELLI. 2Lt C. HELM.	
		4 AM	During the approach march the battalion was shelled intermittently but the enemy was unable to put down his usual heavy barrage on the line CAPTAINS FARM. FOURCHE FARM. due probably owing to the gas shells which our artillery were sending over in a practically continuous steady bombardment. It was the quietest night comparatively that the battalion had ever experienced in that area. Each company on passing Bn HQ. at Signal Farm dumped eight tins of water as a battalion reserve. Just previous to the assault CAPT. W.B. BUTLER was slightly wounded but after going to the aid post returned to his company. 2Lt A.J.F. DANIELLI was also blown up by a shell & knocked unconscious but on recovering consciousness on the way down on the stretcher, got off & rejoined his platoon in time to lead them in the show!!	
		4.45.	Our barrage fell with great precision & the advance started. The enemy put down his barrages on the lines (1) CAPTAINS FARM, FOURCHE FARM (2) SIGNAL FARM. RUISSEAU FARM, but nothing more than an occasional shell on the line of the STEENBEEK.	

Serial No 29. Sheet 7.

Instructions regarding War Diaries and Intelligence Summaries are contained in F. S. Regs., Part II. and the Staff Manual respectively. Title Pages will be prepared in manuscript.

WAR DIARY or ~~INTELLIGENCE SUMMARY~~

(Erase heading not required.)

1/Border Regt. 87 Bde. Belgium

Army Form C. 2118

Place	Date	Hour	Summary of Events and Information	Remarks and references to Appendices
NE of LANGEMARCK	16/8/17	6.40	Visual message was sent through from our advanced signal station at PASSERELLE FARM saying the blue line had been taken.	
		7.20	Another message from the visual station stated that the advance was held up on the blue line by M.G. fire & later a message from Capt Ewbank confirmed this stating that the K.O.S.B. & S.W.B. were held up by M.G. fire from a "pill-box" near what appeared to be MONTMIRAIL FARM. The stokes mortar, which had been pushed forward to Passerelle Farm on the blue line being taken, was accordingly sent forward to engage this obstacle	
		8.50	Lt R E S JOHNSTON o/c C Coy reported that the advance had continued & he had now reached his position in the gun pits near CANNES FM, the opposition from the blockhouse having been overcome by an outflanking movement which caused the garrison to surrender.	
		9.10.	a/Capt H.B. BUTLER reported that the RED LINE had been taken & prisoners captured including 2 machine guns and that he was in touch with A Company on his right.	
		9.30	CAPT. EWBANK M.C. o/c B Coy reported that the block house had been taken by an outflanking movement, forty prisoners being taken from it also a machine gun and a heavy trench mortar. This had enabled him to push on & capture his objective on the RED LINE. Here he took several prisoners and 2 machine guns.	[initials]
		9.35	On receipt of this message Battalion Headquarters was moved forward to WIJDENDRIFT from SIGNAL FARM & at the same time the machine gun section ordered to move forward to take up	

Serial No 29.
Sheet 13.

Instructions regarding War Diaries and Intelligence Summaries are contained in F. S. Regs., Part II. and the Staff Manual respectively. Title Pages will be prepared in manuscript.

WAR DIARY
or
INTELLIGENCE SUMMARY
(Erase heading not required.)

The Border Regt.
BEF Belgium

Army Form C. 2118.

Place	Date	Hour	Summary of Events and Information	Remarks and references to Appendices
			Casualties for the action 16/8/17. Killed. officers NIL other ranks. 14. (including C.S.M. HARRISON. J) Wounded { " 1. } " " 66. { 2Lt M.C. NICHOLSON }	
	17/8/17		Battalion relief was complete by about midnight & the battalion moved to CHARTERHOUSE CAMP near DE WIPPE CABARET behind Elverdinghe spending a restful day	[initials]
	18/8/17		Cleaning up, reorganising and replacing deficiencies of the battalion. Casualties week ending 17/8/17. Killed Officers 1. 2Lt G.F. HAMLETT. 13/8/17 other ranks. 24. Wounded. Officers 3 Capt A FULTON 13/8/17; 2Lt J.B. TROTTER 13/8/17; 2Lt M.C. NICHOLSON 16/8/17 other ranks 105. Missing. officers 1. 2Lt H.T THOMPSON 13/8/17 other ranks 22 Died of wounds — 1 Total 5 officers. 152 other ranks.	[initials]
DE WIPPE CABARET	19/8/17		Moved CHARTERHOUSE CAMP to new site just NE of ELVERDINGHE Maj General Sir Beauvoir De Lisle called on the CO. saw company commanders & congratulated all on the excellent show of 16/8/17	[initials]

Serial No 89 – Sheet 14

Instructions regarding War Diaries and Intelligence Summaries are contained in F. S. Regs., Part II. and the Staff Manual respectively. Title Pages will be prepared in manuscript.

WAR DIARY
or
~~INTELLIGENCE SUMMARY~~

(*Erase heading not required.*)

1/Border Regt
B.E.F. France.

Army Form C. 2118.

Place	Date	Hour	Summary of Events and Information	Remarks and references to Appendices
ELVERDINGHE	20/8/17		In camp near Elverdinghe making the place respectable. Great Boche air activity in the evening dropping bombs around.	[initials]
	21/8/17		Company parades etc. but fairly restful day. The boche again "laid eggs" around the camp this evening no casualties.	[initials]
	22/8/17		Battalion worked for two hours on the dry weather track forward to the canal	[initials]
	23/8/17		Fairly quiet restful day – nothing much doing	[initials]
	24/8/17		Battalion moved into the line opposite CANNES FARM this evening. Major R.P.M. NICHOLS in command temporarily Lt G.B.D. CARGILL adjutant temporarily while Lt Col A.J. ELLIS D.S.O. and CAPT A.W. SUTCLIFFE M.C. being temporarily 10% for a rest. Lt W.S.M. RIXTON took out a special patrol tonight to explore the crossings of the BROEMBEEK & consider the possibility of establishing posts on the far side. also 2Lt A.V.F. DANIELLI made a stout hearted attempt to establish an advanced post near NEY WOOD but was unsuccessful owing to an enemy post having been already established near, a party of about 20 boche being located. One prisoner was taken tonight by D Coy. a German Despatch rider who had lost his way	[initials]
	25/8/17		Considerable shelling of the front line and battalion HQ. at CANNES FARM but fortunately casualties were light. The weather was appallingly wet & raw	
	26/8/17		Another uneventful day. Considerable shelling by day & miserable weather posts were eventually established across the BROENBEEK. Lt RIXTON doing particularly good work again in establish	[initials]

Somme No 29. Sheet 15.

Instructions regarding War Diaries and Intelligence Summaries are contained in F. S. Regs., Part II. and the Staff Manual respectively. Title Pages will be prepared in manuscript.

WAR DIARY
or
~~INTELLIGENCE SUMMARY~~

(Erase heading not required.)

1/Border Regt
R.S.F.
Belgium

Army Form C. 2118

Place	Date	Hour	Summary of Events and Information	Remarks and references to Appendices
	26/8/17		ing posts within 25x of the enemy. Prisoner - a Prussian guard Sergt Major (Feldwebel) being taken by Pte Corran. C.Coy. after Pte Corran had killed 3 & wounded 1 of a patrol of 5 including the feldwebel, by his Lewis Gun	
Trenches.	27/8/17		Battalion moved back from front line & got into support by this morning at dawn the 4th Scots Guards taking over, on the WIJDENDRIFT Line	
	28/8/17		Battalion relieved from the WIJDENDRIFT line & moved back to ELVERDINGHE area & moved at 5pm by rail to beyond PROVEN into the P4 area & into	
CHARTERHOUSE CAMP	29/8/17		POLLARD Camp near HAANDEKOT cross roads. - the men's lines were very sloppy & muddy owing to the heavy rains. Officers lines good glass.	
POLLSHILL CAMP near HAANDEKOT.	31/8/17		Spent the day in reorganising - checking deficiencies & making them up as far as possible - & cleaning up generally.	
"	31/8/17		CO held battalion parade & presented the following medal ribbons. Capt J W Ewbank MC. - bar to MC — Capt W B Butler, Capt F R C Chambers 2/Lt A J F Dawlin - MC. Sergt Shearer DCM and MM. Cpl Gibbs No. 33857 DCM. 9130 CQMS Smith DCM. Military Medals. 10743 Sgt Billington. 2791 L/Sgt Graham. 19797 Sgt Markham. 8281 Cpl Jarvis. 17576 Cpl Moore J. 15988 Cpl Morris J. 10780 L/C Kelly J. 14073 L/C Napron E. 33695 L/C Blow F.A. 240890 L/C Dumay W. 11833 L/C Mason T. 13782 L/C Graham J. 33615 Pte Crooke. 25245 Pte Watson J. 26787 Watson J. 4927 Massey T. 21123 Pte Turner J. 24488 Burton L. 28730 Pte Watt D. 7584 Allen G. 25425 Wrigley G.	[illegible] Capt a/Adjutant

Wt. W593/826 1,000,000 4/15 J.B.C. & A. A.D.S.S./Forms/C. 2118.

Army Form C. 2118

Instructions regarding War Diaries and Intelligence Summaries are contained in F. S. Regs., Part II. and the Staff Manual respectively. Title Pages will be prepared in manuscript.

WAR DIARY
or
INTELLIGENCE SUMMARY

(Erase heading not required.)

Place	Date	Hour	Summary of Events and Information			Remarks and references to Appendices
			Casualties for week ending 31/8/17.			
			Increase.	Off.	O.R.	
			Drafts from base	1	32	
			Rejoined from Hosp.		1	
				1 +	33	
			Decrease. Killed		9.	
			Wounded		22.	
			Missing		2.	
			Evacuated		4.	
			To Corps Sch. HQ		1	
			Total.		38	

Lt Lowthorpe Lutwidge Lt.

[illegible] Capt
Adjutant
1/Border Regt

1875 Wt. W593/826 1,000,000 4/15 J.B.C. & A. A.D.S.S./Forms/C. 2118.

A 1
Shewing posit. of 1 BORDER before & after action 16/8/17
Langemarck
Scale 1:20,000
Advanced Section A.P. & S.S.

Message Pad.

Your Message must be such as will enable the Addressee to know what the Situation is with You and your Neighbours.

NEGATIVE INFORMATION IS ALSO VALUABLE.

Strike out and alter sentences as necessary.

TO..

1. Am advancing to..
2. Am putting out (Have put out) protective parties.
3. Am sending out. Have sent out and am keeping out patrols to keep touch with the enemy.
4. Am (Have) consolidating (ed).
5. Our line now runs...
6. I require (give article or articles and No. required):

   Send the above to..
7. Troops on my right are (give situation)
8. Troops on my left are (give situation)
9. My strength now is......................................
10. Am being shelled from..
11. Am held up by M.G., T.M., rifle, artillery fire from....................................
12. Am now ready to..
13. Enemy line runs..
14. Enemy (strength)..................................at..

    doing..
15. Have captured ....
16. Enemy prisoners belong to..
17. Enemy counter-attack forming up at...
18. Other remarks—

Time a.m. (p.m.)	Name..
Date..	Rank..
Place..	Platoon................. Company.....................
(Map Ref. or mark on back of map).	Battalion..

5TH FIELD SURVEY Co R.E. (1,176)

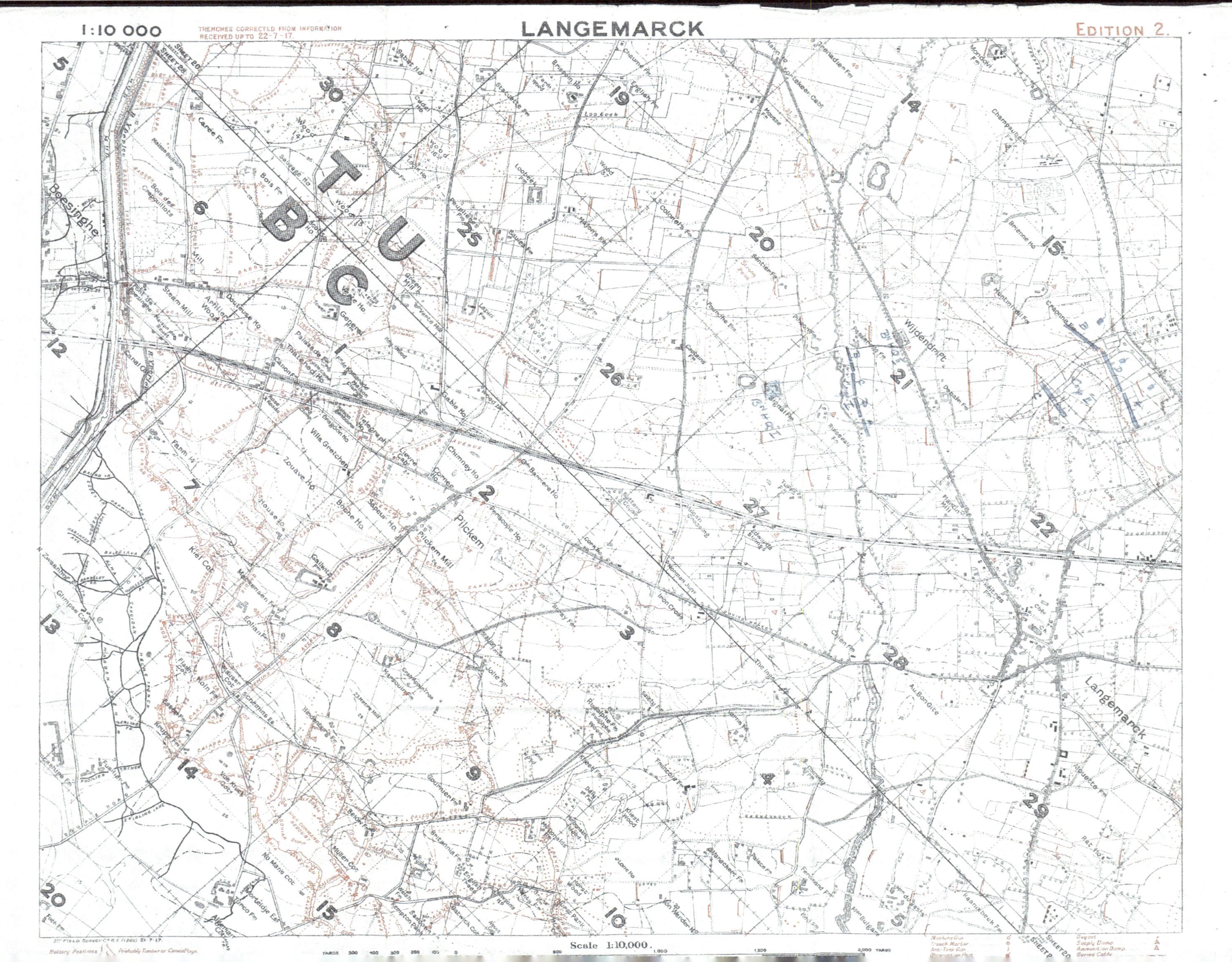

1:10 000
TRENCHES CORRECTED FROM INFORMATION RECEIVED UP TO 22-7-17
LANGEMARCK
EDITION 2.
Langemarck
Pilckem
Wijdendrift
Boesinghe
Scale 1:10,000

Confidential

Vol 18

War Diary

of

1st Bn The Border Regiment.

From:- 1st Sept. 1917. To:- 30th Sept. 1917.

Volume 30.

30 K.

Serial No. 30 September 1917

Instructions regarding War Diaries and Intelligence Summaries are contained in F. S. Regs., Part II. and the Staff Manual respectively. Title pages will be prepared in manuscript.

WAR DIARY
or
~~INTELLIGENCE SUMMARY.~~
(Erase heading not required.)

1st The Border Regt. 87th B[illegible] Belgium.

Army Form C. 2118.

Place	Date	Hour	Summary of Events and Information	Remarks and references to Appendices
Poshill Camp	1st		Training at POSHILL CAMP.	
	2nd		1st Battalion visited 2nd Battalion at OUDEZEELE. – Tug of war & football contest 1st Battalion won the 1st & drew for the second event.	[illegible]
	6th		Brigade Ceremonial Parade under B. G. Gen. Lucas D.S.O. when General De Lisle presented medal ribbons to those who had won decorations 16/8/17	[illegible]
	4th		Inspection parade under C.O.	
	5th		Training parade.	[illegible]
	6th		Do.	
	7th		[illegible] Staff rides & schemes for Co. 2nd in Command & Coy Commanders	
	8th		Battalion moved to WINNEZEELE training ground. billets in village. – very good billets.	
	9th		Field Day Training 9 am – 3 pm with lunch in the open. Divisional day troops worked excellently – most successful & pleasant day [illegible]	[illegible]
	10.			
			Casualties for week ending 9th.	
			Increase – Draft from Base. Off. 6. O.R. 64. 2/Lt L.R. Clapp 2/Lt B. [illegible]	
			Returned from Hospital 2. 2/Lt J.H. Smith 2/Lt C.W. Saynor	[illegible]
			6 – 66 2/Lt [illegible] 2/Lt D. [illegible]	

Sheet 2. Serial No. 30.

Instructions regarding War Diaries and Intelligence Summaries are contained in F. S. Regs., Part II. and the Staff Manual respectively. Title pages will be prepared in manuscript.

September

WAR DIARY
or
~~INTELLIGENCE~~ SUMMARY.
(*Erase heading not required.*)

1st Border Regt
B.E.F.
Belgium

Army Form C. 2118.

Place	Date	Hour	Summary of Events and Information	Remarks and references to Appendices
POLHILL CAMP	9th		Decrease: Evacuated 10. Transferred 1. Total 11 O.R.	
	11th		Brigade training field day. similar to the previous battalion ones.	
near HAANDEKOT	12th		Moved back to POLHILL CAMP again at conclusion of training	
	13th		Brigade sports this afternoon. Battalion won Band Race, Officers' Pick a back race. Despatch Bicycle race 2nd & 3rd. Tug of war 2nd.	
"				
"	14th		Marched to Bandaghinghem station & entrained for Elverdinghe, to MICHEL FARM & supplied working parties to the R.E.	
ELVERDINGHE MICHEL Fm.	15th		Increase during week ending 14/10/17	
			Drafts from base. O.R. 74. — Decrease.	
			Rejoined from Hosp. 2. — To base (under age) 1. O.R.	
			— under arrest 1. — Evacuated. 8. O.R.	
			Total. 77 Other Ranks. Total 9 Other Ranks.	
"	15		Working parties to R.E. as before.	
	16		Battalion returned to POLHILL CAMP today by train to BANDAGHINGHEM.	
to parade →	17th Sunday / 18th		Brigade ceremonial parade before Gen. La CAPELLE, cmdt. 5th French Army Corps - who presented French decorations including CROIX DE GUERRE to PTE MASSEY No 4924. 1st Border Regt.	

2353 Wt. W2544/1454 700,000 5/15 D. D. & L. A.D.S.S./Forms/C. 2118.

Serial. No. 30. Sheet 3.

Instructions regarding War Diaries and Intelligence Summaries are contained in F. S. Regs., Part II. and the Staff Manual respectively. Title Pages will be prepared in manuscript.

September

WAR DIARY
or
~~INTELLIGENCE SUMMARY~~

(Erase heading not required.)

1st Bn Border Regt. Belgium

Army Form C. 2118.

Place	Date	Hour	Summary of Events and Information	Remarks and references to Appendices
PORHILL CAMP	19th		Bathing & inspections	[illegible]
HENLEY CAMP	20		Battalion moved to HENLEY CAMP behind ELVERDINGHE very comfortable camp. Enemy aeroplanes dropped bombs fairly near during night but no casualties nor damage done.	[illegible]
(FOREST AREA)	21st		Training at HENLEY CAMP & started Battalion inter platoon football matches.	
	22nd		Training &c as yesterday 21st.	
			Casualties week ending 21st. Off. O.R.	
			Increase. Rejoined from Hosp. — 1	
			Draft from base 1. 12. 2/Lt R.W. Raine	
			On appointment 1 2/Lt T.S. Gayfer	
			Decrease. Transferred 6/7th Bn on appointment 1. Lt Buckman	
			Transferred 87 T.M.B. 1. 2/Lt R.L. Beck	
			To base under age. 1.	
			Evacuated 10.	
			Promoted to Commission. 1. (Sergt) to 2/Lt Gayfer.	[illegible]
	23rd		Church parade.	
	24th 30th		Training at Henley Camp.	[illegible]

2449 Wt. W14957/M90 750,000 1/16 J.B.C. & A. Forms/C.2118/12.

Serial No 30 Sheet 4.

Instructions regarding War Diaries and Intelligence Summaries are contained in F. S. Regs., Part II. and the Staff Manual respectively. Title Pages will be prepared in manuscript.

WAR DIARY

or

~~INTELLIGENCE~~ SUMMARY

(Erase heading not required.)

1st The Border Regt.
B.E.F. Belgium.

Army Form C. 2118.

Place	Date	Hour	Summary of Events and Information			Remarks and references to Appendices
HENIEF Camp	29.		Casualties for Week ended 29th	Off.	O.R.	
			Arrivals from Corps Depot.		17.	
			Rejoined		2.	
					19.	
			Transferred to 8?th K.R.R.		3.	
			Wounded (Gas.)		1.	
			Wounded		2.	
			Executed.		6.	
					12.	

Arthur B. Sutcliffe Capt.
Adjutant 1st Border Regiment.

2449 Wt. W14957/M90 750,000 1/16 J.B.C. & A. Forms/C.2118/12.

Confidential

81 K.

87
29

War Diary

of

1st Battalion The Border Regiment

From 1st October 1917 To. 31st October 1917

Volume 31.

Instructions regarding War Diaries and Intelligence Summaries are contained in F. S. Regs., Part II. and the Staff Manual respectively. Title pages will be prepared in manuscript.

Dunkirk 31

WAR DIARY
or
INTELLIGENCE SUMMARY.
(Erase heading not required.)

October 1917

1st Bn The Border Regt
B. E. F

Army Form C. 2118.

Place	Date	Hour	Summary of Events and Information	Remarks and references to Appendices
CHARTERHOUSE CAMP	1st		At CHARTERHOUSE CAMP the enemy dropped bombs in evening no casualties.	[illegible]
"	2nd		Bn relieved 2nd SWB's in trenches in WIDJENDRIFT sector no casualties during relief	[illegible]
Trenches	3rd		Day quiet very little enemy shelling.	[illegible]
"	4th		Our barrage dropped 5.45 am, Enemy heavily shelled our sector all day, very few casualties	[illegible]
"	5th		Relieved by Coldstream Gds & Grenadier Gds, Bn marched to CHARTERHOUSE CAMP arrived 2 am	[illegible]
CHARTERHOUSE CAMP	"		Increases & decreases for week ending 5-10-17	
			Increase	
			Arrivals at Corps Dept from Base — Off — / OR 17	
			Decrease	
			Transferred to Base (unfit for further service at front) — OR 1	
			Killed — OR 7	
			Died of wounds (2-10-17) 2nd Lt S B Cropper — Off 1	
			Wounded (4-10-17) 2nd Lt Raine — Off 1, OR 20	
			Missing — OR 1	
			Total — Off 2, OR 29	[illegible]
CHARTERHOUSE CAMP	6th		Bn marched to DUBLIN CAMP (huts) good	[illegible]
DUBLIN CAMP	7th		Kit inspection by Company Officers	[illegible]
"	8th		Resting.	[illegible]
	9th		Bn marched to ELVERDINGHE entrained for PROVEN & marched to PIDDINGTON CAMP (tents) very wet & muddy	[illegible]

T2134. Wt. W708—776. 500000. 4/15. Sir J. C. & S.

Serial 51

Instructions regarding War Diaries and Intelligence Summaries are contained in F. S. Regs., Part II. and the Staff Manual respectively. Title pages will be prepared in manuscript.

October 1917

WAR DIARY
or
INTELLIGENCE SUMMARY.
(Erase heading not required.)

1st Bn The Border Regt
B.E.F.

Army Form C. 2118.

Place	Date	Hour	Summary of Events and Information	Remarks and references to Appendices
FIDDINGTON CAMP	10th		Rested & cleaned up	
"	11th		Rain. Improved camp chiefly draining	[illegible]
"	12th		Rained all day. Increases & decreases for week ending 12-10-17	[illegible]
			Increases — Off / OR	
			Wounded at duty (previously reported wounded 1st Lt [illegible]) — 1 / –	
			Drafts from Base 2nd Lt A [illegible], 2nd Lt G [illegible] — 2 / 129	
			Rejoined from hospital — / 1	
			Total — 3 / 130	[illegible]
			Decreases	
			Killed — 2	
			Wounded — 2	
			Transferred to [illegible] Army [illegible] School — 1	
			Evac from [illegible] — 6	
			Total — 11	
"	13th		Rained all day. State of camp terrible. Troops working all day on drains & road	[illegible]
"	14th		Ditto	[illegible]
"	15th		Bn marched to [illegible] entrained 2 am 16th.	
			Billets good	[illegible]
BAILLEULMONT	16th		[illegible] 5 pm & marched to BAILLEULMONT	[illegible]
"	17th		Settling down in billets & arranging for intensive training	[illegible]
"	18th		Commenced platoon training & training of specialists	[illegible]

2353 Wt. W2544/1454 700,000 5/15 D. D. & L. A.D.S.S./Forms/C. 2118.

Serial 51

October 1917

Instructions regarding War Diaries and Intelligence Summaries are contained in F. S. Regs., Part II. and the Staff Manual respectively. Title pages will be prepared in manuscript.

WAR DIARY
or
INTELLIGENCE SUMMARY.
(Erase heading not required.)

Army Form C. 2118.

1st Bn The Border Regt
B.E.F.

Place	Date	Hour	Summary of Events and Information	Remarks and references to Appendices
BAILLEULMONT	19th		Continued Platoon training. Increase & decrease for week ending 19-10-17 — Increase: Rejoined from 87th T.M.B. 2nd Lt Beckh — Off. 1, OR –; Decrease: Transferred to 87th T.M.B. — 1; To England sick (5-10-17) 2nd Lt Lowther(?) — 1; Evac from Div Area — 6; total 1 / 7	[initials]
"	20th		Col Ellis DSO took command of 87th Bde	
"	"		during Gen Lucas' absence on leave to England	[initials]
"	21st		Church parade.	[initials]
"	22nd		Continued training, Pte Downie wounded rifle grenade (accidently)	[initials]
"	23rd		" "	[initials]
"	24th		" "	[initials]
"	25th		2nd Lt H S Park killed (bombing accident)	[initials]
"	26th		Continued training Gen de Lisle came round	[initials]
"			Increases & decreases for week ending 26-10-17	
			Increases — Offrs. / OR: Draft from Base — / 1; Rejoined ex Hospital — / 1; " from 87th T.M.B — / 1; total 3	[initials]
			Decreases: Killed (accidentally) 2nd Lt Park (25-10-17) 1; Died of wounds accidental — 1; Wounded " — 2; Evac from Div Area — 9; Transferred to 87th T.M.B — 1; " " XIV Corps School — 3; total 1 / 16	[initials]

Instructions regarding War Diaries and Intelligence Summaries are contained in F. S. Regs., Part II. and the Staff Manual respectively. Title pages will be prepared in manuscript.

Diary 31 October 1917

WAR DIARY
or
INTELLIGENCE SUMMARY.
(*Erase heading not required.*)

1st Bn The Border Regt B.E.F.

Army Form C. 2118.

Place	Date	Hour	Summary of Events and Information	Remarks and references to Appendices
BAILLEULMONT	27th		Lt R Canfield & 2nd Lt Devereux-Edgington & Little joined from Base & 2nd Booth rejoined.	[illegible]
"	28th		Anniv des Molinis, special dinner for men & free beer & special dinner for all officers at Bn Mess in the Recreation hut in village. The following officers belonging to the regiment being guests Brig Gen H Nelson DSO Cmdg 88th Bde – A Brig (?) J Ellis DSO Cmdg 87th Bde Lt Col Forbes Robertson DSO Cmdg 16th Middlesex Regt – Lt Col G Harrison DSO Cmdg 6th Corps School & Capt Pierre de Soissons (special attachment) 43 officers in all attended.	[illegible]
"	29th		Continued training	
"	30th		" " also practice Bde ceremonial parade.	[illegible]
"	31st		Continued training	[illegible]

[illegible] Capt
a/Adjutant
1st Border Regt

2353 Wt. W2541/1454 700,000 5/15 D. D. & L. A.D.S.S./Forms/C. 2118.

87/29 32 D

Confidential

War Diary

of

1st Battalion, The Border Regiment

From 1st Nov. 1917 To. 31st Nov. 1917

Folio. 39

1/120

Sheet I Serial No. 32

Instructions regarding War Diaries and Intelligence Summaries are contained in F. S. Regs., Part II, and the Staff Manual respectively. Title Pages will be prepared in manuscript.

November 1917

WAR DIARY
or
INTELLIGENCE SUMMARY
(Erase heading not required).

1st Bn The Border Regt.

Army Form C. 2118.

Place	Date	Hour	Summary of Events and Information	Remarks and references to Appendices
BAILLEULMONT	1st		Brigade ceremonial parade at L'ALLOUETTE near RANSART before the Divisional Commander.	[illegible]
"	2.		Training on Battalion training area.	[illegible]
"	3.		Major R.P.M. NICKOLS left the Battalion to assume duties of chief instructor at IIIrd Corps School. CAPT. H. SUTCLIFFE M/C took over temporary command of Battalion	[illegible]
"	4.		Church parade	[illegible]
"	5		Training as usual.	[illegible]
"	6.		Continued Training	[illegible]
"	7.		Commenced Battalion training in open warfare.	
"	8.		Continued training.	[illegible]
"	9.		Continued battalion training, advanced guards, crossing bridgeheads etc.	[illegible]
"	10.		Training on RANSART training ground.	[illegible]
"	11.		Conference at Divisional H.Q.	[illegible]
"	11.		Brigade field day training at RANSART	[illegible]
"	12.		Continued training in preparation for forthcoming operations.	
"	14.		another field day at RANSART	
"	15.		Divisional field day at RANSART.	[illegible]
"	16.		Battalion marched from BAILLEULMONT at 3PM & marched to BOISLEUX AU MONT & entrained at 1AM. for PERONNE. — detrained	
HAUT ALLAINES	17		about 4 AM and marched to HAUT ALLAINES. into Nissen huts just arriving at dawn.	[illegible]
FINS	18		moved this evening. marched at 6 PM. to FINS into DESSART WOOD huts arriving about 1 AM. ~~[illegible]~~ Everyone very tired	[illegible]

BSD - B. M351/22/11. 12/15 5000.

Sheet 2. Serial 32 November 1917. 1st The BORDER REGT. 87th Bde. France.

Instructions regarding War Diaries and Intelligence Summaries are contained in F. S. Regs., Part II, and the Staff Manual respectively. Title Pages will be prepared in manuscript.

WAR DIARY
or
INTELLIGENCE SUMMARY

(Erase heading not required).

Army Form C. 2118.

Place	Date	Hour	Summary of Events and Information	Remarks and references to Appendices
DESSART WOOD	19th		Rested in DESSART WOOD. Issued all battle stores & completed arrangements for the battle tomorrow.	
	20th	1 AM.	The battalion, less 5% details - moved out of DESSART WOOD to the concentration area BORDERER RIDGE GOUZEAUCOURT arriving there without incident at about 3 AM. Here the batt [illegible] formed close column of companies facing north - bivouacked and lay down to await dawn & zero hour. The night was fine but bitterly cold and troops were simply in battle order so that very little rest was obtained. At 6.20 AM ZERO - the barrage dropped with a crash & everyone watched the show with keen interest. At 7 AM the battalion started to move following the 1st K.O.S.B. and proceeded on the west of the GOUZEAUCOURT MARCOING railway to the "jumping off place" - the sunken road running NORTH from the northern outskirts of VILLERS PLOUICH arriving here about 8 AM and waited eagerly for the permission to advance, which was given at 10.05 AM - immediately news was received that the HINDENBURG support had fallen. During our wait in the sunken road a number of casualties were sustained by the battalion chiefly in the SOUTHERN portion of the sunken road - from shellfire chiefly shrapnel. Here Capt. J.C. CLARKE MC RAMC the regimental M.O. was wounded but he proceeded to obtain a relief M.O. before going to hospital. At 10.05 AM the advance was started in diamond formation of companies. A coy the lead [illegible]	
		6.00	(faint time entry in Hour column, placement uncertain)	

BSD - B. M351/22/11. 12/15 5000.

Sheet II. Serial No 2[illegible] November 1917

Instructions regarding War Diaries and Intelligence Summaries are contained in F. S. Regs., Part II, and the Staff Manual respectively. Title Pages will be prepared in manuscript.

WAR DIARY
or
INTELLIGENCE SUMMARY
(Erase heading not required).

Army Form C. 2118.

1st The Border Regt
B.E.F. France.

Place	Date	Hour	Summary of Events and Information	Remarks and references to Appendices
			under Capt B.H. Chambers M.C. B. Coy right flank coy under 2Lt J.W. JOHNSTON. D.C.M. C. coy left flank coy under Capt R.E.S. JOHNSON and The rear point batt^n H Quarters under Lieut. Col. A.J. ELLIS D.S.O. and D. Coy under Captain B Butler. M.C. A distance of about 400 was kept behind the 1st Bn K.O.S.B. ~~The~~ The first and second objectives were crossed easily. The enemy guns were silent and no infantry opposition was encountered. On reaching the outskirts of MARCOING a short halt was made to enable the 1 K.O.S.B. to get into the village. About 15 min as there appeared to be little opposition, the BORDER REG entered MARCOING close on the heels of the K.O.S.B. and A & D Coys pushed across the railway bridge across the canal. C Company crossing by the bridge at L.23.b.2.9 at 12.12 P.M. A hostile machine gun was in action in the open on the Railway Station platform. The crew of the gun was shot & the gun [illegible] captured and the advance continued. A & D Companies moving by the East side of the railway and C Company by the west. B Coy had been involved in the taking of MARCOING COPSE in conjunction with the ROYAL INNISKILLING FUS. A, D & C Companies had completed the crossing of the canal & were ready to continue the advance on to the final objective by 12.20. P.m.	

BSD - B. M351/22/11. 12/15 5000.

Sheet 4. Serial No. 32 November 1917

WAR DIARY
or
INTELLIGENCE SUMMARY.
(*Erase heading not required.*)

1st The BORDER REGt
B.E.F. France.

Army Form C. 2118.

Instructions regarding War Diaries and Intelligence Summaries are contained in F. S. Regs., Part II. and the Staff Manual respectively. Title pages will be prepared in manuscript.

Place	Date	Hour	Summary of Events and Information	Remarks and references to Appendices
MARCOING			As the enemy appeared to be thoroughly disorganised the order was given to the three companies to push on to the final objective. On the way one platoon of C Coy under 2nd Lt W.G. DENAREAZ silenced and captured two machine guns which were firing in the vicinity of the LOCK BRIDGE at L.23.b.29. The first serious opposition was met with when A Coy on the right flank reached the sunken road running from L.18.b.4.5. towards the ammunition pits in L.19.c. These pits were strongly held by the enemy with machine guns and half a battalion of infantry. As the ROYAL INNISKILLEN FUSILIERS who were to be on our immediate right flank had not yet come up the advance had to be checked and a defensive flank formed facing WEST. This necessitated the employment of D company as A company was in danger of being outflanked. B company in the meantime came across the canal and were placed in battalion reserve – having crossed the canal by the bridge at G.23.d.9.2. This company was held in readiness under the WEST embankment of the Railway Station.	[illegible]

2353. Wt. W2544/1454 700,000 5/15 D. D. & L. A.D.S.S./Forms/C. 2118.

Sheet 5. Serial No 32 November 1917. 1st The BORDER Regt. 87th Brigade.

Instructions regarding War Diaries and Intelligence Summaries are contained in F. S. Regs., Part II. and the Staff Manual respectively. Title pages will be prepared in manuscript.

WAR DIARY or INTELLIGENCE SUMMARY.

(*Erase heading not required.*)

Army Form C. 2118.

Place	Date	Hour	Summary of Events and Information	Remarks and references to Appendices
MARCOING	20th		The O.C. of this company reported that the S.W.B. and Roy. Innis. Fus. had experienced considerable difficulty in effecting a crossing and that therefore the latter regiment was some distance behind the Battalion's right flank. On receipt of this information a message was at once dispatched to O.C. Roy. Innis. Fus. requesting him to push on with all possible speed. At the same time a message asking for the assistance of tanks was sent both to O.C. TANKS and Brigade at 13.30.	
			Shortly after the dispatch of this message, a combined attack of [illegible] and the Roy. Innis. Fus. succeeded in clearing the communication [illegible] and a line was established from the canal at L.7.d.6.4. to L.2.4.a.7.9 slightly in advance of the road.	
			At 14.15 a message was sent to Brigade stating that touch had been gained with Roy. Innis. Fus. on the right and that the leading companies were being reinforced with the remaining company of the Battalion (B Coy) and that an attack would be launched immediately.	
			Shortly after the dispatch of this message the O.C. Roy. Innis. Fus. arrived at Battn. H.Q. in MARCOING Station with the [illegible]	

T2134. Wt. W708—776. 500000. 4/15. Sir J. C. & S.

Sheet 6. Serial No. 32 November 1917

Instructions regarding War Diaries and Intelligence Summaries are contained in F. S. Regs., Part II. and the Staff Manual respectively. Title pages will be prepared in manuscript.

WAR DIARY
or
INTELLIGENCE SUMMARY.

(Erase heading not required.)

1st Battn The Border Regt.
R. E. Jeans

Army Form C. 2118.

Place	Date	Hour	Summary of Events and Information	Remarks and references to Appendices
MARCOING	20th		that his right flank was being heavily engaged by machine gun fire from the northern outskirts of MASNIERES. Capt Raikes o/c TANKS allotted to 87th Infantry Brigade who was also present offered to send four tanks round to assist the Roy. Innis. Fus. This arrangement was agreed upon but by the time the tanks arrived at the required place the o/c Roy. Innis. Fus. considered that it was too dark to carry out the attack and countermanded the order to attack to his battalion informing the right & centre companies of 1 BORDER REGT that he had done so. Meantime at about 4 p.m. orders had been sent to the companies of 1st Border Regiment to start the attack but o/c D & A companies having been informed that the Roy. Innis. Fus. were not going to attack came back to Battn HQ to ask for further instructions. On learning ~~the situation~~ how things stood orders were at once issued to all companies that the attack was postponed. This order did not reach CAPT. R.E.S. JOHNSON o/c C Coy. on the left flank in time to stop his advance. He accordingly attacked the third objective on the frontage from G.13.b.5.6. to G.7.d.2.2. following a tank which was advancing in this sector. He succeeded in penetrating the BOCHE LINE just SOUTH of FOOT FARM capturing two machine guns and a number of prisoners. His exposed right flank was however heavily engaged with machine gun fire from parties of the enemy	

2353 Wt. W2544/1454 700,000 5/15 D. D. & L. A.D.S.S./Forms/C. 2118.

[illegible] / Serial No. 32 November 1917 — 1st [illegible] Border Regt.

Instructions regarding War Diaries and Intelligence Summaries are contained in F. S. Regs., Part II. and the Staff Manual respectively. Title Pages will be prepared in manuscript.

WAR DIARY
or
INTELLIGENCE SUMMARY

(Erase heading not required.)

Army Form C. 2118.

Place	Date	Hour	Summary of Events and Information	Remarks and references to Appendices
MARCOING.			were working round his flank. He was accordingly ordered to return to his original line which he skilfully accomplished, bringing in two enemy prisoners. [illegible] then proceeded to [illegible] [illegible] the Capt. [illegible] [illegible] consolidate on his present front line. [illegible] carried out during the night. Three companies C. A. D. holding a line of strongpoints just NE of the Sunken road from G.13.d.6.1. to the road at G.18.[illegible].2.7. and one company B. in support along the Sunken road near [illegible].3.	
			The enemy did not counter attack during the night and good progress was made in the consolidation.	
	21 Nov		The early part of the morning passed without incident, the enemy being very quiet [illegible] shelling and occasional M.G. bursts [illegible] [illegible] an attack on the third Objective [illegible] [illegible] [illegible] [illegible] [illegible] [illegible] [illegible]	
			[illegible] station. [illegible] over the crest was the signal for a terrific burst of machine gun fire from the enemy's position [illegible] THE N. [illegible] of [illegible] & FLOT FARM. This fire was so intense [illegible] It was evident that the enemy line had been strongly reinforced probably by another machine gun battalion, as many [illegible] appeared [illegible] machine guns in action.	

2449 Wt. W14957/M90 750,000 1/16 J.B.C. & A. Forms/C.2118/12.

Sheet 8 — Serial 32. November 1917. 1st The BORDER REGT. B.E.F. France.

Army Form C. 2118.

Instructions regarding War Diaries and Intelligence Summaries are contained in F. S. Regs., Part II. and the Staff Manual respectively. Title pages will be prepared in manuscript.

WAR DIARY
or
INTELLIGENCE SUMMARY.
(Erase heading not required.)

Place	Date	Hour	Summary of Events and Information	Remarks and references to Appendices
MARCOING.	21.		The Battalion, which had been held in reserve to support the K.O.S.B. attack if necessary was not called upon to take any part in the operations. By about 3.30 P.M. the operations for the day closed. Our lack because of slight near FOOT FARM and those to the right lead to our line were badly shot about by armour piercing bullets & their personnel had suffered heavy casualties. Consolidation of the position was carried on during the night but as the enemy was reported by Brigade to be massing for a counter attack in rafts N. NORTH of ROUMINHL a large number of men were required for patrolling purposes. The night however passed quietly & there was no sign of any counter attack tendencies on the battalion front.	
	22nd		During the morning a daring daylight reconnaissance was carried out by Lt. J.W. JOHNSTON D.C.M. (O/C 1st Coy) & from information received from him it was decided to push the line forward to the line G.13.d.7.1. to L.18.d.5.6. This line afforded a better field of fire & was already marked by an old cable trench dug to a depth of about 1'6". Good progress was made with this during the night & it was possible to occupy it by day on the 23rd.	
	23.		Nothing of interest occurred during the day though enemy shelling became rather pronounced, a certain amount of T.M. and field gun registration on the part of the enemy took place & their air activity – low flying to locate our	

1577 Wt. W10791/1773 500,000 1/15 D. D. & L. A.D.S.S./Forms/C. 2118.

Sheet 9.
Sinal. 32.

Instructions regarding War Diaries and Intelligence Summaries are contained in F. S. Regs., Part II. and the Staff Manual respectively. Title pages will be prepared in manuscript.

November 1917.

WAR DIARY
or
INTELLIGENCE SUMMARY.
(*Erase heading not required.*)

1st R. Inniskilling Fus. [illegible] Regt. France.

Army Form C. 2118.

Place	Date	Hour	Summary of Events and Information	Remarks and references to Appendices
			positions increased. Lewis gun fire was directed on the low flying aircraft but with no apparent result. Counter sniping was instituted with good results & at least two enemy snipers were definitely accounted for. During the night 23/24th work was pushed forward vigorously & the wiring of the whole front was taken in hand. A C.T. was also cut through from the sunken road to the firing line with the result that it was possible to go round the whole front line from our junction on the right with the Royal Inniskilling Fusiliers to the railway by daylight on the 24th. 3 Officers patrols went out during the night to the enemy lines & reported that the enemy was hard at work consolidating the FLOT FARM - RUMILLY line.	
	24th		The day passed uneventfully. The enemy shelling MARCOING and B[illegible] in the Station to a limited extent & leaving the front line alone. His sniping though persistent never became formidable. During the night 24/25th work was continued and wiring of the whole front and by dawn the line was a good deep substantial trench with firesteps and C.T. were 6 feet deep. Also the whole front was covered	

1577 Wt. W10791/1773 500,000 1/15 D. D. & L. A.D.S.S./Forms/C. 2118.

Sheet 10. Serial 32. November 1917. 1st The Border Regt.

Instructions regarding War Diaries and Intelligence Summaries are contained in F. S. Regs., Part II. and the Staff Manual respectively. Title pages will be prepared in manuscript.

WAR DIARY
or
INTELLIGENCE SUMMARY.
(Erase heading not required.)

Army Form C. 2118.

Place	Date	Hour	Summary of Events and Information	Remarks and references to Appendices
MARCOING	24		by a double belt of wire including knife rests. Most of the digging was performed with captured enemy tools and all the wire & knife rests were Boche, collected from the vicinity of a large Dump in the railway Station.	[illegible]
	25.		The day passed quietly, the enemy showing slight artillery, T.M. & air activity – while ours was nil. The battalion was relieved this evening by the 1 Newfoundland Regt. & the relief was carried out without a hitch or a casualty, relief complete being reported by 7.30 P.M. The attached maps shew final dispositions before handing over. The front line was held on the picquet system, each platoon forming a "picquet" and only that portion of the fire trench required by the garrison being firestepped, the intervening portions being used merely for lateral communication. This system was found to work admirably. From the 20th to the 25th the Battalion, with a trench strength of about 400, dug 1500x of trench to an average depth of 4' 6" & wired a front of about 900x with a double belt of wire & knife rest entanglements.	[illegible]

1577 Wt. W10791/1773 500,000 1/15 D. D. & L. A.D.S.S./Forms/C. 2118.

Sheet 11. Serial 32. November 1917

Instructions regarding War Diaries and Intelligence Summaries are contained in F. S. Regs., Part II. and the Staff Manual respectively. Title pages will be prepared in manuscript.

WAR DIARY
or
INTELLIGENCE SUMMARY.
(Erase heading not required.)

1st The Border Regt.
29 Div. [illegible]

Army Form C. 2118.

Place	Date	Hour	Summary of Events and Information	Remarks and references to Appendices
MARCOING	26		The battalion moved into MARCOING and lived in cellars. Cleaning up & resting. Good cellar accommodation for nearly the whole battalion - Thanks to the BOCHE most were heavily protected & beds erected in them, several being nicely boarded & furnished with stoves. Quantities of coal - vegetables etc. were also found & the troops were quite happy. The whole village - which was then practically undamaged - was quite the most comfortable the troops had been in since BAILLEULMONT on the 16th. All the houses contained scores of German rifles, heaps of clothing & equipment - quartermasters' stores of bread & rations were found, also many enormous sheepskin full length greatcoats apparently from the Russian front & the troops utilised these for their comfort as they had no greatcoats being in battle order. The troops thoroughly enjoyed themselves & the morale was at boiling point having worked up higher & higher daily from the commencement of the attack.	

Sheet 12. Serial 32. November 1917

Instructions regarding War Diaries and Intelligence Summaries are contained in F. S. Regs., Part II. and the Staff Manual respectively. Title Pages will be prepared in manuscript.

WAR DIARY *or* INTELLIGENCE SUMMARY

(Erase heading not required.)

1 The Border Regt. 1584 France.

Army Form C. 2118.

Place	Date	Hour	Summary of Events and Information	Remarks and references to Appendices
MARCOING	28.		Moved into the firing line into our old sector in relief of the Newfoundland Regt. taken over from G.13.c.4.2. to ESCAUT RIVER at L.17 b.5.2. The firing line was held by 3 companies as shewn in attached sketch. with 1. coy. in support in the Strongpoint at L.18.d.3.2. The relief was carried out without difficulty & was complete by about 7.30 pm. Work on the firing line & communication & wiring was carried on during the night. Line for a new support line was selected by Lt Col A.J. ELLIS D.S.O. comdg. The night passed uneventfully.	
	29th		Enemy showed increased artillery activity during the day & registered on our front line & communication trenches. The bulk of the shelling however, was on Battn HQ. MARCOING STATION & the village. The Railway bridge across the canal always a favourite target was particularly well strafed at night. With the assistance of 2nd SWB. party of 60, 180x of new support line was dug & completed to dimensions of 3' x 3' x 2'. also firing line deepened & improved & were considerably strengthened.	

Sheet [illegible] November 1917

Instructions regarding War Diaries and Intelligence Summaries are contained in F. S. Regs., Part II. and the Staff Manual respectively. Title Pages will be prepared in manuscript.

WAR DIARY
or
INTELLIGENCE SUMMARY
(Erase heading not required.)

1st The Border Regt.
[illegible] France.

Army Form C. 2118.

Place	Date	Hour	Summary of Events and Information	Remarks and references to Appendices
			C Coy dug a communication trench connecting their front line with their supporting platoon & back to the work crossing at the junction of the railway & the sunken road.	
[illegible]	30		At 7.45 AM., as the C.O. & adjutant were visiting the line the enemy commenced heavy shelling of the whole front line with a good deal of gas shell - lachrymatory & slight mustard oil - for the first time in this sector - causing a certain number of casualties. From the intensity & extent it was obvious that the BOCHE was contemplating attacking somewhere. All lines to the rear were cut & no information came through till about 10.30 when the line to the Roy Innis Fus was working for a few minutes. The O/C Roy Innis Fus first stated that it appeared that our troops had been driven out of MASNIERES & a few moments later stated that the enemy was firing into his own Batt. H.Q. from across the canal at MARCOING COPSE. An order was sent at once to O/C B Coy to send a patrol out to his right flank & find out if the Roy Innis Fus were all right & to [illegible] his company	

2449 Wt. W14957/M90 750,000 1/16 J.B.C. & A. Forms/C.2118/12.

Plat III Series 32 Nov. 1917

Instructions regarding War Diaries and Intelligence Summaries are contained in F. S. Regs., Part II. and the Staff Manual respectively. Title Pages will be prepared in manuscript.

WAR DIARY
or
INTELLIGENCE SUMMARY

(Erase heading not required.)

Army Form C. 2118.

1st The Border Regt. B.E.F. France.

Place	Date	Hour	Summary of Events and Information	Remarks and references to Appendices
			in readiness to form a defensive flank facing MASNIERES. ~~facing~~ MASNIERES.	
			At 11.15 AM. O/c B Coy reported Roy Innis Fus. all right & holding their original line. At 11.25. Sergt LEVITT came down from the front line wounded & reported that no hostile infantry movement had taken place on our immediate front & that everything was all right tho' we were having a fair number of casualties from hostile shelling.	
			At 11.50 hostile shelling died down considerably.	
			Enemy Aircraft were very active & had been from dawn flying ~~low~~ very low & quite unmolested. Very early in the proceedings they flew over & promptly downed the only observation balloon we had, in flames. At one time 17 and at another 23 E.A. were counted over our front. Lewis gunning appeared to have no effect.	
			At 12 noon. O/c D Coy reported that bar a few casualties from shellfire everything was all right on his front & also the Roy Innis Fus on his right.	
			At 12.35 a message was received from the Roy Innis Fus that at about 10 AM the enemy	

2449 Wt. W14957/M90 750,000 1/16 J.B.C. & A. Forms/C.2118/12.

Sheet 16. Serial 32. Nov. 1917 — 1st The Border Regt. B.E.F. France

Instructions regarding War Diaries and Intelligence Summaries are contained in F. S. Regs., Part II. and the Staff Manual respectively. Title Pages will be prepared in manuscript.

Army Form C. 2118.

WAR DIARY
or
INTELLIGENCE SUMMARY
(Erase heading not required.)

Place	Date	Hour	Summary of Events and Information	Remarks and references to Appendices
Marcoing Trenches	20		had broken through beyond his right & had actually been right round MARCOING COPSE & as far as the outskirts of the village. They had however been counterattacked by a part collected by Capt J W EWBANK M.C. from Brigade Headquarters. Then by 2nd SWB & 1 KOSB & finally by units of the 88th Inf. Brigade & driven right out of MASNIERES back to their original line. This message was confirmed by one from Brigade H.Q. which arrived about 12.50 P.M. The shelling on our front died down in the afternoon & almost ceased at dusk, & a fairly quiet night resulted although everyone remained on the alert as no information on the situation generally was obtainable & our present position appeared to be very precarious. Every precaution was taken however & arrangements made to hold everything even to the last including Batt H.Q. who were mobilised & prepared. Total casualties of the month - weekly - & during the battle - daily - are attached.	

Arthur [illegible] Capt & Adjutant

2449 Wt. W14957/M90 750,000 1/16 J.B.C. & A. Forms/C.2118/12.

Sheet 16. Sernac 32. November 917. 1st The Border Regt. B.E.F. France.

Army Form C. 2118.

* Instructions regarding War Diaries and Intelligence Summaries are contained in F. S. Regs., Part II. and the Staff Manual respectively. Title Pages will be prepared in manuscript.

WAR DIARY
or
INTELLIGENCE SUMMARY
(Erase heading not required.)

Place	Date	Hour	Summary of Events and Information	Remarks and references to Appendices
MARCOING.			The officers who took part in the action were as follows.	
			Bn H.Q. Lt Col. A J ELLIS D.S.O. commanding.	
			CAPT A.N. SUTCLIFFE M.C. adjutant	
			Capt G.B. CARGILL. asst adjt & Intelligence offr	
			Lt G.H.S. McDONALD. Signalling Officer.	
			CAPT. J. COURTNEY CLARKE M.C. RAMC. Regtal M.O.	
			A Coy. Capt. B.F.H. Chambers. M.C. o/c coy.	
			2Lt. B. GASH.	
			L.V. LITTLE	
			O DAFFURN	
			B Coy. 2Lt. J.W. JOHNSTON o/c.	
			Lt. R.L. BECKH.	
			W.R. PETTIFER.	
			C.W. SAYNOR.	
			C. Coy. CAPT R.E.S. JOHNSON o/c	
			Lt. J.L.P. GAMON.	
			2Lt S.M. OGDEN	
			2Lt. W.G. DENEREAZ.	
			D. Coy. Capt. W.D. BUTLER M.C.	
			Lt. L. MACHEL.	
			2Lt. M. ELRINGTON.	
			2Lt. C. HELM.	
			[illegible signature] Col.	

2449 Wt. W14957/M90 750,000 1/16 J.B.C. & A. Forms/C.2118/12.

Army Form C. 2118.

Instructions regarding War Diaries and Intelligence Summaries are contained in F. S. Regs., Part II. and the Staff Manual respectively. Title Pages will be prepared in manuscript.

WAR DIARY
or
INTELLIGENCE SUMMARY

(Erase heading not required.)

Place	Date	Hour	Summary of Events and Information	Remarks and references to Appendices

2440 Wt. W14957/M90 750,000 1/16 J.B.C. & A. Forms/C.2118/12.

Sheet 18 Serial 32 November 1917.

Army Form C. 2118.

Instructions regarding War Diaries and Intelligence Summaries are contained in F. S. Regs., Part II. and the Staff Manual respectively. Title Pages will be prepared in manuscript.

WAR DIARY
or
INTELLIGENCE SUMMARY

(Erase heading not required.)

1st/4th BORDER Regt
88 F. Brigade

Place	Date	Hour	Summary of Events and Information	Remarks and references to Appendices
			Casualties for November 1917.	
			Week ending 2/11/17. Increase. Drafts. Off. 4 — men 1. (2/Lt. E. Crutchley, 2/Lt. L. Little, 2/Lt. W. G. Deverenz, 2/Lt. H. Elrington)	
			Rejoined from Hosp. 7.	
			4 8	
			Decrease. 1. (2/Lt. J. G. Ramsay)	
			Transferred to TANK Corps. 1.	
			to 29 Div. HQ. 4	
			Evac. from Div. area [illegible]	
			1 + 5	
			Week ending 9.11.17. Decrease	
			Evac. from Div. area 5.	
			To England. 1. (Capt. A. Campbell)	
			Transf. to 29 Div. HQ 1.	
			XIV Corps. 1.	
			1 + 7.	
			Increase	
			Draft from Base 5.	
			Arrivals at Corps Depot 1.	
			Rejoined [illegible] 1.	
			7	

[Signature illegible]

2449 Wt. W14957/M90 750,000 1/16 J.B.C. & A. Forms/C.2118/12.

Sheet ~~20~~ 19

Period 32. November 1917

1st The Border Regt.

87 I.B.

France.

Army Form C. 2118.

WAR DIARY
or
INTELLIGENCE SUMMARY

(Erase heading not required.)

*Instructions regarding War Diaries and Intelligence Summaries are contained in F. S. Regs., Part II. and the Staff Manual respectively. Title Pages will be prepared in manuscript.

Place	Date	Hour	Summary of Events and Information	Remarks and references to Appendices
			Week ending 16/11/17. Increase. From base. Offr. — O.R. 2.	
			Hosp. 1.	
			3	
			Decrease. Transferred to ... 2	
			To England for Commission 1.	Sergt. ...
			Evacuated. 5.	
			8.	
			23/11/17. Increase. Rejoined from Hosp. 1.	
			4.	
			5	
			Decrease. Killed 22.	
			Wd. 2 92.	
			Missing 26.	
			2 140	
			30/11/17. Increase. Rejoined (previously Missing) 6.	
			Decrease. Killed. 3	
			Wd. 4.	
			Missing 2.	
			Evac. from Div. area 1	
			10	

[signature illegible]

33 K.

Confidential

War Diary

of

1st Battalion The Border Regiment

From: 1st December 1917 To: 31st December 1917

Folio 33.

WO 21

Sheet
Serial No 32 December 1917

Instructions regarding War Diaries and Intelligence Summaries are contained in F. S. Regs., Part II. and the Staff Manual respectively. Title pages will be prepared in manuscript.

WAR DIARY
or
INTELLIGENCE SUMMARY.
(Erase heading not required.)

1st The Border Regt.
B.E.F. France

Army Form C. 2118.

Place	Date	Hour	Summary of Events and Information	Remarks and references to Appendices
Trenches MARCOING	1/12/17		Situation most precarious & indefinite this morning heavy gunning could be heard on our immediate flanks but not very heavy on our own front. Received word from Brigade that the enemy broke through yesterday & captured GOUZEAUCOURT also ~~HESTRUT~~ LA VACQUERIE & LES RUES VERTES but large reinforcements had come up to counterattack & GUARDS retook GOUZEAUCOURT. Received message that 86th Brigade will probably evacuate MASNIERES this evening, & the Roy. Innis Fus. consequently refuse their right flank to conform to this. O/C B Coy therefore was ordered to carry out a reconnaissance of a possible support defensive line behind the Roy. Innis. Fus. this he did with great success. (2Lt J.W. JOHNSTON D.C.M.) At 4 P.m. a message was received from Brig Gen. CHEAPE comdg 86 Inf. Bde. that enemy were in the EAST side of LES RUES VERTES & that he was holding the bridge, but was in a very bad way & would probably be driven back. 2Lt J.W. JOHNSTON was therefore ordered to be ready at once to occupy his defensive flank through the ammunition pits. At 1830 a message from Brigade was received giving details of the arrangements for the withdrawal of 86th Inf Bde from MASNIERES.	

2353. Wt. W2544/1454 700,000 5/15 D. D. & L. A.D.S.S./Forms/C. 2118.

Sheet 2 Serial 33. December 1917

Instructions regarding War Diaries and Intelligence Summaries are contained in F. S. Regs., Part II. and the Staff Manual respectively. Title pages will be prepared in manuscript.

WAR DIARY
or
INTELLIGENCE SUMMARY.
(Erase heading not required.)

1st Bn Border Regt.
87 I.B.
France.

Army Form C. 2118.

Place	Date	Hour	Summary of Events and Information	Remarks and references to Appendices
Trenches MARCOING	1/12/17		The following message was therefore sent to all companies. The 86th Inf. Bde will withdraw from MASNIERES & LES RUES VERTES starting at 11 pm tonight. They will occupy a line running from G. 24. c 8.7 (covering lock bridge) to L 30 central. To conform to this the ROY INNIS FUS will form a defensive flank from their most advanced strongpoint, running East of ammunition pits to canal at about G.19.d 2.8. This flank will be continued by 2 coys of MONMOUTHS down to the railway bridge. 1st BORDER REGIMENT will hold on to its present line until further orders B coy being in readiness to form a defensive flank facing RIGHT. WEST of the ammunition pits, if necessary. These rearrangements were carried out during the night with great success in an orderly manner & without the enemy's knowledge. At 19.13 the Brigade Major sent a situation message stating that the line running South from the lock in G.24.c. ran along ditch through L 30 A & B joined at L.30 c. 8.7. thence S.W. to L.34. c. 8.4 At this time it was learned that CAPT J.H. EWBANK M.C. attached 87th Inf Brigade had been killed whilst gallantly leading a counter attack from MARCOING on the 30th inst. This counter attack consisting of Cooks & [illegible] etc had cleared the situation at MARCOING	[illegible initials]

2353 Wt. W2514/1454 700,000 5/15 D. D. & L. A.D.S.S./Forms/C. 2118.

Sheet 3 Serial 33. Dec 1917 — 1 Bn

Instructions regarding War Diaries and Intelligence Summaries are contained in F. S. Regs., Part II. and the Staff Manual respectively. Title Pages will be prepared in manuscript.

WAR DIARY
or
INTELLIGENCE SUMMARY
(Erase heading not required.)

Army Form C. 2118.

Place	Date	Hour	Summary of Events and Information	Remarks and references to Appendices
Trenches MARCOING	2.		The night passed quietly with only a moderate amount of shelling on our front. Enemy aircraft activity – which had been very marked & harassing during the 30th & 1st (37 enemy planes being over at one time flying at anything down to 150 feet!) was less pronounced, but ours were as little in evidence as they had been before. Got word that we should be relieved by a battalion from the 16th Brigade (6th D.W.) This evening an officer came up to reconnoitre the position. The day was uneventful & about 10.30 o'clock the relieving regiment came up & the relief was complete about 1.20	
Trenches MARCOING (Ribecourt)	3.		We left our original line dug on the 20th & succeeding days being handed over intact. On relief the battalion moved by MARCOING past the church to RIBECOURT & into the HINDENBURG LINE (SUPPORT). The troops were so exhausted on arrival as a result of the strain in the line that they slept on the firestep without coats or blankets in a severe frost as dug out accommodation was insufficient. Throughout the period from the 19th Nov – 3 Dec. they had been in fighting order – without coats or blankets in severe weather. Their fortitude & fighting spirit however were magnificent under most trying conditions.	

Sheet 4
Serial 33

December 1917

Instructions regarding War Diaries and Intelligence Summaries are contained in F. S. Regs., Part II. and the Staff Manual respectively. Title Pages will be prepared in manuscript.

WAR DIARY
or
INTELLIGENCE SUMMARY
(Erase heading not required.)

Army Form C. 2118.

1st Sh. Border Regt
B.E.F. France.

Place	Date	Hour	Summary of Events and Information	Remarks and references to Appendices
HINDENBURG SUPPORT LINE at RIBECOURT	4.		Enemy were attacking heavily on the right endeavouring to get WELSH RIDGE consequently a line of defence was reconnoitred in case WELSH RIDGE fell. Stood to most of the day ready to move if required. Heard BOURLON WOOD & MARCOING were evacuated during the night! Lt Col A J ELLIS who was temporarily commanding the Brigade last night returned to command the battalion today. Relieved this evening by 36th Division & the battalion marched back to SORREL. Everyone thoroughly exhausted & dead tired. arrived SORREL	
	5.		about 2 AM. – chiefly [?] but no accommodation. moved off at 10 AM marched to ETRICOURT entraining at 2 PM & arriving MONDICOURT about 6 PM. being shelled on the way near BAPAUME. marched 9 kilometres to GRAND RULLECOURT where all had comfortable billets & thoroughly appreciated them.	[illegible]
	6.		Rested at GRAND RULLECOURT.	
	7.		" "	
			Casualties week ending 7-12-17	
			Increase. Rejoined from Div[?] Base 5. Joined 1. Total 6.	
			Decrease. Killed: Off. 1, O.R. 1. Wounded: Off. 1, O.R. 18. Missing: O.R. 3. Evacuated: O.R. 15. Total: Off. 2, O.R. 37. Capt J W EWBANK M.C. 2Lt. W J C THOMPSON.	
			[signature] Capt.	

2449 Wt. W14957/M90 750,000 1/16 J.B.C. & A. Forms/C.2118/12.

Instructions regarding War Diaries and Intelligence Summaries are contained in F. S. Regs., Part II. and the Staff Manual respectively. Title Pages will be prepared in manuscript.

WAR DIARY
or
INTELLIGENCE SUMMARY
(Erase heading not required.)

Army Form C. 2118.

Serial 33 Dec. 1917

1st R. Innis. Fus. Regt. (?) B.E.F. France.

Place	Date	Hour	Summary of Events and Information	Remarks and references to Appendices
GRAND RULLECOURT	8		Conference at Divisional H.Q. where complimentary messages were read from everyone from Sir D Haig C in C. downwards complimenting the Division on their work at CAMBRAI. Billets at GRAND RULLECOURT	[illegible]
"	9			
"	10		Battalion Ceremonial parade. Gen Sir H. de Lisle rode on to parade & congratulated the battalion on its work at CAMBRAI.	
"	11		Capt A W SUTCLIFFE M.C. took over duties of a/Brigade major at 87th Bde & Capt E.G. CRAIG took over adjutant.	[illegible]
"	12		Continued training at GRAND RULLECOURT.	[illegible]
"	13		Lt Col A.H. MORRIS D.S.O. took over command of 87th Infantry Brigade temporarily & Maj. M.P.M. NICHOLS took over command of the battalion.	
"	14		Maj. M. NICHOLS went sick. Capt R.E.S. JOHNSON took over command. Battalion continued training.	
"	15		Continued training at Grand Rullecourt. [illegible]	
			Casualties week ending [illegible] Off. O.R.	
			Increase. Drafts from base 3. 91. Lt H.D. LEES M.C., 2Lt J. TURNER, 2Lt A.L. PRIDIcombe.	
			Rejoined from hospital [illegible] 4 — 8 95	
			Decrease. Wounded 2. Missing 1. Evacuated 35. Attached R.F.C. 1. Lt D. ELLIOT. Evac. sick to England 1. E.G. CRAIG. 2 + 38 O.R.	

2449 Wt. W14957/M90 750,000 1/16 J.B.C. & A. Forms/C.2118/12.

Sheet 6. Serial 33. December 1917.

WAR DIARY
or
INTELLIGENCE SUMMARY

(Erase heading not required.)

Instructions regarding War Diaries and Intelligence Summaries are contained in F. S. Regs., Part II. and the Staff Manual respectively. Title Pages will be prepared in manuscript.

Army Form C. 2118.

1st The Border Regt. B.E.F. France.

Place	Date	Hour	Summary of Events and Information	Remarks and references to Appendices
Grand Rullecourt	16		Resting	
FLERS	17		Moved to FLERS by march route. very bad going owing to deep snow. Transport did not get through.	
AZINCOURT	18		Marched to Agincourt. again bad roads & heavy going owing to snow. only a small amount of transport got through.	
CREQUY	19		Marched to CREQUY. similar conditions to the previous two days. but got lorries through today by main roads.	
"	20		CREQUY resting.	
"	21		" "	
			Casualties week ending 21/12/17.	
			Inc. Drafts from base — OR 60	
			Rejoined from Hosp. — 1	
			Total — 61	
			Decrease. Transferred to R.F.C. — Off. — OR.	
			Evac. from Div. Area — 12	
			Total — Off. 1 — OR. 12	
	22		CAPT A W SUTCLIFFE M.C. returned from 87th Inf Bde & took over command of the Battalion. Capt R.E.S. JOHNSON becoming 2nd in Command.	

Sheet 87
Serial 33.

December 1917.

Instructions regarding War Diaries and Intelligence Summaries are contained in F. S. Regs., Part II. and the Staff Manual respectively. Title Pages will be prepared in manuscript.

WAR DIARY
or
INTELLIGENCE SUMMARY
(Erase heading not required.)

1st The Border Regt.
B.E.F. France.

Army Form C. 2118.

Place	Date	Hour	Summary of Events and Information	Remarks and references to Appendices
CREQUY.	23		Resting at CREQUY.	
"	24		" "	
	25		CHRISTMAS DAY. Very excellent day for the battalion. Two pigs & beer etc. bought & excellent dinners were served. Gen Sir Aylmer Hunter Weston K.C.B. visited the battalion & expressed his admiration & wished them a merry Xmas & prosperous new year amid great demonstration & applause.	
"	26		Resting CREQUY. CAPT. W B SUTHERLAND M.C. took over 2nd in Command.	
	27		Training at Crequy.	
	28		Do — Do.	
			Casualties week ending 28/12/17. Off. 2. O.R. 39. 2Lt E.S. Oxley. 2Lt J.B. Trotter.	
			Rejoined from hospital 3.	
			2 42	
			Decrease. Transferred to 11th BORDER. 2. 2Lt T.S. Gayes. 2Lt J.B. Trotter.	
			Sick from Div. Area. 39	
			2 39.	

Sheet 8.
Serial 33. Dec 1917.

Instructions regarding War Diaries and Intelligence Summaries are contained in F. S. Regs., Part II. and the Staff Manual respectively. Title Pages will be prepared in manuscript.

WAR DIARY
or
INTELLIGENCE SUMMARY

(Erase heading not required.)

1st The Border Regt.
BEF France.

Army Form C. 2118.

Place	Date	Hour	Summary of Events and Information	Remarks and references to Appendices
CREQUY	29.		Training – still deep snow.	[illegible]
"	30.		Training weather still severe. snow & frost. Transport difficulties very great.	[illegible]
REMILLY WERQUIN	31.		Marched from Crequy to REMILLY WERQUIN. (32 kilometres) very bad going & deep snow in parts. only one man fell out, – this man fainted.	[illegible]

Arthur R. Sutcliffe Capt.
a/Adjutant, The Border Regt.
BEF France.

2449 Wt. W14957/M90 750,000 1/16 J.B.C. & A. Forms/C.2118/12.

Confidential

War Diary

of

1st Battalion The Border Regiment

From 1st Jan. 1918 To. 31st Jan. 1918

Folio 42.

Sheet 1 Serial 34

Instructions regarding War Diaries and Intelligence Summaries are contained in F. S. Regs., Part II. and the Staff Manual respectively. Title pages will be prepared in manuscript.

January 1918

WAR DIARY or INTELLIGENCE SUMMARY.

(Erase heading not required.)

1st Bn The Border Regt.

Army Form C. 2118.

Place	Date	Hour	Summary of Events and Information	Remarks and references to Appendices
LA CROSSE	1/1/18		Marched from RENTLY-WIRQUIN to LA CROSSE - Very bad going owing to deep snow	
ZERMEZEELE	2/1/18		" " LA CROSSE to ZERMEZEELE.	
HERZEELE	3/1/18		" " ZERMEZEELE to HERZEELE	
PROVEN	4/1/18		" " HERZEELE to PETWORTH CAMP (PROVEN)	
"	5/1/18		The Battalion furnished working parties for C.R.E XIXth Corps - working on defences E of BOESINGHE.	
			Casualties. Week ending 5/1/18. Increase. Draft from Base O/R 5	
			Rejoined from Hospital 2	
			— 7.	
			Decrease. Evac from Div Area. — 6.	
"	6/1/18		Battalion furnished working parties to C.R.E. XIXth Corps	
"	7/1/18		" " " " " "	
"	8/1/18		" " " " " "	
"	9/1/18		" " " " " "	
"	10/1/18		" " " " " "	
CARIBOU CAMP.	11/1/18		Marched to CARIBOU CAMP (DE WIPPE).	
			CAPT. W.B. BUTLER assumed Command of the Battalion	
			Capt. R.E.S JOHNSON took over 2nd in Command.	

2353 Wt. W2544/1454 700,000 5/15 D. D. & L. A.D.S.S./Forms/C. 2118.

Sheet 2. Serial 34

January 1918

Instructions regarding War Diaries and Intelligence Summaries are contained in F. S. Regs., Part II. and the Staff Manual respectively. Title pages will be prepared in manuscript.

WAR DIARY
or
INTELLIGENCE SUMMARY.
(Erase heading not required.)

1st Bn The Border Regt.

Army Form C. 2118.

Place	Date	Hour	Summary of Events and Information	Remarks and references to Appendices
CARIBOU CAMP.	12/1/18		Battalion supplied working parties to CRE. XIXth Corps	
			Casualties week ending 12.1.18. Increase. Rejoined from 87 Bde — O/O: – OR: 1; " " Hospital — OR: 5; Drafts from Base — OR: 6; Total — O/O: – OR: 12	
			Decrease. To England Sick — O/O: 2 OR: –; Evac. from Div Area — OR: 24; Transferred Base (over age) — OR: 1; Total — O/O: 2 OR: 25	Maj R.P.H. NICHOLS 2/Lt W.G. DENEREAZ.
"	13/1/18		Battalion furnished working parties for CRE. XIX Corps.	
	14/1/18		" " " " "	
	15/1/18		" " " " " "	
	16/1/18		" " " " " "	
	17/1/18		" " " " " " "	
BRANDHOEK	18/1/18		Battalion marched to 'B' Camp BRANDHOEK (28 NW. G6 d 4.2)	
"	19/1/18		Training at BRANDHOEK. CAPT A.B. CLAYTON assumed command of Battalion. Capt W.B. BUTLER MC took over 2/in Command.	

2353 Wt. W2544/1454 700,000 5/15 D. D. & L. A.D.S.S./Forms/C. 2118.

Sheet 3. Serial 34 January 1918

Instructions regarding War Diaries and Intelligence Summaries are contained in F. S. Regs., Part II. and the Staff Manual respectively. Title pages will be prepared in manuscript.

WAR DIARY or INTELLIGENCE. SUMMARY.

1st Bn The Border Regt

(Erase heading not required.)

Army Form C. 2118.

Place	Date	Hour	Summary of Events and Information	Remarks and references to Appendices
BRANDHOEK	19/1/18		Casualties week ending 19.1.18. Increase: Drafts from Base — Off 1, OR 7. Decrease: Evac. from Div Area — 6; Transferred Base (under age) — 1; total 7.	Capt. B.R. DURLACHER. M.C.
"	20/1/18		Training at BRANDHOEK	
	21/1/18		" " Capt W.B. BUTLER. M.C. resumed Command of Battalion. Capt R.E.S JOHNSON took over 2/in Command.	
	22/1/18		" " "	
	23/1/18		" " "	
	24/1/18		" " "	
	25/1/18		Brigade Ceremonial Parade – Presentation of ribbons by Maj. Gen. Sir B. de Lisle.	
			Casualties week ending 25.1.18. Increase: Rejoined from Hospital — Off -, OR 5; Draft from Base — 1, 5; Draft from Corps Depot — 2, -; Arrivals Corps Depot — 4; total 3, 17.	Capt. A.B. CLAYTON; 2/Lt W.G. KEELIHER; 2/Lt T.W. BROWN.
			Decrease: Transfer to 11th Border — 1, -; To England Sick — 1, -; Evac Div. Area — 18; total 2, 18.	Capt J.W. JOHNSTON M.C. D.C.M.; 2/Lt B. GASH

2353 Wt. W2544/1454 700,000 5/15 D. D. & L. A.D.S.S./Forms/C. 2118.

Sheet 4. Serine 34

Instructions regarding War Diaries and Intelligence Summaries are contained in F. S. Regs., Part II. and the Staff Manual respectively. Title pages will be prepared in manuscript.

January 1918.

WAR DIARY
or
INTELLIGENCE SUMMARY. — The Border Regt.
(*Erase heading not required.*)

1st Bn

Army Form C. 2118.

Place	Date	Hour	Summary of Events and Information	Remarks and references to Appendices
WIELTJE	26/1/18		Battalion moved to JUNCTION CAMP (WIELTJE) (28 N.W. C27 b 9.5) by rail	
"	27/1/18		Battalion furnished working parties for work in Army Defence Zone.	
"	28/1/18		" " " " " " " "	
			Capt A.W. SUTCLIFFE M.C resumed command of battalion on returning from leave.	
			Capt W.B BUTLER M.C took over 2/i Command	
"	29/1/18		Battalion furnishes working parties for work in Army Defence Zone.	
"	30/1/18		" " " " " " " "	
"	31/1/18		" " " " " " " " "	

Arthur J. [illegible] Capt
a/adj
1st Bn the Border Regt
B.E.F. France.

2353 Wt. W2544/1454 700,000 5/15 D. D. & L. A.D.S.S./Forms/C. 2118.

S E C R E T.

87th. INFANTRY BRIGADE ORDER No.70.
@%@%@%@%@%@%@%@%@ @_@%@%@%@%@%@%@

January Ist.1918.

Ref.Map HAZEBROUCK.
1/100.000.

I. The 87th.Infantry Brigade (less the 87th.M.G.Coy. and 87th.T.M.Battery) will continue its march to the PROOSDY Area tomorrow the 2nd.inst.

2. The following intervals will be observed on the march.
100 yards between Companies.
100 yards between Units and their Transport.
25 yards between each six vehciels.

4. There will be a halt each day from 12.50.p.m.to 1.30.p.m

5. Acknowledge.

(Sd) W.K.Innes. Captain.
A/Brigade Major 87th.Infantry Brigade.

SECRET.

87th. INFANTRY BRIGADE ORDER NO.72.

14th. JANUARY 1918.

Map reference
1/20.000.
Sheet 28.N.W.

I. The 87th. Infantry Brigade will become the Reserve Brigade, 29th. Divisional and will relieve the 23rd. Infantry Brigade in the BRANDHOEK Area on the 18th. inst.

2. On the line of march the following distances will be observed.

Between Companies.	100 yards.
Between Battalions.	500 yards.
Between Units and Transport.	100 yards.
Between every six vehciles.	25 yards.

East of ELVERDINGHE Units will march in file.

3. Completion of move will be reported to these Headquarters which will be established at BRAKE Camp. A.30.C.7.3.

4. ACKNOWLEDGE.

(Sd) E. Brodiemair.
Captain.
Brigade Major. 87th. Infantry Brigade.

S/E C R E T.

87th. INFANTRY BRIGADE ORDER NO.73.

25th. January 1918.

Ref. Map.
1/20.000. Sheets 28. N. W.

I. The 87th. Infantry Brigade will relieve the 88th. Brigade in Divisional Support on Saturday January 26th. 1918.

2. Units will take over all defences schemes, stores, details of work etc,. from Units they relieve.

3. (a) The Officer Commanding Ist. King's Own Scottish Borderers will detail FOUR Lewis Guns and teams to take over from the Ist. ESSEX REGIMENT A. A. Positions at:-
D. 9. d. 3. 1.
D. 9. d. 6. 1.
D. 9. d. 0. 7.
D. 9. b. 4. 3.

(b) The Officer Commanding the Ist. King's Own Scottish Borderers will detail a guard of I N.C.O. and 3 men on NILE DUMP.

Guides for the above (a) and (b) will be at SPREE FARM C. 18. d. 1. 2. at 2. 30. p. m.

4. ACKNOWLEDGE.

(Sd) W. K. Innes. Captain.
A/Brigade Major, 87th. Infantry Brigade.

Confidential.

WO 95/2303 [illegible]

War Diary

of

1st Battalion The Border Regiment.

From: 1st February 1918 To: 28th February 1918

Folio. 35

55 K

Serial No. 35   Sheet 1.   February 1918

Instructions regarding War Diaries and Intelligence Summaries are contained in F. S. Regs., Part II. and the Staff Manual respectively. Title pages will be prepared in manuscript.

WAR DIARY
or
INTELLIGENCE SUMMARY.
(Erase heading not required.)

1st Bn. The Border Regt.

Army Form C. 2118.

Place	Date	Hour	Summary of Events and Information	Remarks and references to Appendices
WIELTJE	1/2/18		Battalion furnishes working parties for work on Army Battle Zone.	
			Casualties. Week ending 1/2/18 Increase. Off. OR	
			Rejoined from Hospital – 2	
			Joined from base 1 – 2/Lt. H. ELKINGTON.	
			Arrivals at Corps Depot. 2	
			Transfer from 8th Bn. 1	
			1 5	
			Decrease	
			To Course 1 –	
			To England for Commn. 1	
			Evac. from Divl Area 5	
			1 . 6.	
	2/2/18		Battalion furnishes working parties for work on Army Battle Zone	
PASSCHENDAELE	3/2/18		Moved into trenches – fairly quiet relief. Bn. held right front line of Brigade sector. Bn. H.Q. at [illegible] CROSS ROADS. A - B - D Coys in front line C Coy in GOUDBERG.	
	4/2/18		Quiet day	

2353 Wt. W2541/1454 700,000 5/15 D. D. & L. A.D.S.S./Forms/C. 2118.

Serial 35. Sheet 2.

Instructions regarding War Diaries and Intelligence Summaries are contained in F. S. Regs., Part II. and the Staff Manual respectively. Title pages will be prepared in manuscript.

February 1918

WAR DIARY
or
INTELLIGENCE SUMMARY.
(Erase heading not required.)

Army Form C. 2118.

1st Bn The Border Regt

Place	Date	Hour	Summary of Events and Information	Remarks and references to Appendices
[illegible]	5/2/18		Fairly quiet day, – Bn HQ shelled from 3 – 5 pm.	
			Bn moved back into support being relieved by 2/S.W.B. Bn HQ BELLEVUE.	
			A B Coys at BELLEVUE. C Coy at GOUDBERG. D Coy at CALIFORNIA CAMP	
BELLEVUE	6/2/18		Working on BELLEVUE Defences Slight shelling	
	7/2/18		do do do	
	8/2/18		do do do D Coy relieved C Coy at GOUDBERG – C	
			Coy going to CALIFORNIA	
			Casualties week ending 8/2/18	
			Increase ~~[illegible]~~ Off OR	
			From 6th Border Regt 5. 100	Capt D.F. RIDLEY MC Lieut E.L. HOLLAND 2/Lieut R. PARKER 2/Lieut D.W. PATTERSON 2/Lieut H. AINSCOUGH
			Arrived Corps Depot – 7	
			From Hospital 1	
			5. 108	
			Decrease Killed 2	
			Wounded 4	
			Evac. Div. Area 5	
			To England for Commn 1	
			To England – Sick 1 –	Capt A.B. CLAYTON
			1 – 12	

2353 Wt. W2544/1454 700,000 5/15 D. D. & L. A.D.S.S./Forms/C. 2118.

Serial 35. Sheet 3

Instructions regarding War Diaries and Intelligence Summaries are contained in F. S. Regs., Part II. and the Staff Manual respectively. Title pages will be prepared in manuscript.

February 1918

WAR DIARY
or
INTELLIGENCE SUMMARY.
(Erase heading not required.)

1st Bn Border Regt

Army Form C. 2118.

Place	Date	Hour	Summary of Events and Information	Remarks and references to Appendices
PASSCHENDAELE	9/2/18		Battalion relieved 1/KOSB in firing line of Brigade sector and the left Coy of 2/SWB who were holding right firing line. D Coy relieved C Coy at GOUDBERG – A, B – C Coys holding the front line – Bn HQ at PRIOR 83 – Two companies 2/SWB at WOLLEMOLLEN and INCH HOUSES came under command of C.O. 1st Border Regt.	
"	10/2/18		A & B Coys with Bn HQ and the two attached Coys 2/SWB were relieved by 1/WORCESTERS (8th Division) and moved back to billets in the WATOU area – C & D Coys passed under command of O.C. 1/WORCESTERS	
"	11/2/18		C & D Coys were relieved and moved back to WATOU	
			Total Casualties in line – 2 OR Killed 12 OR wounded.	
WATOU	12/2/18		Cleaning up – Lt Col A.J. Ellis DSO resumed command of the Bn on return from leave. Major A.V. Sutcliffe MC took over the duties of 2/in Command. Billets good but scattered	
	13/2/18		Refitting at WATOU	
	14/2/18		Bathing " "	
	15/2/18		Training in WATOU area	
	16/2/18		" " "	

2353 Wt. W2544/1454 700,000 5/15 D. D. & L. A.D.S.S./Forms/C. 2118.

Serial No 35 Sheet 4

Instructions regarding War Diaries and Intelligence Summaries are contained in F. S. Regs., Part II. and the Staff Manual respectively. Title pages will be prepared in manuscript. Feb. 1918

WAR DIARY
or
INTELLIGENCE SUMMARY.
(Erase heading not required.)

1st Bn Border Regt

Army Form C. 2118.

Place	Date	Hour	Summary of Events and Information	Remarks and references to Appendices
WATOU			Casualties week ending 15/2/18	
			Increase — Offrs: – ; O.R.: –	
			At Corps Depot — O.R. 9	
			Wounded 9/2/18 now at duty — O.R. 1	
			From hospital — O.R. 1	
			Total — Offrs – ; O.R. 11.	
			Decrease	
			Wounded — Offrs – ; O.R. 8	
			Evacuated sick — O.R. 7	
			Transferred to base — O.R. 1	
			To England for Comm. — O.R. 1	
			Total — Offrs – ; O.R. 17	
"	17/2/18		Training in WATOU Area.	
"	18/2/18		" " "	
"	19/2/18		" " "	
"	20/2/18		" " "	
"	21/2/18		" " " Maj J. FORBES ROBERTSON from 16th Midd[x] Regt took over duties of 2/i Command	
	22/2/18		Brigade Ceremonial Parade. Ribbons presented by Maj Gen Sir Beauvoir de Lisle ...	

2353 Wt W2541/1454 700,000 5/15 D. D. & L. A.D.S.S./Forms/C. 2118.

Serial No 35 Sheet 5

February 1918

Instructions regarding War Diaries and Intelligence Summaries are contained in F. S. Regs., Part II. and the Staff Manual respectively. Title pages will be prepared in manuscript.

WAR DIARY
or
INTELLIGENCE SUMMARY.
(Erase heading not required.)

1st Bn The Border Rgt.

Army Form C. 2118.

Place	Date	Hour	Summary of Events and Information	Remarks and references to Appendices
			Off. OR	
WATOU	22/2/18		Casualties. Week ending 22/2/18 Increase. From 16th Mddx 1 –	Major J. FORBES ROBERTSON DSO MC
			From Base 3	
			" Hospital 1	
			From 6th Border Rgt. 1	
			1 5.	
			Decrease. To England on Duty 2 –	Capt R.E.S. JOHNSON Lt J.N. MORRIS
			Evacuated sick 1 6	Lt A.L. RUDDOCOMBE
			Transfer to MGC 7	
			" TMB. 6	
WATOU	23/2/18		Brigade Sports Day. W/Col A.S. Ellis DSO took command of 86 Inf Bde. Maj J. Forbes Robertson DSO MC took command of the battalion. Captain A.W. Sutcliffe MC took over 2/in command.	
	24/2/18		Training at WATOU	
	25/2/18		" "	
	26/2/18		Marches to POPERINGHE	
	27/2/18		Battalion furnishes working parties on Army Battle Zone.	
	28/2/18		" " " " " "	

[signature] Lt Col
Cmdg 1st Bn Border Rgt

2353 Wt. W2544/1454 700,000 5/15 D. D. & L. A.D.S.S./Forms/C. 2118.

Confidential

War Diary

of

1st Battalion The Border Regiment

From 1st March 1918. To 31st March 1918.

Folio 44.

Serial No 36 Sheet 1

Army Form C. 2118.

Instructions regarding War Diaries and Intelligence Summaries are contained in F. S. Regs., Part II, and the Staff Manual respectively. Title pages will be prepared in manuscript.

WAR DIARY
or
INTELLIGENCE SUMMARY.
(Erase heading not required.)

March 1918.

1st Bn The Border Regt.

Place	Date	Hour	Summary of Events and Information	Remarks and references to Appendices
POPERINGHE	1/3/18		Battalion furnished working parties for work on Army Battle Zone	[illegible]
			Casualties week ending 1.3.1918. Increase Drafts from base. O/ff. — O.R. 11	
			Rejoined ex hospital 1	
			" from 87 T.M.B. 5	
			" " 87 M.G.C. 1	
			18	
			Decrease. Classified 'B' O/ff. 1 O.R. –	Lt. J. TURNER.
			Trans/d 87 T.M.B 4	
			" 87 M.G.C. 5.	
			Evac. from Div. Area 8	
			1 17.	
"	2/3/18		Battalion furnished working parties for work on Army Battle Zone	[illegible]
"	3/3/18		" " " " " " " " "	[illegible]
"	4/3/18		" " " " " " " " "	[illegible]
"	5/3/18		Battalion moved by rail to JUNCTION CAMP. WIELTJE.	[illegible]

D. D. & L., London, E.C.
(A7883) Wt W809/M1672 350,000 4/17 Sch 52a Forms/C/2118/14

Serial No. 36 Sheet 2 1st Bn. The Border Regt. Army Form C. 2118.

WAR DIARY
or
INTELLIGENCE SUMMARY.

(Erase heading not required.)

Instructions regarding War Diaries and Intelligence Summaries are contained in F. S. Regs., Part II, and the Staff Manual respectively. Title pages will be prepared in manuscript.

March 1918

Place	Date	Hour	Summary of Events and Information	Remarks and references to Appendices
WIELTJE	6/3/18		Battalion furnished working parties for work on Divisional Reserve Line and Army Battle Zone	[initials]
"	7/3/18		" " " " " " " " " " "	[initials]
"	8/3/18		" " " " " " " " " " "	[initials]
	8/3/18		Casualties. week ending 8/3/18 Increase Transferred from 6th Bn. — Off. 1, OR – — 2/Lt. A. CHICKEN	
			Arrivals at Corps Depot — OR 3	
			Rejoined from APM. 29 Divn. — OR 1	
			" ex Hospital — OR 1	
			Off. 1, OR 5	
			Decrease To England for 6 months duty — Off. 2, OR – — Lt. J.L.P. GAMON	
			Transfer to Base "Under Age" — OR 1 — 2/Lt. C.W. SMITH	
			To Hospital in England (from base) — OR 5	
			Evac. from Divl Area. — OR 10	
PASSCHENDALE	9/3/18		Battalion relieved 2/SWB in left sector – left Brigade. — Off. 2, OR 16	
			Quiet relief – complete by 12 mid night	
			Bn. H.Q. Pill Box 83	[initials]

D. D. & L., London, E.C.
(A7883) Wt W809/M1672 750,000 4/17 Sch 52a Forms/C/2118/14

Serial No 36 Sheet 3

Army Form C. 2118.

WAR DIARY
or
INTELLIGENCE SUMMARY.
(Erase heading not required.)

1st Bn The Border Regt.

Instructions regarding War Diaries and Intelligence Summaries are contained in F. S. Regs., Part II. and the Staff Manual respectively. Title pages will be prepared in manuscript.

March 1918

Place	Date	Hour	Summary of Events and Information	Remarks and references to Appendices
PASSCHENDAELE	10/3/18		Very quiet day – weather glorious and very sunny – observation good	[initials]
"	11/3/18	6 A.M.	Heavy barrage on our immediate right – 4/SWB raided but put up a gallant defence	[initials]
			We had no casualties although our line was fairly heavily shelled	
			Glorious weather – rest of day very quiet	
"	12/3/18		Very quiet day. weather glorious	[initials]
"	13/3/18		Heavy barrage on right otherwise very quiet – weather still fine	[initials]
"	14/3/18		Fairly quiet. Hostile Trench Mortars unusually active – weather fine	[initials]
"	15/3/18		Quiet day. relieved by 2/SWB and moved into Brigade Reserve at ENGLISH CAMP WIELTJE	[initials]
			Casualties week ended 15/3/18 Increase – Joined from base — Offrs 1 — 2/Lt W. COE	
			Arrivals Corps Depot — O.R. 1	
			Rejoined ex hospital — O.R. 1	
			Offrs 1 — O.R. 2	
			Decrease – To England 6 mos duty — Offrs 1 — O.R. – — Lt G.H.S. McDONALD	
			Killed — O.R. 1	
			Wounded — O.R. 4	
			Missing — O.R. 1	
			To Hospital in England — O.R. 1	
			Committed to Prison — O.R. 1	
			Evac out of Dwl Area — O.R. 2	[initials]
			Offrs 1 — O.R. 13	

D. D. & L., London, E.C. (A7883) Wt W3c9/M1672 250,000 4/17 Sch 52a Forms/C/2118/14

Serial No 36 Sheet 4

March 1918

WAR DIARY
or
INTELLIGENCE SUMMARY.
(Erase heading not required.)

1st Bn The Border Regt

Army Form C. 2118.

Instructions regarding War Diaries and Intelligence Summaries are contained in F. S. Regs., Part II, and the Staff Manual respectively. Title pages will be prepared in manuscript.

Place	Date	Hour	Summary of Events and Information	Remarks and references to Appendices
WIELTJE	16/3/18		Cleaning up and refitting.	
"	17/3/18		Work on KRONPRINZ LINE	
"	18/3/18		Shelled by longrange H.V. gun from 2pm to 7pm. 1 man wounded	
			Relieved 1/KOSB in right sector L. Brigade Bn HQ MUIR LODGE - 4 casualties during relief.	
"	19/3/18		Langemarck - BELLEVUE heavily shelled. Hostile Trench Mortars active against	
			D Coy (GOUDBERG) - 4 Killed three wounded.	
"	20/3/18	2.20am	S.O.S. on right - nothing on our front - Usual shelling of BELLEVUE - Rain.	
	21/3/18		Glorious day again - Lt HILL (U.S.A.) attached to D Coy.	
	22/3/18		Quiet day - relieved by 2/HANTS. - All clear 11.30. Entrained SPREE FARM for VLAMERTINGHE	
			Casualties week ending 22/3/18 — Increase: Off. / OR	
			Rejoined ex hospital — / 1	
			Arrivals at Corps Depot — / 9	
			/ 10	
			Decrease: Evacuated sick — 5	
			To hospital in England — 1	
			Struck off after 7 days - FA — 6	
			To 226 Employment Coy — 2	
			To Base - unfit — 6	
			Killed — 7	
			Wounded — 12	
			Gassed — 1	
			— / 40	

D. D. & L., London, E.C.
(A7883) Wt W809/M1672 750,000 4/17 Sch. 52a Forms/C/2118/14

Serial No 36 Sheet 5

Instructions regarding War Diaries and Intelligence Summaries are contained in F. S. Regs., Part II, and the Staff Manual respectively. Title pages will be prepared in manuscript.

March 1918

WAR DIARY
or
INTELLIGENCE SUMMARY.
(Erase heading not required.)

1st Bn The Border Regt.

Army Form C. 2118.

Place	Date	Hour	Summary of Events and Information	Remarks and references to Appendices
VLAMERTINGHE	23/3/18		WARRINGTON CAMP - resting - good Camp.	[initials]
"	24/3/18		Cleaning up and refitting - Boiling hot day.	[initials]
"	25/3/18		Work on Army Line	[initials]
"	26/3/18		" " " "	[initials]
"	27/3/18		" " " "	[initials]
"	28/3/18		" " " "	[initials]
"	29/3/18		" " " "	[initials]
"	30/3/18		Relieved 1 R.G.L.I. in Left Sector - R Brigade. Quiet relief - but very wet	[initials]
PASSCHENDAELE	31/3/18		Fairly quiet - weather changeable -	[initials]
			Casualties week ending 29.3.18. Increase — Offrs. / O.R.	
			Rejoined ex hospital — - / 5	
			from Corps Depot — 35	
			Draft from Base — 4	
			Rejoined from T.M.B. — 1	
			— - / 45	
			Decrease — Wounded. — 1 / 1	CAPT. W.B. BUTLER M.C.
			Medical Board Orders — 1 / -	Hon Lt & Qm. H. IRELAND
			Trans to M.G. Bn — 9	
			" " 87 T.M.B. — 1	
			" 1 Divl. HQ — 1	
			" " Signal Coy — 1	
			Evac. from Divl Area — 19	[initials]
			— 2 / 32	

Arthur J. Ha[illegible] Capt. Adjt. 1st Bn The Border Regt

D. D. & L., London, E.C. (A7883) Wt W809/M1672 250,000 4/17 Sch. 52a Forms/C/2118/14

87th Brigade.

29th Division.

1st BATTALION

THE BORDER REGIMENT

APRIL 1918.

W A R D I A R Y.

OF

1st BN. The BORDER REGIMENT.

FROM :- 1st APRIL, 1918.

TO :- 30th APRIL, 1918.

Instructions regarding War Diaries and Intelligence Summaries are contained in F. S. Regs., Part II. and the Staff Manual respectively. Title pages will be prepared in manuscript.

Serial 37

(1)

WAR DIARY
or
INTELLIGENCE SUMMARY.
(Erase heading not required.)

Army Form C. 2118.

Place	Date	Hour	Summary of Events and Information	Remarks and references to Appendices
PASSCHENDAELE	1/4/18		Raiding party went back to JUNCTION CAMP for training under Major A. W. Sutcliffe M.C. Quiet day.	
	2/4/18		Quiet day - inter Company Relief. A Coy relieved C in R. firing line. B Coy relieved D Coy in L firing line. C Coy in reserve at BELLEVUE	
	5/4/18		Battalion relieved on night of 5/6th by 1/KOSB.	
	6/4/18		Quiet relief.	
WIELTJE	6/4/18		Details rejoined from BRAKE CAMP. Cleaning up and refitting.	
	7/4/18		Cleaning up and refitting. Relieved by 20th D.L.I. 41st Division	
ST JAN TER BIEZEN	8/4/18		Moved by rail to QUINTIN (POPERINGHE) and marched to ROAD CAMP (ST. JAN DER BIEZEN)	
	9/4/18		Battalion under orders to entrain for St POL area - Billeting party sent in advance.	
		5.30 pm	Orders received to entrain at 8.30 pm for MERVILLE area. Conference of Commanding Officers at Brigade H.Q.	J.B.

(A9175) Wt W2355/P360 600,000 12/17 D. D. & L. Sch. 52a. Forms/C2118/15.

837

2

Army Form C. 2118.

WAR DIARY
or
INTELLIGENCE SUMMARY.
(Erase heading not required.)

Instructions regarding War Diaries and Intelligence Summaries are contained in F. S. Regs., Part II. and the Staff Manual respectively. Title pages will be prepared in manuscript.

Place	Date	Hour	Summary of Events and Information	Remarks and references to Appendices
NEUF BERQUIN	10/4/18	2.30am	Battalion embussed at Cross Roads PROVEN-POPERINGHE-WATOU roads - 10% details were left at ROAD CAMP under Major A.W. Sutcliffe M.C.	
		8.00am	Battalion debussed N of NEUF BERQUIN and marched into close billets in the village. The Battalion was ordered to throw out an outpost line to cover the Brigade in NEUF BERQUIN. Battalion H.Q. established at L22.c.9.5 (sheet 36a) the outpost line extending from L20.b central to L8.c.5.9	
		10am	Battalion, with H.M.Gs. attached under orders of O.C. Border Regt placed at disposal of 50th Division and ordered to take up a position across the ESTAIRES - NEUF BERQUIN ROAD from Lys canal L28 to the METEREN BECQUE at L24 c central - the outpost line in front of NEUF BERQUIN being taken over by the 1st K.O.S.B. Packs and overcoats dumped at Brewery NEUF BERQUIN. Bn H.Q. was established at L22 c.3.8 and the line was held by A-C-D Coys from Right to Left with B Coy in support in L22.a. Fighting continuing in ESTAIRES and to the North but no shelling in Battalion area.	
		5pm	Hand over line to XV Corps Reinforcement Battalion. Orders also	JFR.

(A9475) Wt W2359/P360 600,000 12/17 D. D. & L. Sch. 52a. Forms/C2118/15.

837 3

WAR DIARY
or
INTELLIGENCE SUMMARY.
(Erase heading not required.)

Army Form C. 2118.

Instructions regarding War Diaries and Intelligence Summaries are contained in F. S. Regs., Part II. and the Staff Manual respectively. Title pages will be prepared in manuscript.

Place	Date	Hour	Summary of Events and Information	Remarks and references to Appendices
NEUF BERQUIN	10/4/18	5pm	received that Battalion would be relieved by 2nd R. Fus (86th Bde) but	
			relief was not completed by Reinforcement Bn and 2nd R. Fus. until	
			6.30pm when the Battalion moved off in reserve to the 1/KOSB and	
			2/SWB. The relief being complete the Battalion came back again	
			under orders of the 29th Division and marched to 36(A) L.12 in Brigade	
			Reserve, the 1/KOSB and 2/SWB forming a line facing E. sheet 36.	
			squares G2 and 8. This was a support line to the 50th Division who	
			were in the firing line. The situation was very obscure.	
		9pm	Distribution of Battalion. D Coy under 2/Lt G. H. Baller along the	
			road G11a 9.5 to G11 c 3.3 facing SE. the 50th Division held a	
			B Coy under Capt [illegible] G7 b 6.3 facing east and south	JSM
			line further South. C Coy under Lieut W. S. H. Ruxton M.C. L12 c 5.5	
			across the road facing S.E. A Coy under Capt H. F. H. Chambers MC	
			along the road L12 a 3.5 to L12 c 5.6 facing E. The 4 M.Gs in G7 d	
			Battalion H.Q. farmhouse at L12 c 5.4. The night was very dark	
			but passed very quietly rations came up by limber to Coys	
			Owing to the distances to be covered 2 mounted orderlies with	JSM

(A9173) Wt W2355/P560 650,000 12/17 D. D. & L. Sch. 52a. Forms/C2118/15.

4

WAR DIARY
or
INTELLIGENCE SUMMARY.
(Erase heading not required.)

Army Form C. 2118.

Instructions regarding War Diaries and Intelligence Summaries are contained in F. S. Regs., Part II. and the Staff Manual respectively. Title pages will be prepared in manuscript.

Place	Date	Hour	Summary of Events and Information	Remarks and references to Appendices
NEUF BERQUIN	10/4/18	9pm	3 horses were kept at Bn H.Q.	
	11/4/18	10am	Information was received that the 40th Division on the left were being driven in but that the 2/S.W.B. and 1st K.O.S.B. had engaged and stopped the enemy	
		12.30pm	The Battalion was ordered to move up on the Right of the 1 K.O.S.B. and prolong the line to the METEREN BECQUE. TROU BAYARD appeared to be occupied by the enemy so C Coy was ordered to prepare to attack these farm houses and A Coy to line up as a second wave in support if necessary. C Coy dribbled across and formed a line along the road L17 d 4.8 to L18 a 2.6 and A Coy formed up behind the road at L12 c 2.6 in preparation for the advance on TROU BAYARD	
		12.45pm	Troops of 50th Division were driven in on our right flank and the Lancs Fus were ordered to withdraw to take up a position on the left flank near DOULIEU L 5 d. Their withdrawal caused disorganisation among the troops on the right of METEREN BECQUE and these began to withdraw. Consequently the advance of	JFR.

(A9175) Wt W2358/P360 600,000 12/17 D. D. & L. Sch. 52a. Forms/C2118/15.

Instructions regarding War Diaries and Intelligence Summaries are contained in F. S. Regs., Part II. and the Staff Manual respectively. Title pages will be prepared in manuscript.

WAR DIARY
or
INTELLIGENCE SUMMARY.
(Erase heading not required.)

Army Form C. 2118.

Place	Date	Hour	Summary of Events and Information	Remarks and references to Appendices
Near [illegible]	11.4.18	2.45pm	C Coy was stopped and Bn. H.Q. informed and verbal orders received to stand fast. A counter attack of some of our troops about L.5.d. and L.11.c was seen to make progress.	
		3pm	About this time the line on the left was apparently driven in, men were seen retiring across the open N and S of 'B' Coy in G.7.b. Capt Chambers was at once given verbal orders to left form A Coy to advance East and counter attack and hold the edge of the [illegible] in G.7.b. the H.Q. of the [illegible] being about G.7.b central.	
			Having given the orders to A Coy the Commanding Officer rode across and organized a line of the troops retiring from L.12.a central north to L.6.a central where the line was in touch with 4/R. Fus. who had not been attacked E of [illegible]. The C.O. returned to Bn. H.Q. and reported situation by telephone to Brigade H.Q., by this time B Coy in G.[illegible] were heavily engaged and men of the 50th Division had come back and were stopped at Bn. H.Q. The counter attack of A Coy had made good headway.	[illegible]

(A9175) Wt W2357/P360 600,000 12/17 D. D. & L. Sch. 52a. Forms/C2118/15.

S37

6

Army Form C. 2118.

WAR DIARY
or
INTELLIGENCE SUMMARY.
(Erase heading not required.)

Instructions regarding War Diaries and Intelligence Summaries are contained in F. S. Regs., Part II. and the Staff Manual respectively. Title pages will be prepared in manuscript.

Place	Date	Hour	Summary of Events and Information	Remarks and references to Appendices
NEUF BERQUIN	11/4/18	3pm	and got into the Copse in F.7.b. reinforced B Coy and fighting was	
		3.30.	proceeding. The C.O. then rode the line to the S.W. and found "C" Coy	
			firm on the line in 17b with the 1/Lancs Fus on their right but the	
			troops in front of them coming back. On the way back the C.O.	
			reported to Bde H.Q. in L10. and was informed that the enemy had	
			made progress on the right and that in the event of having to	
			withdraw, to do so in conjunction with the Lancs Fus. and fight	
			on the line of the road L7a to Doulieu.	
		4pm	By the time C.O. returned to Bn. H.Q. D Coy were very much in the	
			air. So a cycle orderly was despatched ordering them to retire on	
			Battalion H.Q. 2/Lt Bates had already been brought back wounded.	
			2 Platoons of D Coy could not be extricated and were last	
			seen surrounded but still fighting. The Adjutant under a	
			nucleus garrison was sent back to take up another position L11 d.3.7	
			to L12 a.2.3. The retirement of D Coy was effected under cover	
			of the M.Gs. D Coy were loaded up with the ammunition	J.F.R.

(A9175) Wt W2355/P360 600,000 12/17 D. D. & L. Sch. 52a. Forms/C2118/15.

537

7

Instructions regarding War Diaries and Intelligence Summaries are contained in F. S. Regs., Part II. and the Staff Manual respectively. Title pages will be prepared in manuscript.

WAR DIARY
or
INTELLIGENCE SUMMARY.
(Erase heading not required.)

Army Form C. 2118.

Place	Date	Hour	Summary of Events and Information	Remarks and references to Appendices
NEUF BERQUIN	11th	11pm	from the dump at Bn H.Q distributed to the troops in the firing line	
			and then D Coy reorganised in the rear position under the Adjutant.	
		5.10pm	The 4 M.G. were withdrawn to this position. O.C. Lanes [illegible] notified	
			and finally Bn H.Q withdrawn to L.4.b.8.8. The line towards	
			DOULIEU [illegible] apparently again giving way. The Commanding Officer	
			again rode the line and found that the men of the 50th Division	
			were being ordered by their Officers to withdraw, the reason being	
			given that they had been relieved by the 29th Division. This was	
			stopped as it looked like the beginning of another rot and report	
			made to Bde H.Q then established at L.3.a.1.5. The counterattack	
			delivered by A Coy held the enemy up at L.2.b. for 2 hours at the	
			end of which time heavy T.Ms were brought into action. The	
			position for A and B Coys being untenable with both flanks in	
			the air they were ordered to withdraw to a new line in L.2.a.	
		[illegible]	Heavy attack on the new line repulsed with heavy loss generally.	
			The enemy were caught in the open with Vickers and Lewis	J.F.N.

(A9175) Wt W2355/P360 600,000 12/17 D. D. & L. Sch. 52a. Forms/C2118/15.

8

Army Form C. 2118.

Instructions regarding War Diaries and Intelligence Summaries are contained in F. S. Regs., Part II. and the Staff Manual respectively. Title pages will be prepared in manuscript.

WAR DIARY
or
INTELLIGENCE SUMMARY.
(Erase heading not required.)

Place	Date	Hour	Summary of Events and Information	Remarks and references to Appendices
NEUF BERQUIN	11/4/18	5.30pm	Guns fire.	
		7 pm	Second attack was repulsed but many casualties were caused from accurate shelling	
		7.30	Second line of defence was dug through F.5.d.	
		8 pm	The firing line from DOULIEU to METEREN BECQUE was reconnoitred by C.O. and report sent in to Brigade of dispositions of units	
		8.45pm	holding the line R. Guernsey Light Inf F.30.c. central 2/R. Fus to L6.a.4.0. 1/K.O.S.B. 2/S.W.B. and some of 150th Brigade to L6.c.8.0 Border Regt less 1 Coy to L11.d.2.6. 1 Coy Border Regt and 1/Lancs Fus forward L.16 central.	
		11 pm	The enemy had made no further impression on our line but had made good progress on both flanks. Orders were received from Brigade to withdraw. 1/KOSB and 2/SWB to hold the line from L7.a.2.7 to L3.a.4.0. Border Regt in Brigade Reserve F.27.d. Evacuation of this position was carried out in conjunction with the Lancs Fus and R. Fus. From the position occupied	GTR

(A9475) Wt W2358/P360 600,000 12/17 D. D. & L. Sch. 52a. Forms/C2118/15.

937 9

Instructions regarding War Diaries and Intelligence Summaries are contained in F. S. Regs., Part II. and the Staff Manual respectively. Title pages will be prepared in manuscript.

WAR DIARY
or
INTELLIGENCE SUMMARY.
(Erase heading not required.)

Army Form C. 2118.

Place	Date	Hour	Summary of Events and Information	Remarks and references to Appendices
NEUF BERQUIN	11th/4	11pm	by the Guards Regt all [illegible] of other Units were sent back first.	
			Two Vickers Guns were placed at L5.c.3.2 and 2 others at L5.a.1.0	
			to cover withdrawal. Coys withdrew leaving one sentry post on	
			each of the tracks and roads through the position till 3am	
			which was fortunate as two enemy patrols were driven off by	
			rifle fire during the withdrawal.	
	12th/4	3am	Evacuation complete. Battalion HQ withdrawn and marched	
			back successfully without interference from the enemy through	
			L4.b central L3.c. central F26.d to F25.d.	
		5.30am	Battalion reached new position just as it was getting light.	
			One Company having taken the wrong road was shelled	
			while moving across the open at L2.a by enemy guns in NEUF	
			BERQUIN. No movement was possible outside the cover in F25.d.	
			so position could only be dug in Copse and in [illegible].	
			Dispositions. C. Coy F25.d.3.3 D. Coy F25.d.8.1. A Coy F25.a.2.9	
			B Coy F25.d.8.5. Bn HQ. F25.d.9.7. The 4 Vickers M.Gs.	[illegible]

(A9175) Wt W2352/P360 600,000 12/17 D. D. & L. Sch. 52a. Forms/C2118/15.

837

10

Instructions regarding War Diaries and Intelligence Summaries are contained in F. S. Regs., Part II. and the Staff Manual respectively. Title pages will be prepared in manuscript.

WAR DIARY
or
INTELLIGENCE SUMMARY.
(Erase heading not required.)

Army Form C. 2118.

Place	Date	Hour	Summary of Events and Information	Remarks and references to Appendices
NEUF BERQUIN	12/4/18	5.30am	on the withdrawal reported back to their Company. The 86th	
			Brigade held the line to the left of the 87th Brigade as far as	
			DOULIEU. The 1st Lancs Fus Brigade reserve F26 central. The 92nd	
			Brigade were in line on the left of the 86th Brigade 149th Bde	
			on the right of the 87th Bde in the Northern portion of NEUF BERQUIN	
			86th and 87th Bde H.Q. at BLEU.	
		7am	Enemy attacking along the whole line	
		10a.m. to 11am	The enemy forced the line and pushed down the roads towards	
			F26 central and K6.b central. The Brigade H.Q. withdrew to LYNDE	
		about 2pm	The enemy had M.Gs at the Cross Roads at F26.d.2.8 and K6.b.5.8	
			and light field Guns in action in L2.c.7.d. The Commanding	
			Officer ordered withdrawal to BLEU. "A" Coy got in touch with	
			K.O.Y.L.I the pioneer Battalion of the 31st Division at F19.c central	
			who connected up with Guards Brigade about LA COURONNE	
			B.C. and D Coys held South edge of BLEU. The O.C. 1/Lancs Fus	
			and O.C. 1/R. Fus asked for reinforcements. Two platoons of	GSR

(A9175) Wt W2358/P560 600,000 12/17 D. D. & L. Sch. 52a. Forms/C2118/15.

Instructions regarding War Diaries and Intelligence Summaries are contained in F. S. Regs., Part II. and the Staff Manual respectively. Title pages will be prepared in manuscript.

WAR DIARY
or
INTELLIGENCE SUMMARY.
(Erase heading not required.)

Army Form C. 2118.

Place	Date	Hour	Summary of Events and Information	Remarks and references to Appendices
NEUF BERQUIN	12/4/18	about 2pm	C Coy. under 2/Lt Chicken were sent to fill a gap about F20.a.0.2 [illegible] had withdrawn to LE PARADIS.	
		4pm	[illegible] came and reported he was digging a line from FME LABIS in the direction of LA COURONNE. The position on the left was now obscure and the enemy appeared to be very near MERRIS.	
		4.30pm	Three orderlies arrived from Brigade within 10 minutes of one another with detailed orders, some of which should have been received 4 hours previously.	
		8pm	O.C. 1st Lancs Fus and 2nd R. Fus reported at Bn. H.Q. F19 b 5.0 bringing with them the remnants of their Battalions about 30 men of the Lancs Fus [illegible] men of the R. Fus. 2/Lt Chicken (wounded) and 3 men who were the remnants of C Coy's 2 platoons arrived reporting that the 9th Bde on their left had retired. Battalion withdrew to the line FME LABIS to about E24.b central. The enemy had MGs in position [illegible] the road North of PLEU[illegible]	[illegible]

837

12

Army Form C. 2118.

Instructions regarding War Diaries and Intelligence Summaries are contained in F. S. Regs., Part II. and the Staff Manual respectively. Title pages will be prepared in manuscript.

WAR DIARY
or
INTELLIGENCE SUMMARY.
(Erase heading not required.)

Place	Date	Hour	Summary of Events and Information	Remarks and references to Appendices
NEUF BERQUIN	12/4/18	5pm	about F20.a.0.8 also light artillery at close range which caused a great many casualties during the withdrawal. A line was formed chiefly in a new railway cutting under construction.	
		6pm	The line from F14.c & 8. to E24 b.0.7. was held by the remnants of the Battalion mixed up with a few K.O.S.B. S.W.B. Lancs Fus and elements of 31st Division and 50th Division. The K.O.Y.L.I on the right having withdrawn in touch with our right ie LA COURONNE. G.O.C. 86th Bde came into the firing line with Col Forbes[?] Lt. Col. Raikes in Command of the remnants of 86th & 87th Bde and ordered O.C. 1st Border back to Bde H.Q. The enemy did not attack this position that evening and the line was organized in the night. The strength of the 2 Brigades being 352 OR with 11 Officers including 12 L. Gs and 2 Vickers Guns. Detail of the Brigade being Border Regt 195 OR. with 8 Officers and 11 Lewis Guns. S.W.B. 24 OR K.O.S.B. 47 OR. Situation 86th Bde in touch with K.O.Y.L.I. in VIEUXBERQUIN about E24 a central	J.F.

(A9175) Wt W2355/P360 600,000 12/17 D. D. & L. Sch. 52a. Forms/C2118/15.

157 13

Army Form C. 2118.

WAR DIARY
or
INTELLIGENCE SUMMARY.
(Erase heading not required.)

Instructions regarding War Diaries and Intelligence Summaries are contained in F. S. Regs., Part II. and the Staff Manual respectively. Title pages will be prepared in manuscript.

Place	Date	Hour	Summary of Events and Information	Remarks and references to Appendices
NEUF BERQUIN	12/4/18	6 pm	and 87th Bde in touch with 92nd Bde North of FME LYNDE. Night of 12/13th passed quietly, the R.E. were sent to help consolidate the line and rations taken up to the firing line by limber.	
NEUF BERQUIN	13th		Dispositions B Coy E12 d 9.1 to F13 a 1.6. A barricade was built across the railway cutting S.W. of FME LABIS. 'C' 'D' Coys occupying the railway cutting in F13 c and A Coy in a trench in front. On the left the 92nd Brigade prolonged the line Northwards towards MERIS. On the right the K.O.Y.L.I. connected up with the Guards Brigade.	
		9 am	Small parties of enemy were seen coming from direction of FME [illegible] moving Northwards. They deployed from F13 b 1.1 to F13 LESAGE.	
		[illegible]	Enemy started moving forward towards [illegible] but were met with very heavy Lewis Gun fire from C Coy at [illegible]. Heavy casualties were inflicted on enemy. The attack then	JSM

(A9175) Wt W2357/P360 600,000 12/17 D. D. & L. Sch. 52a. Forms/C2118/15.

Instructions regarding War Diaries and Intelligence Summaries are contained in F. S. Regs., Part II. and the Staff Manual respectively. Title pages will be prepared in manuscript.

A37

WAR DIARY
or
INTELLIGENCE SUMMARY.
(Erase heading not required.)

Army Form C. 2118.

Place	Date	Hour	Summary of Events and Information	Remarks and references to Appendices
VIEUX BERQUIN	13/4/18	7.30am	broke up, enemy coming on in small parties.	
		10.0am	Small parties crossed VIEUX BERQUIN – OUTTER STEENE road at F13.a.8.3 These were heavily engaged by 2 Vickers and 4 Lewis Guns from C and D Companies at barricade across Railway cutting F13.c.4.8. Small party of enemy occupied house at F13 a 7.2	
		10.30	Parties of enemy scattered and retired towards FME LESAGE. Enemy evacuated house at F13 a 7 2 the blowing up of one of our ammunition dumps by our Artillery making it untenable No more was seen of enemy on left	
		11am	Throughout the morning the machine guns and Lewis Guns were fully employed firing at good targets and caused the enemy considerable losses.	
		2.30pm	K.O.Y.L.I were French mortared out of their posts and withdrew some 300 yards while the Lancs Fus. were shelled out of VIEUX BERQUIN	
		3pm	A Coy pushed a post out to the Right and another to the Right	g.B.R.

15

A37

Instructions regarding War Diaries and Intelligence Summaries are contained in F. S. Regs., Part II. and the Staff Manual respectively. Title pages will be prepared in manuscript.

WAR DIARY
or
INTELLIGENCE SUMMARY.
(Erase heading not required.)

Army Form C. 2118.

Place	Date	Hour	Summary of Events and Information	Remarks and references to Appendices
VIEUX BERQUIN	13th	3pm	[illegible] & connected up with some Lancs Fus. who were holding [illegible] about F19 a.8.2.	
		5pm	Very large forces of enemy in 4 waves appeared at F19 c.8.9 moving towards LE COURONNE. These were fired on by A & D Coys. Our heavy artillery came into action at this point doing great execution.	
		11.0a	Two Companies of enemy advanced from FME BLEU to F19 a.5.2 in small parties. These were heavily engaged by rifle and Lewis Gun fire and stopped but they dug in under very heavy rifle fire. Throughout the afternoon the trench was heavily trench mortared while snipers and M.Gs were very troublesome both from immediate front and from both flanks. Brigade H.Q. had withdrawn in the morning to FME MOLNEGHIN. E.6.c. Communication for most of the day was cut off. In the afternoon the 92nd Brigade on the left withdrew pivoting their right back to [illegible]. This was seen by one of the	J.P.D.

837

16

Instructions regarding War Diaries and Intelligence Summaries are contained in F. S. Regs., Part II. and the Staff Manual respectively. Title pages will be prepared in manuscript.

WAR DIARY
or
INTELLIGENCE SUMMARY.
(Erase heading not required.)

Army Form C. 2118.

Place	Date	Hour	Summary of Events and Information	Remarks and references to Appendices
VIEUX BERQUIN	13/4/18		Brigade Staff who was on the spot who got them back into position but this withdrawal again took place in the evening which was followed up by the enemy. This left both flanks of the Battalion and the other small remnants of the two Brigades very much in the air	
		10pm	The remnants of the two Brigades withdrew. Orders for this withdrawal had been issued by Division but had not been received at the time by the troops. Marched back unmolested through new line of defence being dug by 92nd Brigade from about E12 central to E17 central through a 2nd line of defence being dug by 1st Australian Division. E19 b. Bde H.Q. then established at E3.d.1.1. The march was then continued according to orders back to the ST SYLVESTRE area	
			Casualties.	
			Officers / Other Ranks	
			Killed 1 / 42	
			Missing 3 / 185	
			Wounded 7 / 160	
			11 / 387	J.F.M.

(A9175) Wt W2358/P360 600,000 12/17 D. D. & L. Sch. 52a. Forms/C2118/15.

Instructions regarding War Diaries and Intelligence Summaries are contained in F. S. Regs., Part II. and the Staff Manual respectively. Title pages will be prepared in manuscript.

831

WAR DIARY
or
INTELLIGENCE SUMMARY.
(Erase heading not required.)

Army Form C. 2118.

Place	Date	Hour	Summary of Events and Information	Remarks and references to Appendices
ST SYLVESTRE	14th	1pm	Billeted in F36 a with Brigade H.Q.	
CAPPEL		4.	Moved to W.1 a.1.9. Comfortable billets with good barns	
	15th		Reorganising and refitting. Composite Battalion moved	
			forward. Major A.N. Sutcliffe M.C. 2nd in Command of Battalion	
			Capt. [illegible] M.C. and 2 Coy. Border	
	17th		Remainder of Battalion moved back by march route to BANDRINGHEM	
			Good billets.	
	[illegible]		[illegible] under Capt. [illegible] moved back by lorry to LA BREARDE V.5.C.	
	19th		[illegible] moved back by march route to LA BREARDE where	
			the Battalion reformed, the Composite Battalion being broken	
			up. Bn. H.Q. V5 c.[illegible]	JBn.

(A9175) Wt W2352/P363 600,000 12/17 D. D. & L. Sch. 52a. Forms/C2118/15.

18

Army Form C. 2118.

Instructions regarding War Diaries and Intelligence Summaries are contained in F. S. Regs., Part II, and the Staff Manual respectively. Title pages will be prepared in manuscript.

WAR DIARY
or
INTELLIGENCE SUMMARY.
(Erase heading not required.)

Place	Date	Hour	Summary of Events and Information	Remarks and references to Appendices
ST SYLVESTRE CAPPEL	14/4/18	1pm	Billetted in P36a with Brigade H.Q.	
		4.	Moved to W.1.a.1.9. Comfortable billets with good barns.	
	15/4/18.		Reorganising and refitting. Composite Battalion composed of Battalions of 87th Brigade made into Coys. Lt Col Murray 1/K.O.S.B. Commanding and Major A.W. Sutcliffe M.C. 2nd in Command.	
	16/4/18		Capt Cowburn M.C. commanded Border Regt portion which was organized into 2 Coys. Composite Battalion received orders to move forward into close billets near LE PEUPLIER and arrived 7.30 pm in support to an impending attack on METEREN by the French that evening.	
	17/4/18.		No attack materialised. Stood by till 4 am moved into close support to French Right and Australian left taking up position behind hedges etc near COURTE CROIX sheet 27. W.18. by 5.30 am in response to urgent request of French Commander. Very quiet till 8 am when considerable air activity took place low flying scouts carrying apparently British markings flew over, ie first appearance of enemy planes marked with circle and	J.R.

D. D. & L., London, E.C.
(A7883) Wt. W5031/M1672 350,000 4/17 Sch. 52a Forms/C/2118/14

19

Instructions regarding War Diaries and Intelligence Summaries are contained in F. S. Regs., Part II. and the Staff Manual respectively. Title pages will be prepared in manuscript.

WAR DIARY
or
INTELLIGENCE SUMMARY.
(Erase heading not required.)

Army Form C. 2118.

Place	Date	Hour	Summary of Events and Information	Remarks and references to Appendices
COURTECROIX	17/4/18	8 am	Faint Iron Cross.	
		9 am	Crash barrage on whole position and extending North and South indefinitely - all High Explosive of all calibres. Combing barrage in depth searching particularly farms hedges and nullahs	
		12 noon	Barrage continued till 12 noon inflicting casualties as follows. 10 Officers 60 men in 87th Composite Battalion. Border casualties Officers 3 OR. 31. Relieved at 8 pm by 5th Bde Australians and moved back to ST SYLVESTRE CAPPEL area arriving 2 am 18th inst. Remainder of Battalion moved back by march route to BANDRINGHEM. Good billets	
	18/4/18		110 OR under Capt Cargill moved back from BANDRINGHEM by lorry to LABREARDE V.5.c. 87th Composite Battalion rested	
	19/4/18		Remainder moved back by march route to LABREARDE where the Battalion reformed, the Composite Battalion being broken up Bn HQ V 5 c 4.0	
	20/4/18 to 26/4/18		Battalion in good billets in Sheet 27.V.10 a c.d. men employed	

D. D. & L., London, E.C. (A7883) Wt. W593/M1672 350,000 4/17 Sch. 52a Forms/C/2118/14

20

Instructions regarding War Diaries and Intelligence Summaries are contained in F. S. Regs., Part II. and the Staff Manual respectively. Title pages will be prepared in manuscript.

WAR DIARY
or
INTELLIGENCE SUMMARY.
(Erase heading not required.)

Army Form C. 2118.

Place	Date	Hour	Summary of Events and Information	Remarks and references to Appendices
LA BREARDE	20/4/18 to 26/4/18		on digging reserve lines E of HAZEBROUCK under R.E. supervision	
	27/4/18		Night 27th/28th Battalion relieved 18/D.L.I. 31st Division in SEC BOIS area moving by march route from LA BREARDE. Quiet relief. Two Coys 4th Tank Corps L. G. Bn in sector came under	
	28/4/18		orders of Commanding Officer. 1st Border Regiment organised in 2 Coys with 15 Lewis Guns No. 1 Coy (1 Pl. A Coy and 2 Pls. C. Coy) under Capt Chambers No 2 Coy (2 Pls B Coy & 1 Pl. D Coy) under Capt Cargill. Front line 2 platoons B Coy Support 1 platoon D Coy and 2 platoons C. Coy, in billets GRAND SEC BOIS 1 platoon A Coy Battalion HQ in farm (36a) E 2 c 5.1. 1 Coy Tank Corps front line 1 Coy support line.	
	29/30/4/18		Patrol under 2/Lt Olden and 2/Lt Holt, object to get prisoner and reconnoitring with view of making a raid	
	30/4/18		Quiet day Major A.W. Sutcliffe came to Bn HQ to train raiders.	[initials]

D. D. & L., London, E.C. (A7883) Wt. W593/M1672 350,000 4/17 Sch. 52a Forms/C/2118/14

1 Border Regt

No. 38

Instructions regarding War Diaries and Intelligence Summaries are contained in F. S. Regs., Part II. and the Staff Manual respectively. Title pages will be prepared in manuscript.

WAR DIARY
or
INTELLIGENCE SUMMARY.
(Erase heading not required.)

Army Form C. 2118.

Vol 28

Place	Date	Hour	Summary of Events and Information	Remarks and references to Appendices
SEC Bois	1918 May 1		Quiet day. During night 1/2nd. an inter Coy. relief was carried out. "A" & "D" Coys in front line "B" Coy & "C" Coy less 1 pl. in support. One pl. "C" Coy to be trained as raiding party moved back to Bn. HQ. Quiet relief. Coy Comdrs did not change over. Capt. G.B.D. CARGILL remaining in firing line HQ. & Capt W.F.H. CHAMBERS, M.C in support.	
			Afternoon patrol under 2/Lt. S.M. OLDEN unsuccessful in finding Germans.	
	2		Quiet day. Coy Comdrs. changed over.	
	2/3		Raiding party under 2/Lt. S.M. OLDEN went out North of farm at E11 d 3.4. Sunken road was found to be full with about 200 Germans at work. A hostile covering party prevented the capture of any isolated enemy.	
	3.		Quiet day generally. About 5.20 pm a crash barrage was put on Bn. HQ & HQ moved back to shell holes in rear for 1½ hours. 2/Lt. HOLT wounded, two other ranks. Bn HQ was again shelled about 8 pm. 2 transport men wounded and one mule had to be destroyed.	

(A9175) Wt W2359/P560 600,000 12/17 D. D. & L. Sch. 52a. Forms/C2118/13.

Instructions regarding War Diaries and Intelligence Summaries are contained in F. S. Regs., Part II. and the Staff Manual respectively. Title pages will be prepared in manuscript.

WAR DIARY
or
INTELLIGENCE SUMMARY.
(Erase heading not required.)

Army Form C. 2118.

Place	Date	Hour	Summary of Events and Information	Remarks and references to Appendices
			Casualties week ending May 3rd 1918. (12 noon).	
			INCREASE: — Drafts from Base 1 officer 7 OR. (2/Lt. E. FISHER) DECREASE: — Evac. Sick - -	
SEC BOIS	3/4		Raiding Party found German working party again in Sunken road, but could not get a prisoner.	
	4		Quiet day.	
	4/5		Raid on sunken road in E 11 d. Raiders consisted of 20 OR. under CAPT. B.R. DURLACHER, M.C, Lt. H. HAYMAN JOYCE & 2/Lt. R. RAE. O.C. raid 2/Lt. S.M. OLDEN. Zero hour 1.5 am. Artillery barrage went down correctly to time with good density, advancing eastwards by 100x lifts every 2 minutes, forming a box barrage. No counter-barrage was put down by the enemy but a few bursts of machine gun fire were opened. Firing of red Very lights was used as signal for raiders to return. Enemy casualties one man and a light machine gun captured, 5 bayonetted & several who ran back into the barrage were	JW

(A9175) Wt W2358/P360 600,000 12/17 D. D. & L. Sch. 52a. Forms/C2118/15.

Instructions regarding War Diaries and Intelligence Summaries are contained in F. S. Regs., Part II. and the Staff Manual respectively. Title pages will be prepared in manuscript.

WAR DIARY
or
INTELLIGENCE SUMMARY.
(Erase heading not required.)

Army Form C. 2118.

Place	Date	Hour	Summary of Events and Information	Remarks and references to Appendices
	MAY			
SEC BOIS	4/5		seem to feel. 2/Lt S.M. OLDEN was killed by shell fire, being hit by	
			one or two shrapnel. 2 OR. were slightly wounded by M.G. fire	
	5		Front line lightly shelled.	
	5/6		Bn. relieved by 1st WORCESTER RGT. "A" Coy sustained 10 casualties	
			coming out by front line Coy. HQ. a shell falling among a	
			party of men. 2/Lt. L.A. HUBBART wounded. Otherwise a quiet relief.	
			Bn. moved by march route to Nissen Hut camp at LE GRAND	
			HASARD. Good billets.	
			Casualties 27/4/18 to 6/5/18.	
			Officers. OR.	
			Killed 1 3 2/Lt S.M. OLDEN	
			Wounded. 2 9 2/Lt F. HOLT, 2/Lt L.A. HUBBART.	
			Missing – –	
			Total 3 12	
LE GRAND	6.		Batn. rested. Refitting & bathing.	
HASARD	7-12		Men employed on digging & making breastworks about LA MOTTE.	[initials]

(A9175) Wt W2353/P560 600,000 12/17 D. D. & L. Sch. 52a. Forms/C2118/15.

Instructions regarding War Diaries and Intelligence Summaries are contained in F. S. Regs., Part II. and the Staff Manual respectively. Title pages will be prepared in manuscript.

WAR DIARY
or
INTELLIGENCE SUMMARY.
(Erase heading not required.)

Army Form C. 2118.

Place	Date	Hour	Summary of Events and Information	Remarks and references to Appendices
LE GRAND HASARD	7-12		under R.E. Classes of L.G. Signalling & scouting carried on as far as working parties would allow. "[illegible]" remained with 29th Div. Re. Bn.	
			Casualties week ending May 10th 1918 (12 noon).	
			INCREASE:- Drafts from Base — Officers – , OR. 17	
			DECREASE:- KILLED O. 1, OR. 3 — 2/Lt. S.M. OLDEN.	
			WOUNDED O. 2, OR. 10 — 2/Lt. F. HOLT & 2/Lt. W.A. HUDDART.	
			SICK O. 1, OR. 2 — 2/Lt. T.W. BROWN.	
			To PRISON O. –, OR. 1	
			TOTAL O. 4, OR. 16	
	12/13		Hostile aircraft bombed Bn. Transport. No casualties.	
	13		Coys. bathed. Bn. relieved 2ND. HANTS in right sector of left Bde. front starting to move from LE GRAND HASARD at 7 pm. Relief complete 11.30 pm 14/5/18. No casualties. No. 1 Coy. in firing line (from R.G.L. No. 5 & 4 pls. C Coy., No 1 pl. 'A' Coy under CAPT. J.W. HOOD M.C.	
SWARTENBROUCH			No. 2 Coy. in support 6 pl. 'D' Coy. & 3 & 2 pls 'B' Coy. Bn. HQ at SWARTENBROUCH E 15 d 36.	[initials]

(A9175) Wt W2353/P360 600,000 12/17 D. D. & L. Sch. 52a. Forms/C2118/15.

Instructions regarding War Diaries and Intelligence Summaries are contained in F. S. Regs., Part II. and the Staff Manual respectively. Title pages will be prepared in manuscript.

WAR DIARY
or
INTELLIGENCE SUMMARY.
(Erase heading not required.)

Army Form C. 2118.

Place	Date	Hour	Summary of Events and Information	Remarks and references to Appendices
SWARTEN-	14		Quiet during day. Very fine weather with much air activity.	
BRUCH	14/15		2nd R.F's on our right carried out a raid at 1 am. Vigorous enemy reply from 1 am to 2 am. One casualty (slight wound) in our front line from own shell falling short.	
	15.		Hostile artillery more active. Bn. HQ registered with 5.9s at 11.30 am. Very fine day with much air activity. At 7 pm. Bn. HQ moved back to farm at E 14 d 5.3. Major A W SUTCLIFFE, M.C., reported to take over from C.O.	
	16.		Quiet day. Very fine but hazy. C.O returned to Transport Lines. MAJOR A.W. SUTCLIFFE, M.C., assumed command of the Bn. in the line. Heavy T.M. fired on E 22 b.	
	17		Quiet day. Support Coy HQ lightly shelled.	
	17/18		No 2 Coy relieved No. 1 Coy in front line. D Coy pl on right & plts "B" Coy on left. No 1 Coy moved back to support. Quiet relief.	
			Casualties week ending May 17th 1918 (12 noon).	
			INCREASE — O. OR. — Drafts from Base 7 21. DECREASE — O. OR — Sick - 2; Wounded - 5; Transferred - 4; Total - 11	
			2/LTs. J. ROBERTSON, W. McINTYRE, J. McLACHLAN, A. CHICKEN, J. L. FINLAYSON, G. MARSHALL, W. H. YOUDALE.	[initials]

(A5015) Wt. W5535/P690 600,000 12/17 D. D. & L. Sch. 52a. Forms/C2118/15

Instructions regarding War Diaries and Intelligence Summaries are contained in F. S. Regs., Part II. and the Staff Manual respectively. Title pages will be prepared in manuscript.

WAR DIARY
or
INTELLIGENCE SUMMARY.
(Erase heading not required.)

Army Form C. 2118.

Place	Date	Hour	Summary of Events and Information	Remarks and references to Appendices
SWARTEN-BROUCH	18		Low flying E.A. dropped small bombs on firing line at dawn. No damage. F.L. HQ. shelled by H.V. gun. E.A. attempted several times to fly low over lines but were driven off by A A L. Gs. 2/Lt. G.S. BLACKBURN slightly wounded but remained at duty.	
	19.		F.L. HQ again shelled by H.V. gun. Artillery generally more active & light shelling of both front & support line took place. During the night 19/20 the right F.L. pl. in SECLIN relieved by a pl. of 2 LEINSTERS. The pl under 2/Lt. J. McLACHLAN moved back to support line & came temporarily under command of CAPT. J.W. HOOD M.C.	
	20		Hostile artillery fairly active. Fine day & much air work carried on.	
	20/21		Bn relieved by 2 S.W.Bdrs. Quiet relief. No casualties. Coys moved back to billets in SWARTENBROUGH with Bn.H.Q. at E7c77. No. 2 Coy standing to in SWARTENBROUGH defences. No. 1 Coy in trenches of reserve line temporarily under OC 2 S.W.B. 6 L. Gs under 2/Lt. W McINTYRE placed in PT. SEC BOIS defences under orders O.C. 1 K.O.S.B.	
	21		Quiet day. ~~Coys found working parties~~ Men rested. News was received	

(A9175) Wt W2358/P360 600,000 12/17 D. D. & L. Sch. 52a. Forms/C2118/15.

Instructions regarding War Diaries and Intelligence Summaries are contained in F. S. Regs., Part II. and the Staff Manual respectively. Title pages will be prepared in manuscript.

WAR DIARY
or
INTELLIGENCE SUMMARY.
(Erase heading not required.)

Army Form C. 2118.

Place	Date	Hour	Summary of Events and Information	Remarks and references to Appendices
SWARTEN-BROUCK	21		in the Battn. that the C.O. had been awarded the V.C. for the part played by him in the fighting in April. Great rejoicing in the Battn.	
	21/22		7/S.W.B. carried out a successful raid. 1 pl. "D" Coy under 2/Lt. G.S. BLACKBURN was moved up to support line in E.1.a ready to proceed to garrison front line posts in case of need but was not called on to do so. During retaliation a direct hit from 5.9 shell occurred at Bn. HQ.	
	22		Quiet day. Coys. found working parties for R.E. making shelters & improving trenches.	
	23		Quiet day. Work as on 22nd.	
	24		Quiet day. Night 24/25 No. 2 Coy. relieved by 4 WORCESTER REGT. & moved to Northern portion of Reserve line in E.8.b & E.9.a & E.3.c and No. 1 Coy. moved without being relieved to reserve line in E.8.d & E.14.a & b, the men being in billets in GRAND SEC BOIS during the day. The L.G.s attached to 2 S.W.B. & 1 K.O.S.B. were not relieved. Bn. HQ shelled at 10 pm. 2 direct hits	

(A9175) Wt W2351/P560 600,000 12/17 D. D. & L. Sch. 52a. Forms/C2118/15

Instructions regarding War Diaries and Intelligence Summaries are contained in F. S. Regs., Part II. and the Staff Manual respectively. Title pages will be prepared in manuscript.

WAR DIARY
or
INTELLIGENCE SUMMARY.
(Erase heading not required.)

Army Form C. 2118.

Place	Date	Hour	Summary of Events and Information	Remarks and references to Appendices
SWARTEN-BROUCH			Casualties week ending 24th May 1918 (12 noon).	
			INCREASE:- O. OR. / Drafts from Base 3 10 / (2/Lt. J.W. CRAIG, 2/Lt. A.R. DICK, 2/Lt. W.C. KING.) — DECREASE:- O OR / Sick - 2 / Wounded 2 / Total 4	
	25		Work continued under RE - construction of shelters Bn. H.Q. Cookhouses, Aid posts, etc were burnt to the ground. Otherwise quiet	
	26.		Quiet day. Work continued under RE. Night 26/27 1 K.O.S.B carried out a successful raid capturing 3 prisoners & a M.G. No casualties in the Bn.	
	27		Quiet day.	
LE GRAND HASARD	27/28		Bn was relieved by 2 Coys 1 R.D.F & moved back by march route to bivouac camp at LE GRAND HASARD.	
	28		Bn rested. Fine weather & men comfortable in their bivouacs under hedges. Baths.	
	29/31		100 men employed daily working about LA MOTTE under RE. Remainder training in Rifle Grenade, L.G. & patrolling.	[initials]

(A9175) Wt W2358/P360 600,000 12/17 D. D. & L. Sch. 52a. Forms/C2118/15.

Instructions regarding War Diaries and Intelligence Summaries are contained in F. S. Regs., Part II, and the Staff Manual respectively. Title pages will be prepared in manuscript.

WAR DIARY
or
INTELLIGENCE SUMMARY.
(Erase heading not required.)

Army Form C. 2118.

Place	Date	Hour	Summary of Events and Information	Remarks and references to Appendices
LE GRAND HASARD	31.		Casualties during tour in line 14/5/18 – 28/5/18.	
			KILLED Off. – OR. 1	
			WOUNDED 1 8 2/LT. G.S. BLACKBURN (remained at duty)	
			MISSING – –	
			TOTAL 1 – 9	
			Casualties week ending 31st. May 1918 (12 noon).	
			INCREASE:– O. OR. DECREASE:– O. OR.	
			Drafts from Base 2 12 Sick – 15	
			2/LT. E.W. CHICKEN. Wounded – 2	
			LT. J. PATTINSON. To Base – 2	
			" England – 1	
			– 20	

J.H. Smith [?] 2/Lt.,
Asst. Adj. 1st. Bord. Rgt.

Serial No 38

Instructions regarding War Diaries and Intelligence Summaries are contained in F. S. Regs., Part II. and the Staff Manual respectively. Title pages will be prepared in manuscript.

WAR DIARY
or
~~INTELLIGENCE SUMMARY.~~
(Erase heading not required.)

Army Form C. 2118.

1 Border Regt
Vol 27

Place	Date	Hour	Summary of Events and Information	Remarks and references to Appendices
LE GRAND HASARD	1918 JUNE 1		Working parties and training. Regimental Dinner of all officers invited by Lt Col J FORBES-ROBERTSON V.C. DSO. MC. in camp at GRAND HASARD.	
	2		Working parties and training	
	3		do do	
SWARTENBROUCH	4/5		Bn relieved 2 LEINSTER R. in trenches in left of Bde Sector East of NIEPPE FOREST. A Coy & 2 plts B Coy in firing line. C Coy & 2 plts B Coy in support. D Coy in reserve at E 20 central. BN Hd Qrs at E14 c 8.0 SWARTENBROUCH. Quiet relief.	
	5		Working parties under R E on Bn Hd Qrs & Coy Hd Qrs making splinter-proof shelters. E.A. flying low driven off by A A Lewis Gun fire.	
	5/6		Fighting patrol under 2/Lieut W. YOUDALE came in touch with enemy at E22 d 8.4. but withdrew as they were outnumbered	
	6		Quiet day. 6/7 Bn Hd Qrs shelled slightly with gas. L G posts dug in front of support lines. Grass cut away in front of posts. Patrol under	JM

D. D. & L., London, E.C. (A7883) Wt. W803/M1672 350,000 4/17 Sch. 52a. Forms/C/2118/14

2

Instructions regarding War Diaries and Intelligence Summaries are contained in F. S. Regs., Part II. and the Staff Manual respectively. Title pages will be prepared in manuscript.

WAR DIARY
or
INTELLIGENCE SUMMARY.
(*Erase heading not required.*)

Army Form C. 2118.

Place	Date	Hour	Summary of Events and Information	Remarks and references to Appendices
SWARTENBROUCH	6/7		Lt E TOWLE and Lieut J. PATTINSON swept our wire. Fighting patrol under 2/Lieut W. YOUDALE did not get in touch with enemy. Lt-Col	
	7		J FORBES-ROBERTSON VC DSO MC assumed command of 87 Bde (temporarily) & MAJOR A.W. SUTCLIFFE MC took command of the Bn	
	~~7/8~~		~~D Coy relieved A Coy in front line~~ Casualties Week ending 7/6/18	
			INCREASE — Off. / OR; DECREASE — Off. / OR	
			Granted Commission: 2/Lieut A J SMITH — Off. 1; Killed — OR 1	
			Sick — OR 7	
			Draft (from Manch R) — OR 14; CQMS A J SMITH Granted Commn — OR 1	
			Transferred to England — OR 1	
			Total increase: Off. 1, OR 14; Total decrease: OR 10	
	7/8		D Coy relieved A Coy in front line. Quiet relief. Work continued on trenches. Patrol under 2/Lieut W YOUDALE reconnoitred consolidated shell-holes & were engaged by party of enemy about 20 strong. They lay in wait for	[initials]

D. D. & L., London, E.C. (A7883) Wt. W509/M1672 350,000 1/17 Sch. 52a Forms/C/2118/14

3

Army Form C. 2118.

Instructions regarding War Diaries and Intelligence Summaries are contained in F. S. Regs., Part II. and the Staff Manual respectively. Title pages will be prepared in manuscript.

WAR DIARY
or
INTELLIGENCE SUMMARY.
(Erase heading not required.)

Place	Date	Hour	Summary of Events and Information	Remarks and references to Appendices
SWARTEN-BROUCH	7/8		these, but were also attacked on left flank. Fire fight ensued & patrol retired to trench as they were outnumbered. One man reported missing. Lieut J PATTINSON took out wire-sweeping party but found no enemy. Proposed raid was cancelled.	
	8		Enemy artillery active during day on front & support lines. E A flew low over our lines.	
	8/9		Patrol under 2/Lt L V LITTLE came in touch with enemy & engaged them with bombs. Broke off engagement in face of superior numbers. Patrol consisting of Sjt MOORE & Cpl ELLIS (B Coy) kept watch on BEAULIEU FARM from 7.30 am until 9.30 pm. Enemy movement seen in the farm. Lieut J MARSHALL took out patrol to reconnoitre consolidated shell-holes. No enemy seen.	
	9		Quiet day.	
	9/10		Work continued on wire. Patrols swept wire but found no enemy.	
	10		Very quiet	
	10/11		"C" Coy relieved 1. KOSB in front line on right of Bde sector. A Coy in support. 1. LANCS FUS. took over Reserve line of whole sector. Quiet relief	[signature]

D. D. & L., London, E.C. (A7883) Wt. W80/M1672 350,000 4/17 Sch. 52a Forms/C/2118/14

4

Army Form C. 2118.

Instructions regarding War Diaries and Intelligence Summaries are contained in F. S. Regs., Part II, and the Staff Manual respectively. Title pages will be prepared in manuscript.

WAR DIARY
or
INTELLIGENCE SUMMARY.
(Erase heading not required.)

Place	Date	Hour	Summary of Events and Information	Remarks and references to Appendices
	1918 June			
SWARTENBROUCK	10/11		Gas cylinders installed on left of BOIS D'AVAL. 'D' Coy evacuated 3 left posts but gas was not liberated. Usual working parties.	
	11		Quiet day	
	12		E.A flying low over lines.	
	12/13	12 m.	Bn Hd Qrs shelled with gas shells	
	13		Quiet day	
	13/14		Bde dump of RE material formed in front of Support line. 200 men employed. Patrol under 2/Lieut E.W. CHICKEN reached enemy post in consolidated shell holes, engaged them with bombs, but were unable to cross enemy wire.	
	14		Casualties week ending 14/6/18	
			INCREASE: Drafts (from Manchester R) — Off. —, O.R. 305; total 305	
			DECREASE: To England O.R. 2; Killed 1; Wounded 1; Missing 1; Sick 1; total 6	RM

D. D. & L., London, E.C. (A7883) Wt. W593/M1672 350,000 1/17 Sch. 52a Forms/C/2118/14

5

Instructions regarding War Diaries and Intelligence Summaries are contained in F. S. Regs., Part II. and the Staff Manual respectively. Title pages will be prepared in manuscript.

WAR DIARY
or
INTELLIGENCE SUMMARY.
(Erase heading not required.)

Army Form C. 2118.

Place	Date	Hour	Summary of Events and Information	Remarks and references to Appendices
SWARTEN BROUCH	1918 June 14/15		Bn relieved by 2. S.W.B on left + 1. KOSB on right. Quiet relief. Two fighting patrols were sent out under 2/Lieut E.W. CHICKEN + Lieut H. J HAYMAN-JOYCE. Enemy not encountered. Bn returned by march route to old bivouac camp at LE GRAND HASARD.	
GRAND HASARD	15.		Bn in Brigade reserve. Ordered to be ready to move at one hour's notice in case of attack. Bivouac lines shelled by H.V. guns. "C" + "D" Coys moved to new lines north of HAZEBROUCH - MORBEQUE road. One man wounded (C. Coy) Baths + pay.	
	16		Church parade + inspection of Coys by C.O. Bn warned to prepare to take part in offensive to capture enemy front line system about GARS BRUGGHE, GOMBERT FARM + VERT RUE. Conference for C.O.s at Bde Hd Qrs at 12 noon. Lt-Col J. FORBES-ROBERTSON VC. DSO. MC appointed to command a Bde in 52 Div	
	16/17		"A" + "D" Coys total strength 300 men under Capt G B D CARGILL proceeded to BOIS D'AVAL at 11 pm to dig trenches under R.E. On completion of task this working party took up positions in Reserve Line	[initials]

(A9175) Wt W2358/P562 600,000 12/17 D. D. & L. Sch. 52a. Forms/C2118/15.

6

Army Form C. 2118.

Instructions regarding War Diaries and Intelligence Summaries are contained in F. S. Regs., Part II. and the Staff Manual respectively. Title pages will be prepared in manuscript.

WAR DIARY
or
INTELLIGENCE SUMMARY.
(Erase heading not required.)

Place	Date	Hour	Summary of Events and Information	Remarks and references to Appendices
GRAND HASARD	1918 June 16/17		about the LITTLE BORRE for precautionary measures & returned to camp after "stand down"	
	17		Baths. Training. CO's Conference at Bde Hd Qrs. The C O (Major A W SUTCLIFFE MC) & OCs "A" & "D" Coys. selected assembly positions for Bn in front of BOIS D'AVAL	
	17/18		The assembly positions were dug by A & D Coys. (One killed, one wounded)	
	18		Dress Rehearsal of attack at LE GRAND HASARD. DIVISIONAL COMDR'S conference at Bn Hd Qrs. for COs & Coy Comdrs.	
	19		Final preparations made to move up to assembly positions in evening. At 12 noon orders received that operations were cancelled.	
	20		Quiet day. Preliminary arrangements made to move further back.	
EYK HAUT CASTEEL	21		Bn relieved at 3 30 pm by 11 E. YORKS. & moved by route march to camp near EYK HAUT CASTEEL	
RACQUINGHEM	22		Bn moved by route march to HURLINGHEM CAMP at RACQUNGHEM Good canvas camp. Officers messes in village.	
	23		COs conference re. Training at Divisional Hd Qrs, & reconnaissance of positions	[initials]

(A9175) Wt W2355/P360 650,000 12/17 D. D. & L. Sch. 52a. Forms/C2118/15

7

Army Form C. 2118.

Instructions regarding War Diaries and Intelligence Summaries are contained in F. S. Regs., Part II. and the Staff Manual respectively. Title pages will be prepared in manuscript.

WAR DIARY
or
INTELLIGENCE SUMMARY.
(Erase heading not required.)

Place	Date	Hour	Summary of Events and Information	Remarks and references to Appendices
	1915 June 21		Casualties for week ending 21/6/18	
			INCREASE. — DECREASE.	
			Increase: OFF. —; O.R. — / Decrease: OFF. —; O.R. —	
			Drafts (casuals): OFF. —; O.R. 8 / Killed: OFF. —; O.R. 1	
			Wounded: OFF. —; O.R. 10	
			Sick: OFF. —; O.R. 6	
			To England Sick 2/Lieut C. W. SAYNOR: OFF. 1; O.R. —	
			To England to M.G.C. 2/Lieut E. FISHER: OFF. 1; O.R. —	
			Total decrease: OFF. 2; O.R. 17	

[signature]

D. D. & L., London, E.C. (A7883) Wt W809/M1672 250,000 4/17 Sch. 52a Forms/C/2118/14

Instructions regarding War Diaries and Intelligence Summaries are contained in F. S. Regs., Part II, and the Staff Manual respectively. Title pages will be prepared in manuscript.

WAR DIARY
or
~~INTELLIGENCE~~ SUMMARY.
(*Erase heading not required.*)

8

Army Form C. 2118.

Place	Date	Hour	Summary of Events and Information	Remarks and references to Appendices
RACQUING-HEM.	1918 June 23		to be taken up in case of enemy attack	
	24		Bathing & training.	
	25		Training on training area. Individual & Platoon	
	26		do do	
	27		Bn practice in Ceremonial drill on Polo ground	
	28		Bde do do	
			Casualties week ending 28/6/18	
			Increase / Decrease	
			Increase: OFF — O R — / Decrease: OFF. — OR —	
			Drafts (Casuals): OFF —, O R 13 / To 155th Bde Lt Col J FORBES ROBERTSON VC DSO MC: OFF. 1.	
			To 155th Bde: OR 1	
			Sick: OR 13	
			To England for cadet school: OR 3	
			Decrease total: OFF. 1, OR 17	
	29		Bde ceremonial before Corps & Divisional Comdrs.	[initials]

D. D. & L., London, E.C. (A7883) Wt W869/M1672 750,000 4/17 Sch. 52a Forms/C/2118/14

9

Army Form C. 2118.

Instructions regarding War Diaries and Intelligence Summaries are contained in F. S. Regs., Part II. and the Staff Manual respectively. Title pages will be prepared in manuscript.

WAR DIARY

or

~~INTELLIGENCE SUMMARY.~~

(Erase heading not required.)

Place	Date	Hour	Summary of Events and Information	Remarks and references to Appendices
RACQUING-HEM	1918 June 30		Bde Church parade at HURLINGHEM CAMP, Corps Comdr ~~attending~~.	DM

R. Holland Capt
a/adjt. 1 Border R.

D. D. & L., London, E.C.
(A7883) Wt W809/M1672 350,000 4/17 Sch. 52a Forms/C/2118/14

Army Form C. 2118.

Instructions regarding War Diaries and Intelligence Summaries are contained in F. S. Regs., Part II. and the Staff Manual respectively. Title pages will be prepared in manuscript.

Volume No. 39.

WAR DIARY
or
INTELLIGENCE SUMMARY.
(Erase heading not required.)

July 1918.

1 Border Regt

Vol 28

Place	Date	Hour	Summary of Events and Information	Remarks and references to Appendices
RACQUINGHEM	1/3		Training - tactics in PONT ASQUIN area.	
	4		Brigade Sports on Polo Ground at B 20 d. Bn. won Bde. championship on points.	
	5		Training. Lecture by Col. CAMPBELL, A.G. Staff.	
			CASUALTIES - N.C. JULY 5TH 1918	
			INCREASE. O. OR. — DECREASE. O. OR.	
			Drafts from base 1 6 — Batman to G.O.C., 115 Bde 1	
			(CAPT C H WALKER M.C.) — Trac. from Div. Area. 2	
			" to England (Mr L. V. LITTLE) 1	
			Re-posted to 5th Bn. (CAPT. C. H. WALKER) 1	
			Totals 1 6 — 2 3	
	6		Training.	
	7.		Divine service. Bn. Soccer team beat K.O.S.B. in Bde. championship.	
	8		Bde. Ceremonial Parade for inspection by G.O.C. 2nd Army on ground at A 11 c 13. Medal Ribbons presented. Bn. Football team beat 4th WORC. RGT. in Divisional Championship at LUMBRES. No. 3655 C.S.M. KEEFE, M.M. won Div. Army middle-weight championship (boxing) at WARDRECQUES.	JW

(A9175) Wt W2355/P360 600,000 12/17 D. D. & L. Sch. 52a. Forms/C2118/13.

Army Form C. 2118.

WAR DIARY
or
INTELLIGENCE SUMMARY.
(Erase heading not required.)

Instructions regarding War Diaries and Intelligence Summaries are contained in F. S. Regs., Part II. and the Staff Manual respectively. Title pages will be prepared in manuscript.

Place	Date	Hour	Summary of Events and Information	Remarks and references to Appendices
RACQUINGHEM	9		Divisional Horse Show on Polo Ground. No Battn. parades. Bn. won Second prize in Light Draught Horse Event.	
	10		Bn. in practice attack. Dinners on ground. Intensive digging & rapid wiring in afternoon.	
	11		Training. 1 Coy. on range. Battn. team beat 29th M.G. Bn. at Soccer.	
HAZEBROUCK	12		Organisation. Sudden orders to move at 12 noon. Bn. proceeded by march route to HAZEBROUCK into camp about V.21 b 9 0.	
			CASUALTIES – 1st to 12th JULY 1918.	
			INCREASE. O. OR. — DECREASE O. OR.	
			Draft from Base (CAPT. A.S.M. KENNEDY) 1 – — Trac. from Div. Area 6	
			From Hospital – 1 — Deserter 1	
			Trans. to S.W.B. 1	
			To Base (Lt. J. McLACHLAN) 1	
			Total 1 1 — 1 8	
	13		Fitting up for line. Bn. & Coy. Guides reconnoitred front line occupied by 3rd AUSTRALIAN BATTN.	
TIFLIS HOUSE STRAZEELE	14/15		Bn. proceeded by march route to trenches relieving 3rd Bn. A.I.F.	[initials]

(A9175) Wt W235/P360 600,000 12/17 D. D. & L. Sch. 52a. Forms/C2118/15.

3

Instructions regarding War Diaries and Intelligence Summaries are contained in F. S. Regs., Part II and the Staff Manual respectively. Title pages will be prepared in manuscript.

WAR DIARY
or
INTELLIGENCE SUMMARY.
(Erase heading not required.)

Army Form C. 2118.

Place	Date	Hour	Summary of Events and Information	Remarks and references to Appendices
TIFLIS HOUSE	14/15		with "A" Coy on right, "B" Coy middle sector, and "C" Coy relieving 1 Coy 2nd Bn A.I.F on left. "D" Coy in support at GOTHA FM. Line extended from E 11 d 4 2 to E 36 a 9 8. Bn HQ. TIFLIS HOUSE. Quick relief.	
	15		Quiet day. Little gas shelling at 10.30 pm. Wiring & deepening trenches. Lt. R. RAE took out patrol.	
	16		Our artillery & aircraft very active. MERRIS St. heavily shelled at intervals. Wiring & improvement of trenches. 2/Lt J MARSHALL took out patrol at 4 pm.	
	17		Usual artillery activity. Enemy M.G. active from CELERY COPSE. Wiring & work on trenches continued. 2/Lt. A.T. SMITH, D.C.M. & 17 OR. carried out raid with artillery co-operation to capture enemy posts at E 12 c 2 4 but found post evacuated. M.G. spare parts bag captured. Patrol could not penetrate further owing to our barrage. Patrol again went out to another post without success. Advance party of 13th. R. INNISKILLING FUS. (40th DIV.) reconnoitred trenches preparatory to taking over.	T.H.S.

(A9175) Wt W2355/P360 600,000 12/17 D. D. & L. Sch. 52a. Forms/C2118/15.

Instructions regarding War Diaries and Intelligence Summaries are contained in F. S. Regs., Part II. and the Staff Manual respectively. Title pages will be prepared in manuscript.

WAR DIARY
or
INTELLIGENCE SUMMARY.
(*Erase heading not required.*)

Army Form C. 2118.

4

Place	Date	Hour	Summary of Events and Information	Remarks and references to Appendices
TIFLIS HOUSE.	18		Quiet day. 2/Lt A. J. SMITH, D.C.M. took out patrol at 3 pm. in conjunction with R. W. FUS. (31st DIV) on right to enemy post at E 18 a 85. Enemy very alert & on seeing patrol approach fired a spray rocket. M.Gs opened fire from about 6 different posts. Patrol had to withdraw to our line under very heavy fire. Identification of 89th R.I.R. & 393 I.R. obtained from clothing found in post. No casualties.	
	18/19		Bn relieved by 12th R. INNIS FUS. During relief our guns put down a barrage on right sector. Enemy replied with a heavy barrage on front line & supports especially heavy on MONT DE MERRIS. 2/Lt A.R. DICK & 3 other ranks killed and 10 other ranks (including R.S.M. J. MALIA, D.C.M.) wounded. On relief, Bn moved by march route to L'HOFFAND where lorries were waiting to convey troops to BLARINGHEM area. Billets very scattered.	

Casualties during tour

	O.	OR.
Killed	1	4
Wounded	—	19
Missing	—	1
Total	1	24

2/Lt. A.R. DICK.

[signature]

(A9175) Wt W2358/P360 600,000 12/17 D. D. & L. Sch. 52a. Forms/C2118/15.

Instructions regarding War Diaries and Intelligence Summaries are contained in F. S. Regs., Part II. and the Staff Manual respectively. Title pages will be prepared in manuscript.

WAR DIARY
or
INTELLIGENCE SUMMARY.
(Erase heading not required.)

Army Form C. 2118.

5

Place	Date	Hour	Summary of Events and Information	Remarks and references to Appendices
			Casualties [illegible] July 19th. 1918	
			INCREASE O. OR. ; DECREASE O. OR.	
			Draft from Base 2 – ; Evac from Div. Area	6.
			2/Lt. W.H. CRAICK, CAPT. J. H. PROCTOR) ; Wounded	19
			Missing	1
			Killed (2/Lt. W.R. DICK) 1	4
			Total 2 – ; 1	30.
BLARINGHEM	19		Bn resting.	
	20		Reorganising & re-fitting, Inspections etc. C.O's conference on coming training.	
	21		Divine Service. Bn. Training.	
St MARIE CAPPEL.	22		Bn moved north by march route. Halted near LONG CROIX for dinner & tea as billets had not been allotted. Billets in & about St MARIE CAPPEL & widely scattered.	
	23/24		Training.	
	25		2i/c. C.O., Adjutant, O.C. Coys reconnoitred battle positions in Army Line about MONT DES CATS.	
	26		Training. 5 officers reconnoitred line as yesterday.	
			Lt. Col. R.E. [illegible], D.S.O. assumed command of the Bn.	W

(A9175) Wt W2353/P360 600,000 12/17 D. D. & L. Sch. 52a. Forms/C2118/15.

6

Army Form C. 2118.

Instructions regarding War Diaries and Intelligence Summaries are contained in F. S. Regs., Part II. and the Staff Manual respectively. Title pages will be prepared in manuscript.

WAR DIARY
or
INTELLIGENCE SUMMARY.
(Erase heading not required.)

Place	Date	Hour	Summary of Events and Information	Remarks and references to Appendices
			Casualties for w.e. July 26th 1918.	
			INCREASE O. OR. — DECREASE O. OR.	
			Struck off strength * 2	
			From Base - 4 — Trans. to T.M.B. 6	
			" Hospital - [illegible] — " " M.G.C. (Ylt. J. Marshall) 1	
			From 87th Bde (Lt. Col. H.E. Festing D.S.O.) 1 — Evac from Div. Area 2	
			Total 1 [illegible] — Total 3 8	
			* 2/Lts M. Carrington & H.E. Pattifer.	
St. Marie Cappel	27		Training.	
	28		Divine Service.	
	29/30		Coys. bathing. Training. Brig. [illegible]. Lecture to officers & N.C.O's.	
	31		Training.	
			J. Smith Capt. Asst. Adj. 1st Bn. Border Regt.	[initials]

(A9175) Wt W2358/P366 600,000 12/17 D. D. & L. Sch. 52a. Forms/C2118/15.

D.A.G. 3rd Echelon 17/3

Herewith War Diary (original) for period 26 – 31 August 1918 which has been returned to this unit in error

D1607

[illegible] Capt
Cmdg 1st Bn Border Regt

War Diary

Serial No. 40.

for the month of

August 1918

1st Bn The Border Regt

295

Instructions regarding War Diaries and Intelligence Summaries are contained in F. S. Regs., Part II. and the Staff Manual respectively. Title pages will be prepared in manuscript.

WAR DIARY
or
INTELLIGENCE SUMMARY.
(*Erase heading not required.*)

1st Border Regt.

Army Form C. 2118.

Place	Date	Hour	Summary of Events and Information	Remarks and references to Appendices
ST MAREI CAPPEL	1918 Aug 1/2		Training under OC Coys.	
	2		Week ending 2 Aug 1918. 2/Lieut ER CHICKEN + 40 OR proceeded St SYLVESTRE CAPPEL to be attached 3rd Canadian Tunnelling Coy	
			INCREASE: Drafts — Off / O.R; 2/Lt ER FREW, " T CLAYTON — 3 / 20; 2/Lt NM CLAYTON from Hospital — / 3; Total 3 / 23. DECREASE: — OFF / OR; Sick — / 7; Transferred to MGC 2/Lt J MARSHALL — 1 / ; Total 1 / 7	
LA KREULE AREA	3		Training under OC Coys. Lieut J PATTINSON + 48 OR proceeded to Divisional Reception Camp EBLINGHEM as "personnel over 900". Bn moved by Route march to camp at V15d 9.3 leaving old billets at 9.30 p.m. A very good camp. Bn officers' mess + Sergeants' mess established.	
	4		Lieut A.L PUDDICOMBE MC + 14 O.R. represented the Bn at a Special Divine Service at TERDEGHEM, church Parade of 2nd Army Troops. ~~....~~ Army Comdr present. Bn church parade in camp.	[signature]
	5		Baths. Training.	

(A9175) Wt W2357/P360 600,000 12/17 D. D. & L. Sch. 52a. Forms/C2118/13.

Instructions regarding War Diaries and Intelligence Summaries are contained in F. S. Regs., Part II. and the Staff Manual respectively. Title pages will be prepared in manuscript.

WAR DIARY
or
INTELLIGENCE SUMMARY.
(Erase heading not required.)

Army Form C. 2118.

Place	Date	Hour	Summary of Events and Information	Remarks and references to Appendices
LA KREULE	1918 Aug 6		Training. Baths. The Bn lined the LA BRÉARD - LONG CROIX Road in unceremonial manner while his Majesty THE KING passed in his royal car accompanied by Army Corps & Divisional Commanders, during heavy rain about 4pm Inter-Company sports commenced	
	7		Training & sports	
	8		Bn. on working party burying cable in BORRE area	
	9+10		Training & sports Party under Lieut E W CHICKEN rejoined Bn	
			Week ending 9/8/18	

INCREASE		DECREASE	OFF	OR
From hospital	1 OR	Sick		6
" 87 Bde	1 "	Killed Lieut W J KEELIHER	1	
	2	For commission		1
		Struck off strength (TMB)		2
			1	9

[signature]

(A9175) Wt W2355/P360 600,000 12/17 D. D. & L. Sch. 52a. Forms/C2118/15.

Instructions regarding War Diaries and Intelligence Summaries are contained in F. S. Regs., Part II. and the Staff Manual respectively. Title pages will be prepared in manuscript.

WAR DIARY
or
INTELLIGENCE SUMMARY.
(Erase heading not required.)

Army Form C. 2118.

Place	Date	Hour	Summary of Events and Information	Remarks and references to Appendices
LARRIVILLE	1918 Aug 11		Bn. church parade in camp. Major AW SUTCLIFFE commds	
			29 Divisional party & 8. OR 1 Border R attended Special Church parade at TERDEGHEM at which His Majesty the KING was present.	
	12/14		Training & Inter Coy Sports. Sports won by "D" Coy.	
STRAZEELE Sector	14/15		Bn moved into support system of trenches. Bn Hd Qrs at PRADELLES, D Coy STRAZEELE defences A B & C Coy in Support line & COURT CROIX SWITCH. in relief of 4/WORCESTER R	
	15		Quiet day	
	15/16		Working parties consisting in all of 9 officers and 380 OR employed carrying material to forward dumps, digging & laying out mule track	
	16		Quiet day	
			Week ending 16/8/18	
			INCREASE: Nil — DECREASE: Sick 9 O.R.	[initials]

Instructions regarding War Diaries and Intelligence Summaries are contained in F. S. Regs., Part II. and the Staff Manual respectively. Title pages will be prepared in manuscript.

WAR DIARY
or
INTELLIGENCE SUMMARY.
(Erase heading not required.)

Army Form C. 2118.

Place	Date	Hour	Summary of Events and Information	Remarks and references to Appendices
STRAZEELE SECTOR	1918 Aug 16/17		Bn found working parties consisting of 6 officers & 300 O.R carrying to front line. Considerable hostile M.G. fire.	
	17		Quiet day. 1 Border R. order No 21 issued re attack on 18th.	
	17/18		Bn relieved by one Coy 4/WORCESTERSHIRE R in STRAZEELE defences & by 2 HAMPSHIRE R in remainder of Support positions & moved as follows A Coy W24c.9.2. to W24d 7.7. C Coy X19c 25.75 to X19a 7.2. D Coy X25d 2.6 to X25b 45.50, B Coy X25b 2.7 to X19d 1.3. Bn Hd Qrs were established in the same house as Bde Hd Qrs at IONIC HOUSE W18d.1.5 & the Bn Aid post at X19a 15.70. The front line was occupied by 2/SWB on right & 1/KOSB on left.	
OUTTERSTEENE	18		Till Zero hour morning was quiet. At 11.01 am barrage fell satisfactorily & attack commenced. Zero + 3 Enemy SOS put up. Zero + 28 enemy were shelling the BECQUE behind the advance in region of old front line, and METEREN heavily. Our smoke was working well on OUTTERSTEENE and very little hostile retaliation took place on back areas. German shrapnel bursting high	Appendix One

(A9175) Wt W2358/P360 600,000 12/17 D. D. & L. Sch. 52a. Forms/C2118/15.

Instructions regarding War Diaries and Intelligence Summaries are contained in F. S. Regs., Part II. and the Staff Manual respectively. Title pages will be prepared in manuscript.

WAR DIARY
or
INTELLIGENCE SUMMARY.
(Erase heading not required.)

Army Form C. 2118.

Place	Date	Hour	Summary of Events and Information	Remarks and references to Appendices
OUTTERSTEENE	1918 Aug 18		At 11.40 am telephone communication was intact to all companies The hostile barrage was reported to be thickening especially round SCARPE COTTAGE X26d.	
		11.40 am	At Zero+40 B + D Coys moved forward D Coy in artillery formation to the original front line from GARBEDOEN FARM to about X26c central & B Coy in artillery formation in a South Easterly direction to X26d 4.7, thence along the track running West & across the BECQUE by RE bridge at X27c 5.5, formed up in depth facing South between BELLE CROIX FARM & the BECQUE by Zero+74. The enemy was shelling the ground thus crossed, casualties - 8 OR OC B Coy now came under orders OC 1/KOSB. "C" Coy also left its trench at Zero+40 and advanced in artillery formation to the position X25b 1.7 to X19d 1.3 where it was established by 12.10 pm.	
		11.46 am	Message received from A Coy that it was OK but could see nothing of the fight owing to smoke	[signature]

(A9175) Wt W2355/P362 600,000 12/17 D. D. & L. Sch. 52a. Forms/C2118/15.

Instructions regarding War Diaries and Intelligence Summaries are contained in F. S. Regs., Part II. and the Staff Manual respectively. Title pages will be prepared in manuscript.

WAR DIARY
or
INTELLIGENCE SUMMARY.
(Erase heading not required.)

Army Form C. 2118.

Place	Date	Hour	Summary of Events and Information	Remarks and references to Appendices
OUTTER-STEENE	1918 Aug 18		At 12.55 pm the BLUE LINE was reported captured and a report was received by Brigade from an Artillery Observer that our patrols were moving towards OUTTERSTEENE, but appeared to be held up about ½ mile N.W. of the village, in F.2.d.	
			On arrival in assembly position between the BECQUE and BELLE CROIX FARM at 12.14 pm Capt J.H. PROCTOR, OC B Coy went forward to get in touch with 1/KOSB & to reconnoitre the ground, accompanied by Lieut A L PUDDICOMBE M.C. Touch was obtained with A Coy 1/KOSB who were digging in on BLUE LINE about F3a. OC A Coy 1/KOSB stated that the enemy had apparently retired from OUTTERSTEENE & that he was going to push forward patrols. Capt PROCTOR decided to advance & establish his positions South of the village.	
			The Company was ordered to advance in the following order. No 8 Pl to the right of the village under Lieut A L PUDDICOMBE M.C. No 5 Pl (2/Lieut C H DAVIES) to the left of the village, Nos 6 & 7 Pls (2/Lieut W W CRAIK) & 7 Pl followed by Coy Hd Qrs to push through & mop	

(A9475) Wt W2358/P360 600,000 12/17 D. D. & L. Sch/52a. Forms/C2118/15.

Instructions regarding War Diaries and Intelligence Summaries are contained in F. S. Regs., Part II. and the Staff Manual respectively. Title pages will be prepared in manuscript.

WAR DIARY
or
INTELLIGENCE SUMMARY.
(Erase heading not required.)

Army Form C. 2118.

Place	Date	Hour	Summary of Events and Information	Remarks and references to Appendices
OUTTER-STEENE	1918 Aug 18		up the village. During the advance only slight opposition was encountered. No 5 Pl. on the left passed thro' one Pl 1/KOSB digging in in the enclosure at F3c central, who informed them that enemy snipers still remained in the village.	
			About 1.15 pm positions were taken up as follows – No 5 Pl F19a central, No 6 Pl astride the road F9a 2 3, No 8 Pl about F8b83 + No 7 Pl in support in the village. Coy Hd Qrs were with No 7 Pl till about 1.30 pm when they moved to F8b72.	
			At 1.15 pm ground flares were lighted in response to calls from contact aeroplanes. At 1.30 pm a message was sent to OC 1/KOSB notifying him of these positions. During the advance dugouts were searched + bombed + prisoners taken as follows, No 7 Pl 5, No 6 Pl 10, Coy Hd Qrs 4. German telephone wires were cut. On arrival at above positions, South of OUTTERSTEENE patrols were at once sent out by Nos 5, 6, + 8 Pls which crossed the Railway line. The house South of SCANDAL CROSSING was searched + a deserted M.G. emplacement discovered in it.	

Instructions regarding War Diaries and Intelligence Summaries are contained in F. S. Regs., Part II. and the Staff Manual respectively. Title pages will be prepared in manuscript.

WAR DIARY
or
INTELLIGENCE SUMMARY.
(Erase heading not required.)

Army Form C. 2118.

Place	Date	Hour	Summary of Events and Information	Remarks and references to Appendices
OUTTERSTEENE.	1918 Aug,		The enemy were seen retiring South in small numbers, and fire was opened on them sparingly. Patrols from No 5 + No 6 Pls reported 2 enemy Field guns about F9a 7.2.	
			After OC "B" Coy had established his Hd Qrs in OUTTERSTEENE at F8b7.2. a patrol of 1KOSB under Lieut KEIR reported to Capt PROCTOR + was absorbed by him into the line. About this time Lieut BUNCE, No 4 Sectn A Coy 29th MG Bn who was trying to get in touch with 2/SWB reported to Capt PROCTOR + took up a position in his line.	
			At 1.15 pm "A" Coy was ordered to move forward + occupy a position in our old front line from the left of D Coy to SCARP COTTAGE, this Coy being subsequently ordered to extend its left along the RED LINE to the BECQUE + get in touch with the 9th Division.	
			At 1.36 pm "C" Coy was ordered to move forward + take up a position in our old front line South of D Coy from about F1d 23 to GARBEDOEN FARM.	
			About 7.30 pm 2 hostile MGs came into action on the Railway	[initials]

(A9175) Wt W2358/P360 600,000 12/17 D. D. & L. Sch. 52a. Forms/C2118/15.

Instructions regarding War Diaries and Intelligence Summaries are contained in F. S. Regs., Part II. and the Staff Manual respectively. Title pages will be prepared in manuscript.

WAR DIARY
or
INTELLIGENCE SUMMARY.
(Erase heading not required.)

Army Form C. 2118.

Place	Date	Hour	Summary of Events and Information	Remarks and references to Appendices
OUTTERSTEENE	1918 Aug 18		line East of SCANDAL CROSSING, and some of the enemy crossed the line under cover of their fire. Fire was opened on these parties & they were prevented from advancing. About dusk 8.45 pm as there was considerable enemy movement South of the Railway, it appeared a hostile counter-attack was imminent, & an SOS signal was put up & MG, LG, & rifle fire opened on the enemy. The artillery barrage fell at once on his position & the MGs East of SCANDAL CROSSING gave no further trouble.	
		8.45pm	At this time the Bn was disposed as follows. B Coy in the front line South of OUTTERSTEENE, C D & A Coys in our old front line.	
			At about 10.45pm a patrol was sent out under Lieut KEIR 1/KOSB to the Railway line which reported that the enemy had again retired South of the line.	
			At 11pm a patrol under Lieut HOLLES MC was sent forward by C Coy to locate position of B Coy, & at about 2.30 am C Coy carried forward rations for B Coy. About midnight a further patrol	[initials]

(A9175) Wt W2359/P360 600,000 12/17 D. D. & L. Sch. 52a. Forms/C2118/15.

Instructions regarding War Diaries and Intelligence Summaries are contained in F. S. Regs., Part II. and the Staff Manual respectively. Title pages will be prepared in manuscript.

WAR DIARY
or
INTELLIGENCE SUMMARY.
(Erase heading not required.)

Army Form C. 2118.

Place	Date	Hour	Summary of Events and Information	Remarks and references to Appendices
OUTTER-STEENE	1918 Aug 18/19		from D Coy under 2/Lieut E W CHICKEN DCM brought forward ammunition for B Coy.	
	[illegible]		At 3.30 am on 19th a message was received from OC 1/KOSB stating that D Coy 2/SWB was to relieve B Coy 1/Borders. Relief was carried out under heavy artillery fire + B Coy was withdrawn to trench in X 19 c. During the relief Lieut A.L. PUDDICOMBE M.C. + 3 ORs were wounded.	
	19.		At 5 pm. the 86th Bde in conjunction with 31st Div carried out an attack on the right of the 87th Bde + captured their objectives.	
	19/20		Orders were received from Bde for the Bn to relieve 1/KOSB on the night 19/20. This relief was carried out between 9 pm + 12 midnight under considerable artillery fire. 16 casualties were suffered by D Coy + 2/Lieut J McINTYRE was severely wounded + afterwards died of wounds. Bn Hd Qrs moved forward to X 25 d 6 3. where Bn Aid Post was also formed. On completion of relief the Bn. was disposed as follows — "A" Coy Right firing line, D Coy left firing line,	[initials]

(A9175) Wt W2352/P360 600,000 12/17 D. D. & L. Sch. 52a. Forms/C2118/15.

Instructions regarding War Diaries and Intelligence Summaries are contained in F. S. Regs., Part II. and the Staff Manual respectively. Title pages will be prepared in manuscript.

WAR DIARY
or
INTELLIGENCE SUMMARY.
(Erase heading not required.)

Army Form C. 2118.

Place	Date 1918	Hour	Summary of Events and Information	Remarks and references to Appendices
OUTTER-STEENE	Aug 19/20		"C" Coy right support B Coy left support, the Bn being in position on the OUTTERSTEENE ridge on immediate left of the village. B Coy during the period of the relief made 2 trips carrying wiring material from X 19c 20.25. Rations were successfully brought up + distributed to the front line Coys by "C" Coy + work was commenced on consolidation.	
			At 2 30 am the 20th the enemy opened a heavy artillery barrage with guns of large calibre on the position held by the Bn which continued till 5 am. Touch was maintained with the ROYAL SCOTS of the 9th Div on the left + the 2/SWB on the Right. In spite of this extremely heavy bombardment there were practically no casualties.	
	20		During the day the enemy with lulls of only about ¼ of an hour continued to barrage the ridge, but again there were very few casualties. Hostile aeroplanes flew very low over the sector at frequent intervals. Towards evening patrols were sent out	[initials]

(A9175) Wt W2357/P363 600,000 12/17 D. D. & L. Sch. 52a. Forms/C2118/15.

Instructions regarding War Diaries and Intelligence Summaries are contained in F. S. Regs., Part II. and the Staff Manual respectively. Title pages will be prepared in manuscript.

WAR DIARY
or
INTELLIGENCE SUMMARY.
(Erase heading not required.)

Army Form C. 2118.

Place	Date	Hour	Summary of Events and Information	Remarks and references to Appendices
OUTTERSTEENE	1918 Aug 20		from A & D Coys under 2/Lieuts J. ROBERTSON & E W CHICKEN DCM to KISMET HOUSE & DERMOT HOUSE respectively to find out whether they were occupied, & the former was found to be held by MGs and snipers. Total casualties in battle, Killed 1 off 15 OR. Wounded 1 off 58 OR Sick 6 OR.	
"Z" line	20/21		The Bn was relieved by 2/Leinster R, relief being completed without casualties by 3.10 am. The Bn was withdrawn to "Z" line, Coys being disposed in the order A C B D from Right to Left. Bn came under orders GOC 88th Bde, Bn HdQrs were established at BRICK WORKS, STRAZEELE. Aid post at X19a 15.50	
	21		Reorganisation & refitting commenced. Bn rested	
	22		A C & D Coys worked on "Z" line under RE supervision. ESTAMINET CORNER & ERIN COTTAGE shelled ~~with~~ by heavy howitzers all day. No casualties	
	22/23		The left of the Bn in "Z" line was extended to X13d 1.9 & companies took over more of the trench to conform during the night	
	23.		A C & B Coys worked on "Z" line under RE supervision	

(A9175) Wt W2358/P360 600,000 12/17 D. D. & L. Sch. 52a. Forms/C2118/15.

Instructions regarding War Diaries and Intelligence Summaries are contained in F. S. Regs., Part II. and the Staff Manual respectively. Title pages will be prepared in manuscript.

WAR DIARY
or
INTELLIGENCE SUMMARY.
(Erase heading not required.)

Army Form C. 2118.

Place	Date	Hour	Summary of Events and Information	Remarks and references to Appendices
"Z" line STRAZEELE	1918 Aug 23/24		Bn was relieved by 2/SWB & moved by march route to camp at V17c72 at L'HOFFAND. In good bivouac camp.	
L'HOFFAND	24/26		Bn rested. Baths & pay. Bn officers & Sgts messes.	
			Week ending 24/8/18	

INCREASE	OFF.	OR.	DECREASE	OFF.	OR.
From base	4	3	Killed	1	15
Capt E J G SMITH			2/Lt J McINTYRE		
Lieut GEH SLATER			Wounded	1	58
2/Lt W PENNINGTON			Lieut PUDDICOMBE		
P SCOTT			Sick	~~1~~	12
From hospital		4	Capt KENNEDY		
			Struck off Strength	1	2
	4	7		3	87

(A9175) Wt W2355/P565 600,000 12/17 D. D. & L. Sch. 52a. Forms/C2118/15.

Serial to continue

Instructions regarding War Diaries and Intelligence Summaries are contained in F. S. Regs., Part II. and the Staff Manual respectively. Title pages will be prepared in manuscript.

WAR DIARY
or
INTELLIGENCE SUMMARY.
(Erase heading not required.)

Army Form C. 2118.

1 Border Regt 29

Aug 26 – 31st 1918

Vol 34

Place	Date	Hour	Summary of Events and Information	Remarks and references to Appendices
GERBEDOEN FM.	26/27		Bn moved to front line trenches in front of OUTTERSTEENE ridge in relief of 1st WORC. RGT. Coys disposed as follows:- "A" Coy. - Firing & Support line; "C" Coy. - Close Support OUTTERSTEENE LINE; "B" Coy. - Southern Sector of COURT CROIX SWITCH. "D" Coy. remained in camp near LA KREULE. Quiet relief. Bn HQ. E 6 a 7.8. GERBEDOEN FD.	
	27		Heavy shelling of the BECQUE with gas and 5·9's during the afternoon.	
"Y" LINE. HOOGENACKER MILL SECTOR	27/28		Division side-stepped to the left. "B" & "D" Coys relieved 1st YORK & LANC RGT (?) in the HOOGENACKER MILL SECTOR with "D" Coy. on left & "B" Coy. on right in the firing line. "A" & "C" Coys were relieved by the 2nd ROYAL FUS. & "C" Coy moving into empty trenches at RAE FM. in support, & "A" Coy. [illegible] in the "Y" line near ESTAMINET CORNER. Bn H.Q. relieved by 2nd S.W.B. H.Q. & moved to dugouts in communication trench at X 25 d. 3.8. Very quiet relief.	
	28.		Quiet day. "A" Coy. working under R.E. in "Y" line. Very wet weather. "Lt. PENNINGTON" took out small patrol at 11.0 pm to AUK HOUSE and was fired on by M.G. from enclosure about F 4 a 5.5, F 4 a 3.4, and F 4 a 7.7. Patrol having gained contact with enemy, returned to our lines at 12.30 am.	
	29.		Very quiet day. Working parties as yesterday.	

(A9175) Wt W2353/P360 600,000 12/17 D. D. & L. Sch. 52a. Forms/C2118/15.

Instructions regarding War Diaries and Intelligence Summaries are contained in F. S. Regs., Part II. and the Staff Manual respectively. Title pages will be prepared in manuscript.

WAR DIARY
or
INTELLIGENCE SUMMARY.
(Erase heading not required.)

Army Form C. 2118.

Place	Date	Hour	Summary of Events and Information	Remarks and references to Appendices
HOOGENACKER MILL SECTOR	29/30		Numerous dumps being blown up behind enemy line & huge fires. Lt J PATTINSON,	
			2/Lts. [illegible] CHICKEN & W.E. KING took out their platoons and established posts at F.a.6.1,	
			[illegible] 5.15 and F.4.a 6.7. No enemy encountered. 2/Lt W.E. KING pushed out to	
			cross roads at F.4.a.9.1 & found no signs of occupation. At 2 a.m. [illegible]	
			[illegible] reported that enemy was withdrawing from our front and that patrols	
			were to push forward at 5 a.m. with Coys. following in support, with	
			BAILLEUL STATION, CEMETERY (STEENWERCK) & [illegible] as objective for Brigade.	
			[illegible] of the [illegible] which had [illegible] forward of [illegible] during the	
			night and the places named above [illegible] accordingly pushed forward at 5 a.m.	
			[illegible] of [illegible] following in support. C Coy. moved up to	
			[illegible] in 1st line. Bn H.Q. moved to [illegible] passed through	
			AVE FARM, [illegible] FM. across the railway at [illegible] CROSSING to the CEMETERY	
			at STEENWERCK. There was no opposition, but owing to the bad nature of the	
			ground it became very difficult to maintain touch with flanks.	
			Communications to Bn H.Q. from front line were very poor, & the situation	
			in front was obscure during the whole of the morning. At 10 a.m. all	

(A9175) Wt W2358/P360 600,000 12/17 D. D. & L. Sch. 52a. Forms/C2118/15.

Instructions regarding War Diaries and Intelligence Summaries are contained in F. S. Regs., Part II. and the Staff Manual respectively. Title pages will be prepared in manuscript.

Army Form C. 2118.

4

WAR DIARY
or
INTELLIGENCE SUMMARY.
(Erase heading not required.)

Place	Date	Hour	Summary of Events and Information	Remarks and references to Appendices
HOOGENACKER MILL	30		objectives of the Brigade had been reached, except NOOTE BOOM on the right where 2nd S.W.B. found considerable opposition from M.G. rear-guard. At 1.30 p.m. O.C. "B" (2/LT C.H. DAVIES) & O.C. "D" (LT SLATER) reported that they were on the E. side of the CEMETRY & digging in. An enemy aeroplane, spotting for artillery, dropped lights on the position. This was followed by fairly heavy shelling with shrapnel, resulting in three casualties only – slightly wounded. One E.A. was brought down by one of our battle machines at 2 p.m. near VERITY CROSSING. As the Coy. were not in touch with either Bn on their flanks, MAJOR A.W. SUTCLIFFE, M.C. (commanding the Bn. for the time) went forward & organised the positions & digging in was continued on the following line:– A & C central, – due South to E. side of CEMETRY – thence to A.7.b.2.0. Touch was gained with flanks & line was as laid down in orders. [illegible] was occupied by 1 K.O.S.B. & troops of 38th DIV. – the latter also captured MONT [illegible]. At 6 p.m. Brigadier held C.O's conference at BELLE CROIX & issued orders for the Bns to withdraw to "Y" line at dusk & 2nd S.W.B. to take over our front. 1 K.O.S.B. & 2 S.W.B. to form an outpost line along the objectives gained. "C" Coy. was therefore withdrawn from	[initials]

(A9175) W1 W2358/P360 600,000 12/17 D. D. & L. Sch. 52a. Forms/C2118/15.

6

Army Form C. 2118.

Instructions regarding War Diaries and Intelligence Summaries are contained in F. S. Regs., Part II. and the Staff Manual respectively. Title pages will be prepared in manuscript.

WAR DIARY
or
INTELLIGENCE SUMMARY.
(Erase heading not required.)

Place	Date	Hour	Summary of Events and Information	Remarks and references to Appendices
[illegible]	30/1 [?]		"Y" Coy. back to EWE FARM to give depth of room in trenches for "D" & "B" Coy. so that they could get a good night's rest. Bn. HQ moved back to X.25.d.3.8. [illegible] Relief [illegible] carried out and [illegible] the outpost line [illegible]. In the meantime the enemy was destroying farms & dumps behind the line & apart from one battery firing shrapnel at intervals into TERRAIN [illegible] M.G. fire from the vicinity of NORTHBOOM [?] on the right the night was extremely quiet. Our 18 pdr batteries were moving forward all night. In the [illegible] forward to the outpost line, roads & tracks were absolutely impassable for transport due to our heavy shelling during the [illegible] of the war.	
	31		Bn detailed as Outpost Bn for the Brigade front for the night. [illegible] during the day. Bn was [illegible] at 8 am [illegible]. 1 Coy M.G. Bn attached to Bn & [illegible] moved forward in artillery formation at 6.45 am [illegible] & assuming positions on a general line just North of the road from Rly Crossing at A.3.b.99.99 running S.W. to CEMETERY CORNER at A.7.d.2.8. Bn HQ at	[initials, illegible]

Instructions regarding War Diaries and Intelligence Summaries are contained in F. S. Regs., Part II. and the Staff Manual respectively. Title pages will be prepared in manuscript.

WAR DIARY
or
INTELLIGENCE SUMMARY.
(Erase heading not required.)

Army Form C. 2118.

Place	Date	Hour	Summary of Events and Information	Remarks and references to Appendices
BOOK FM.	31/1		BOOK FM. A3 a.2.0. [illegible] in position at 10 p.m. Orders received at 9.30 p.m. to take up outpost positions on a line from [illegible] (running S.E. in front of PONT DE NIEPPE astride BAILLEUL–ARMENTIERES Rly. West of LA CRECHE thence to PONT DE PIERRE, CORT DE SAULE, LA BECQUE & LAROSE FM. in A.14 d.1.2 – a frontage of [illegible] yards. Forward troops [illegible] through outpost position as follows (from left to right) 17th [illegible] through 'B' Coy; 2nd [illegible] through 'C' Coy; 2nd Royal Fus. through 'A' Coy. 'D' Coy remained in support in vicinity of [illegible] at BOOK FM. Very wet & miserable night. Enemy shelled BOOK area with shrapnel at intervals. Relief	
	[illegible]		complete at 5 am without interference from enemy.	JH
			Casualties during Oct – Officers Nil. Other Ranks 1 Killed 10 wounded. Total 11	

Variation

Increase	O.	O.R.	Decrease	O.	O.R.
Drafts from base (CAPT J. F. DUGGAN, M.C., D.C.M.)	1	1	Killed	–	1
From hospital		6	Wounded	–	10
	1	7	To Hospital	–	23
			To Ch. Column	–	1
					35

J Smith Lt. Adjutant.
1st Bn. The Border Regt.

(A9175) Wt W2358/P360 600,000 12/17 D. D. & L. Sch. 52a. Forms/C2118/15.

Appendix I

1st Battalion The Border Regiment

Account of action of the Battalion in operations leading up to and including the capture of STEENWERCKE.

Ref Map 1/20000 MERRIS Ed 2a Local

On the night of Aug 26/27 the Battalion moved to the front line trenches forward of OUTTERSTEENE RIDGE in relief of the 4th Bn The WORCESTER REGT. The Coys took up positions as follows

A Coy. Firing Outpost line
C Coy. Close Support OUTTERSTEENE LINE
B Coy Southern Sector COURTE CROIX SWITCH
D Coy remained in Camp at LA KREULE.

On the following night 27th/28th the Division side stepped to the left.

B & D Coys relieved the 13th YORKS & LANCS (31st Division) in HOOGENACKER MILL Sector with D Coy on the left
B " " Right
in the firing line.
with C Coy in Support at EWE FARM.
A Coy in Reserve in 'Z' line near ESTAMINET CORNER.

Bn Hd Qrs in dugouts in trench at X25.d.3.8

On the night of 29th/30th B & D Coys advanced their positions

B Coy to F3.b.6.6 – F4.a.5.1
D " to X28.c.8.1 – F4.a.9.1

This advance was carried out without opposition and with no casualties.

At 5 a.m. on the 30th a second forward movement was commenced by B & D Coys with C & A Coys following in Support and reserve respectively. while Bn Hd Qrs moved forward to BELLE CROIX FARM.

The objectives were BAILLEUL STATION, STEENJE CEMETRY and NOOTE BOOM.

There was no opposition but owing to the extremely bad nature of the ground it became very difficult to maintain touch on the flanks

At 10 am all objectives except NOOTE BOOM which was stubbornly defended had been gained; by 1.30 pm this resistance was overcome and B & D Coys reported that they were on the East side of STEENJE CEMETRY and were digging in. They were observed by enemy aeroplanes and shortly after were heavily shelled by shrapnel; there were however only 3 casualties, wounded. The following line was then established from A1 c central due South to the East side of the cemetry and thence to A7. b. 2. 0.

At dusk the Battalion was relieved by the 2nd S. W. BORDERERS and C Coy was withdrawn to EWE FARM, B & D Coys withdrew into the Y Line while Bn Hd Qrs moved back to X 25. d. 3. 8.

On August 31st the Battalion was detailed for Outpost Duty for the Brigade and took up the following positions occupying positions to cover the whole X Corps front (3, 530x)

Right A Coy A4 c. – A15. a. 4. 6.
Support Platoon A8. d. 6. 3.
Coy Hd Qrs WORRY HOUSE.

Centre C Coy PITCH FARM – ORGY HOUSE
Support Platoon Cross Rds. A4 c 7. 5.
Coy Hd Qrs NAPPER HOUSE

Left B Coy S29. c. 30 — S29 a 50. 99.

Support D Coy A2. d. 7. 8. – A3. a. 2. 4.
Coy Hd Qrs DOOKE HOUSE A3. a. 2. 3

Bn Hd Qrs DOOK HOUSE A3 a. 2. 3

On the night of Aug. 31st/ Sept 1st orders were received from the Brigade for the Coys to make an advance at 9 am September 1st. and to establish themselves on a line LA KIRLEM STEENWERKE MIRE FARM THE STATION DE SEULE.

To each Company the following arms were attached

1 Gun RFA
1 Trench Mortar
2 M. Guns.
2 Platoons Cyclists.

On the morning of September 1st the advance was commenced without any barrage as follows

Right A Coy Capt F. J. GEMMELL. SMITH.

On the morning of Sept 1st the Coy moved forward at 11.15 am (there was some delay as the cyclists had not arrived) having for its objectives STEENWERCKE and LA KIRLEM. After advancing 1000 yards the left platoon of this Company was held up at 1.15 pm by enemy M.G. fire at A16. a. 6. 0 while the centre platoon was held up by enemy M.G. fire at A21. b. 2. 7. This resistance was overcome by a flanking movement and the cyclists passed through STEENWERCKE at 2-15 pm. the Coy pushed forward and established itself on a line A29. a 2. 2 – A17. d. 9. 3.

Centre C Coy Capt B. R. DURLACHER. M.C.

At 10 am C Coy commenced its advance having as its objective MIRE FARM. The advance had not proceeded far before resistance was met with on the right from a strong point A11 a. 2. 7 and from MUTTON FARM. The Field Gun and Trench Mortar were used to overcome this but without success. MUTTON FARM was eventually cleared by No 12 Platoon with a section of Rifle Grenadiers and Lewis Guns working up the ditches on either side of the road. Meanwhile No 9 Platoon worked along the BAILLEUL RAILWAY and thus both flanks of the strong point at A11. a. 2. 7 were turned and the occupants surrendered. The advance was now able to be carried on fairly quickly and by 4.30 pm the Coy had [illegible] its objectives. Consolidation was [illegible] out at once and the Coy established itself on a line running from

A12.a.3.3 to A18 a. 3.4

Left B Coy 2/Lieut C. H. DAVIES

On the night of Aug 3rd the OC Coy received orders to move the Coy from the Right of the outpost line and to take up a position on the Left as follows.

from S29.C.2.3 – S29.a.8.7.

having the Support Platoon at S28.b.1.8

Coy Hd Qrs at S28 b.2.8.

The Coy had for its objectives

DE SEULE B1 central.

JAIL HOUSE B1.C.3.5.

THE STATION A12.a.6.3.

After a few rounds of H.E. had been fired at PEGASUS FARM S29.d.5.8. and also on A5.a.5.2 (reported MG positions, the cyclists advanced at 10.30 am and got in touch with the enemy.

At 11 am three platoons moved forward to S30.C.1.8.

At 12.30 pm the platoons in the centre and Right were held up by M.Gs. in LA CRECHE. The resistance was very obstinate and caused considerable casualties among the cyclists.

The Coy was reinforced by two platoons of D Coy. the Support Coy and eventually the village was captured by the Coy turning its flanks and a frontal attack by the cyclists.

The Coy pushed forward and established itself on a line running from

A6 a.5.9 – A6.c.5.7.

Coy Hd Qrs at A5 a.4.1

Support Platoon A5.a.9.1

Support Coy D Coy Lt G.E.H. SLATER.

The Support Coy was called upon to assist B Coy in the attack on LA CRÈCHE and sent up two platoons. The enemy fell back from the Village and the two platoons established

themselves with B Coy on the line above mentioned.
The Battalion had thus carried out an advance of an average depth of 5000x on a frontage of 3500x
Their original position had been on a line running from

A14.c – S29.a.8.7.

The final position was on a line running from A29.a 2.3. – A6.a 5.7.
During these operations there were 10 casualties and 11 prisoners were captured.
On the evening of Sept. 1st the Battalion was relieved by the 2nd S.W. BORDERERS and withdrew to the Reserve Line

[illegible] LT., COLONEL,
COMMANDING 1st BN. THE BORDER REGT.

1 Border Regt

1ST BATTALION THE BORDER REGIMENT.

Account of action of the Battalion in operations at OUTTERSTEENE VILLAGE, and SPUR 18/19th August 1918.

On 16th August 1918 orders were received from 87th Brigade that an attack was to be made on the 18th at 11 a.m., to capture enemy front line system, approximately on an East and West line between GARBEDOEN FARM and the METEREN BECQUE with the ultimate object of exploiting success and making good the OUTTERSTEENE RIDGE.

On the night of the 17/18th August the Battalion was re--lieved from its positions in STRAZEELE defences, COURT FARM SWITCH, and support line by the 88th Brigade, and the following approximate positions were taken up.

B & D Coys X.24.b. and d in close support.

C & A Coys in the support line X.19.c. and W.24.d.

Battalion Headquarters were established at IONIC HOUSE.

Battalion Aid Post at X.19.a.15.50.

At 11 a.m on the 18th the attack commenced.

At 11-1 a.m the barrage fell on the enemy line.

At 11-40 a.m B. D & C.Coys moved forward in artillery formation. B Coy passed through our original front line just to the North of SCARPE COTTAGE, thence East, crossing the BECQUE by an R.E. bridge at X.27.c.5.5. and formed up in depth facing South between the BECQUE and BELLE CROIX FARM.

On arrival in this position at 12-14 p.m they came under the orders of 1/K.O.S.B. D Coy took up a position in our old front line from about GARBEDOEN FARM to X.26.c.5.2. just South West of SCARPE COTTAGE, arriving there at 12 noon. C Coy occupied trench vacated by B Coy, arriving there at 12-10 p.m.

Casualties during this advance, B Coy 8, C & D Coys nil.

At 12-55 p.m the BLUE LINE was reported captured and a report was received by Brigade from an Artillery Observer that our patrols were moving towards OUTTERSTEENE, but appeared to be held up about ½ a mile N.W. of the village in F.2.d.

On arrival in assembly position between the BECQUE and BELLE CROIX FARM at 12-14 p.m Capt. J.H.PROCTOR, O.C. "B" Coy, went forward to get in touch with 1/K.O.S.B. and to reconnoitre the ground, accompanied by Lieut A.L.PUDDICOMBE, M.C.

Touch was obtained with A Coy, 1/K.O.S.B. who were digging in on BLUE LINE about F.3.a. O.C. "A" Coy, 1/K.O.S.B. stated that the enemy had apparently retired from OUTTERSTEENE and that he was going to push forward patrols to reconnoitre.

Capt. J.H.PROCTOR (Commanding B Coy, 1/Borders) decided to advance and established his positions South of the village.

The Company was ordered to advance in the following order:- No.8 Platoon to the right of the village, No.5 Platoon to the left of the village, Nos 6 & 7 Platoons followed by Coy Hd.Qrs to push through and mop up the village. During this advance, only slight opposition was encountered. No.5 Platoon on the left passed through one Platoon of the 1/K.O.S.B. digging in in the enclosure at F.3.c. central, who informed them that enemy snipers still re--mained in the village.

About 1-15 p.m positions were taken up as follows:- No.5 Platoon F.19.a. central, No.6 Platoon astride the Road F.9.a.2.3 No.8 Platoon about F.8.b.8.3. and No.7 Platoon in support in the village. Coy Hd.Qrs were with No.7 Platoon till about 1-30 p.m when they moved to F.8.b.7.2.

At 1-15 p.m ground flares were lighted and blue smoke grenades sent up. At 1-30 p.m a message was sent to O.C. 1/K.O.S.B. notifying him of these positions. During this advance dugouts were searched and bombed and prisoners taken as follows, No.7 Platoon 5, No.6 Platoon 10, Coy Hd.Qrs 4.

At 1-10 p.m the Division reported that our patrols were seen South of OUTTERSTEENE and that the village was practically surrounded.

On arrival at positions above indicated, South of OUTTER-

-STEENE, patrols were at once sent out by Nos 5, 6 and 8 Platoons.

All patrols crossed the Railway line. The house South of SCANDAL CROSSING was searched and a deserted M.G.emplacement dis--covered in it.

The enemy was seen retiring South in small numbers, and fire was opened on them sparingly as the expenditure of ammunition was an important consideration.

Patrols from No.5 and No.6 Platoons reported 2 enemy Field guns about F.9.a.7.2.

After O.C."B" Coy had established his Hd.Qrs in OUTTERS--STEENE at F.8.b.7.2., a patrol of 1/K.O.S.B. under Lieut KEIR reported to Capt. J.H.PROCTOR, and was absorbed by him into the line. This Platoon of 1/K.O.S.B. had been passed by No.8 Platoon 1/Borders N.W. of OUTTERSTEENE during the advance on the village.

About this time Lieut BUNCE, No.4 Section, A Coy, 29th M.G.Bn, who was trying to get in touch with 2/S.W.B., reported to Capt. J.H.PROCTOR, and took up a position in his line.

At 1-15 p.m "A" Coy was ordered to move forward and occupy a position in our old front line from the left of D Coy to SCARPE COTTAGE, this Coy being subsequently ordered to extend its left along the RED LINE to the BECQUE and get in touch with the 9th Division.

At 1-35 p.m C Coy was ordered to move forward and take up a position in our old front line South of D Coy from about F.1.d.2.3. to GARBEDOIN FARM.

About 7-30 p.m 2 hostile M.Gs came into action on the Railway line East of SCANDAL CROSSING, and some of the enemy crossed the line under cover of their fire. Fire was opened on these parties and they were prevented from advancing.

About dusk, 8-45 p.m as there was considerable enemy move--ment South of the Railway, it appeared a hostile counter-attack was imminent, and an S.O.S. signal was put up and M.G. L.G. and rifle fire opened on the enemy. The artillery barrage fell at once and the M.Gs East of SCANDAL CROSSING gave no further trouble.

At this time the Battalion was disposed as follows:-
B Coy in the front line South of OUTTERSTEENE, C D & A Coys in our old front line.

At about ½ to 11 p.m a patrol was sent out under Lieut KEIR 1/K.O.S.B. to the Railway line which reported that the enemy had again retired South of the line.

At 11 p.m an Officers' patrol was sent forward by C Coy to locate position of B Coy, and at about 2-30 C.Coy carried forward rations for B Coy.

About midnight a further officers' patrol from D Coy, brought forward ammunition for B Coy.

At 3-30 a.m on the 19th, a message was received from O.C. 1/K.O.S.B. stating that D Coy, 2/S.W.B. was to relieve B Coy, 1/Borders. Relief was carried out under heavy artillery fire and B.Coy was withdrawn to trench in X.19.c.

During this relief Lieut A.L.PUDDICOMBE, M.C. and 3 O.Rs were wounded.

<u>Night 19/8/18.</u>

Orders were received from Brigade for 1/Borders to relieve 1/K.O.S.B. on the night 19/20. This relief was carried out between 9 p.m and 12 midnight under considerable artillery fire, 16 casualties being suffered by D Coy.

Battalion Hd.Qrs moved forward to X.25.d.6.3. where Battn Aid Post was also formed. On completion of relief the Battalion was disposed as follows:-

A Coy Right firing line.
D " Left " "
C " Right Support.
B " Left "

<u>20/8/18.</u>

Orders were received from Brigade that 1/Borders were to be relieved on night 20/21st by 2/Leinster Regt. This relief was com--pleted by 3-10a.m. 21/8/18.

The Battalion was withdrawn to "Z" Line, Coys being disposed in the following order, from Right to Left, A C B D.

Battalion Hd.Qrs BRICK WORKS STRAZEELE. Aid Post X.19.a.15.50

On arrival in the new position, the Battalion came under orders of the G.O.C. 88th Brigade as garrison to "Z" Line.

At about 2 p.m on the 18th the enemy commenced his artillery fire on the OUTTERSTIENE RIDGE and the METEREN BECQUE. This fire rapidly increased in intensity and assumed the character of barrage fire carried out entirely by guns of heavy calibre.

This concentration of heavy artillery fire made the initial consolidation of B Coy, an extremely difficult matter. Movement on the ridge, supply of ammunition and rations, evacuation of the wounded and the maintenance of touch being all extremely difficult.

Continuous heavy barrage fire was put down on the ridge from about 2-30 a.m on the 20th till dawn on the 21st.

It was continued in burst every ½ of an hour until about 3 p.m 21st, when a period of quiet followed until 7 p.m when a continuous heavy barrage was kept on the ridge for about 1 hour.

In this latter case the enemy fire appeared to be cross fire from an Easterly and South Easterly direction.

The casualties incurred by the Battalion were 2 Officers and 74 O.Rs (including 12 O.Rs gassed). Considering the intensity of the hostile artillery fire, they appear to be extremely light.

Lieut-Colonel,
Commanding 1st Battn The Border Regiment.

SECRET

H.Q.
87th Inf. Bde

Herewith War Diary for month of September 1918, Volume No 41 Pages 1 – 10.

11/x/18

J.Harris, Lt for Major
Commdg. 1st Border Regt.

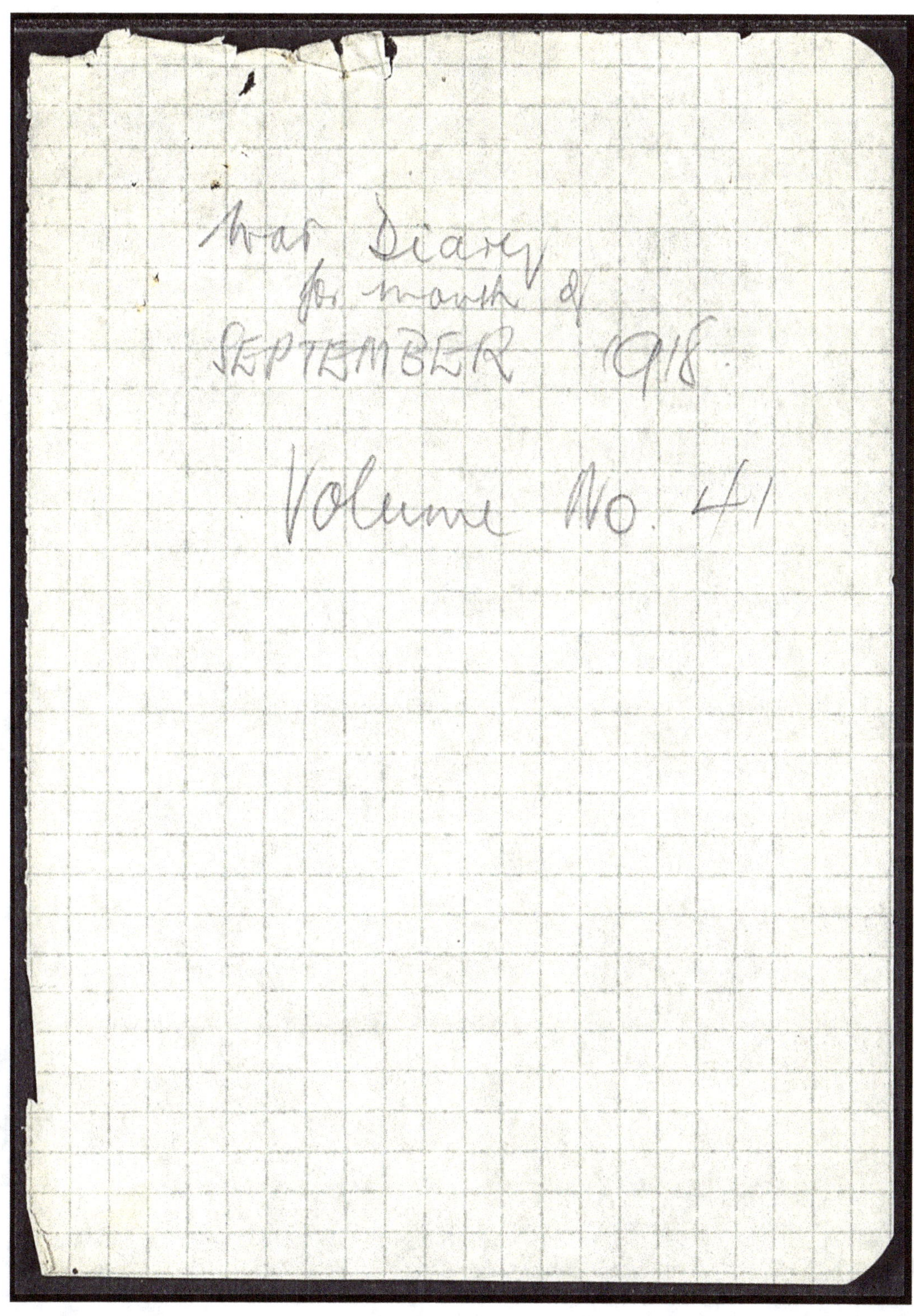
War Diary
for month of
SEPTEMBER 1918
Volume No. 41

Volume No. 41

1 Border Regt

87/29 1

Army Form C. 2118.

Instructions regarding War Diaries and Intelligence Summaries are contained in F. S. Regs., Part II. and the Staff Manual respectively. Title pages will be prepared in manuscript.

WAR DIARY
or
INTELLIGENCE SUMMARY.
(Erase heading not required.)

Sept 30

Place	Date	Hour	Summary of Events and Information	Remarks and references to Appendices
	1918 Sept			
DOOK HOUSE	1	5am	Orders rec'd from Bde to advance at 10 a.m. & establish a line LA KIRLEM,	
Near BAILLEUL			STEENWERCK, MIRE FM, DE SEULE. 1 Batty R.F.A., 1 Batty T.M., 2 M.G. sections & 1 Coy.	Appendix I
		10am	Cyclists attached to Bn. Advance commenced at 10 a.m. without artillery	
			preparation or barrage — from North to South 'B' 'C' & 'A' Coys, 'D' Coy	
			in support at Bn HQ. E. Machine guns held up advance on right	
			at A16a 6.0 & A21 b 7.7; 'C' Coy held up by strong point A11a 2.7. Field	
			guns & TM's dealt with this without success. Rifle grenadiers & Lewis gunners	
			of No. 12 Platoon charged MUTTON Fm, & No. 9 Platoon working along the BAILLEUL	
			Ry. outflanked the strong point. 14 men of the 182 R.I.R. surrendered. 3	
			prisoners of war (2 Italian & 1 Portuguese) were also caught at MUTTON FM.	
			On the left, 'B' Coy met with stubborn resistance from M.Gs in LA CRECHE.	
			They were reinforced by 2 platoons of 'D' Coy.	
		PM 2.15	STEENWERCK & LA KIRLEM captured by 'C' and 'A' Coys. Advance now continued	
			more rapidly.	
		4pm	LA CRECHE entered by 'B' Coy & cyclists.	
		5	Large mine in LA CRECHE exploded. Fortunately, our troops had	JM

(A9175) Wt W2358/P560 600,000 12/17 D. D. & L. Sch. 52a. Forms/C2118/15.

2

Army Form C. 2118.

WAR DIARY
or
INTELLIGENCE SUMMARY.
(Erase heading not required.)

(6) Instructions regarding War Diaries and Intelligence Summaries are contained in F. S. Regs., Part II. and the Staff Manual respectively. Title pages will be prepared in manuscript.

Place	Date	Hour	Summary of Events and Information	Remarks and references to Appendices
STERNWERCK	Sept 1		advanced beyond this point.	
		6pm	MAJOR A.W. SUTCLIFFE, M.C. went forward and established a line of outposts as follows :- North to South A 6 a 5.9. - A 6 c 5.7 - A 12 a 3.3. - A 18 a 3.4 - A 29 a 2.2 ~~[illegible]~~	
			The Battalion had carried out an advance to an average depth of 5.000x on a frontage of 3.500x	
			During the operations there were only 10 casualties. 14 prisoners captured.	JW
			Casualties during tour - 26.8.18 to 1.9.18	
			Officers / O.Ranks.	
			Killed — / 1	
			Wounded — / 21	
			Missing	
			Total. ✓ / 22.	

(A9173) Wt W2358/P360 600,000 12/17 D. D. & L. **Sch. 52a.** Forms/C2118/15.

3

Army Form C. 2118.

WAR DIARY
or
INTELLIGENCE SUMMARY.
(Erase heading not required.)

Instructions regarding War Diaries and Intelligence Summaries are contained in F. S. Regs., Part II. and the Staff Manual respectively. Title pages will be prepared in manuscript.

Place	Date	Hour	Summary of Events and Information	Remarks and references to Appendices
	1918 Sept			
STEENJE	1/2		The Bn. was relieved by 2/S.W.B. and bivouacked about STEENJE. Bn Hd Qrs at F11G 85.95.	
			Lt-Col H.E. FESTING D.S.O. resumed command taking over from Major A.W. SUTCLIFFE M.C.	
	2		Resting.	
	3		Ammtn &c made up ready to proceed back into Outpost line. Warning order received at 11. a.m. that the Brigade would be relieved. Relief was carried out by 92nd Bde, the 11th E. YORKS relieving the Bn. about 4 pm. in Brigade Reserve, bivouacked about A2c The BORDER R remained in their own camp	
	4.		Resting and refitting. Enemy continued his retirement & Q.M. Stores &c commenced moving up to STEENJE.	
	5.		Bn provided working party for R Es at LA BARRIÈRE DES CALVERDANS	
	6 & 7		Training Platoon and Coy tactical schemes.	

Week ending Sept 7th 1918

INCREASE	OFF.	OR.
Draft from Base		75
Rejoined from Hospital		4
		79

DECREASE.	OFF.	OR
Wounded		13
Evacuated sick		8
To England for Comn		1
To 87th T M B		1
		23

(A9175) Wt W2355/P360 600,000 12/17 D. D. & L. Sch. 52a. Forms/C2118/15.

4

Army Form C. 2118.

Instructions regarding War Diaries and Intelligence Summaries are contained in F. S. Regs., Part II. and the Staff Manual respectively. Title pages will be prepared in manuscript.

WAR DIARY
or
INTELLIGENCE SUMMARY.
(Erase heading not required.)

Place	Date	Hour	Summary of Events and Information	Remarks and references to Appendices
STEENJE	1918 Sept 8		Bn provided 300 men for work on repairing roads near BAILLEUL under RE. Congratulations received from Divisional Comdr. on work done during advance. Warning order received that Bn would move back to STRAZEELE area on 9th	
	9		Owing to wet weather move postponed till 10th. Advanced party & heavy baggage despatched to new area	
FLETRE	10		Bn moved by route march to near FLETRE about W11b+d & bivouacked	
	11		Very wet morning. The Army Comdr. 2nd Army visited the Bde in the afternoon & inspected Hd Qr Coy & B Coy	
WALLON CAPPEL	12		Bn moved by Route March to WALLON CAPPEL area. Tent & bivouac camp at V 24 c 2. 4.	
	13+14		Baths & pay. Coys under Coy Comdrs for refitting, inspections &c.	

Week ending 14 Septr 1918

INCREASE	OFF	OR	DECREASE	OFF	OR
Draft from Base		36	Evacuated sick		21
Rejoined from Hospital		14	To hospital while on leave in England		1
		50	To UK sick 2/Lt J. ROBERTSON	1	
				1	22

[signature]

(A9375) Wt W2358/P360 600,000 12/17 D. D. & L. Sch. 52a. Forms/C2118/15.

(5)

5

Instructions regarding War Diaries and Intelligence Summaries are contained in F. S. Regs., Part II. and the Staff Manual respectively. Title pages will be prepared in manuscript.

WAR DIARY
or
INTELLIGENCE SUMMARY.
(*Erase heading not required.*)

Army Form C. 2118.

Place	Date	Hour	Summary of Events and Information	Remarks and references to Appendices
WALLON CAPPEL	1918 Sept 15		Bn Church parade.	
	16		Bn moved by Metre guage railway to ROAD CAMP, ST JAN-TER-BIEZEN entraining at HONDEGHEM, ½ Bn at 10.30 am, remainder at 12.30pm	
ROAD CAMP			Transport moved by road.	
	17		Training under Coy arrangements.	
	18.		do. Reconnoitring party, C.O, Adjt Coy Comdrs went forward.	
ORILLIA CAMP	19	7.30pm	Bn entrained on light railway at LANCASTER Siding & proceeded to camp at ORILLIA CAMP H2a. Skeleton Hd Qrs with C.O. to COMPASS FARM.	
	20		Reconnaissance by C.O. Skeleton Hd Qrs moved forward at 8pm to the RAMPARTS YPRES. Bn, training under Coy Comdrs	
	21		Training. Coy Comdrs conference at the RAMPARTS.	
			Week Ending 21 Sept 1918	

INCREASE	OFF	OR	DECREASE	OFF	OR
From Hospital		13	To Hospital		8
			To base, auth 29 Div c/100 d/12 9/18	2	
			2/Lieut T CLAYTON, " N.M.CLAYTON		
				2	8

(6)

Instructions regarding War Diaries and Intelligence Summaries are contained in F. S. Regs., Part II. and the Staff Manual respectively. Title pages will be prepared in manuscript.

Army Form C. 2118.

WAR DIARY
or
INTELLIGENCE SUMMARY.
(Erase heading not required.)

Place	Date	Hour	Summary of Events and Information	Remarks and references to Appendices
	1918 Septr			
ORILLIA CAMP			Training ~~at~~ by Companies	
	22+23 24		Bn entrained at ORILLIA CAMP 4pm & returned to old billets in ROAD CAMP	[initials]
ROAD CAMP	25		Battn. did practice attack under creeping barrage on ground near camp	
POPERINGHE	26		Bn. moved by march route to billets in POPERINGHE, reaching there about 9pm. Very comfortable quarters.	
	27		Preparing for trenches. Lt. H.R. CLUCAS, M.C reconnoitring march route to assembly area. Bn. entrained on light railway at POPERINGHE & detrained at MACHINE GUN FARM, YPRES. Railhead shelled a little. Proceeded by march route to assembly positions, east of YPRES. Bn. HQ. at THE MOATED GRANGE. Quiet night. Bn. in position by 12 mn.	
	28	2.30am	Preliminary bombardment on Belgian front.	
		5.30	Zero hour. Enemy replied very weakly to our barrage. Drizzling rain.	
		7.30	JACKDAW TUNNELS high ground captured by 'C' & 'D' Coys.	
		8.30	Final objective (INVERNESS COPSE & UNKNOWN COPSE) reached by 2 platoons	[initials]

(A9175) Wt W2358/P360 600,000 12/17 D. D. & L. Sch. 52a. Forms/C2118/15.

(7)

Instructions regarding War Diaries and Intelligence Summaries are contained in F. S. Regs., Part II. and the Staff Manual respectively. Title pages will be prepared in manuscript.

WAR DIARY
or
INTELLIGENCE SUMMARY.
(*Erase heading not required.*)

Army Form C. 2118.

Place	Date	Hour	Summary of Events and Information	Remarks and references to Appendices
MENIN ROAD	28	am. 7.30	"A" Coy, "C" Coy under CAPT J. W. HOOD, M.C. and "D" Coy. under CAPT. J. DUGGAN, M.C., D.C.M. met with little opposition. Enemy M Gs easily overcome. About this time, 2 platoons "A" Coy. under CAPT. W. F. H. CHAMBERS, M.C. and Bn. HQ. captured Bn. HQ. of 13TH BAVARIAN RGT. including C.O., Adjt., Medical Officer and about 110 other ranks. 1ST K.O.S.B. leap-frogged Bn. and pushed on to TOWER HAMLETS.	
		11am	Bn. ordered to hold STIRLING CASTLE high ground for the night, assisted by 8 Vickers guns.	
		6.30pm	Received orders to move to GHELUVELT. Reached PERTH AVENUE about 10.30 pm. and spent night there. 2 Coys. K.O.S.B. at TOWER HAMLETS attached to Battn. Bn. HQ. in pill box about J 21 a 7.4. Total captures for the day – 200 prisoners (including 7 officers) 2 Field Guns, 2 T.M's & 15 Machine Guns. Casualties 1 Officer wounded; other ranks killed 18 wounded 53 Missing 1	
GHELUVELT	29		Orders received in the afternoon to take over line held by S.W.B & 2 Coys. K.O.S.B. 6 M Gs & 2 Coys. K.O.S.B. attached to Bn.	[initials]

(A9175) Wt W2358/P360 600,000 12/17 D. D. & L. Sch. 52a. Forms/C2118/15.

(8)

Instructions regarding War Diaries and Intelligence Summaries are contained in F. S. Regs., Part II. and the Staff Manual respectively. Title pages will be prepared in manuscript.

WAR DIARY
or
INTELLIGENCE SUMMARY.
(Erase heading not required.)

Army Form C. 2118.

Place	Date	Hour	Summary of Events and Information	Remarks and references to Appendices
GHELUVELT	29/10		Relief complete about 4 am, without casualties. Line ran J35 b 8 7 to J35 d 8.4 – thence South west to P5 b 8.0. Bn HQ. in pillbox J35 a 3 8. Coys. disposed as follows N. to S. B, C. D. A Coys. 1 Coy. K.O.S.B on right with 1 Coy. K.O.S.B. echeloned in rear of right flank.	
KRUISEKE	30	6.30 am	From patrols it appeared that Bosche had withdrawn, and orders were given to push forward to the line P5 d 0.0 to X roads in P6 b. Bn HQ. moved to J36 c 1.6. Line was then ordered to swing forward, pivoting on the left to make good the road from AMERICA on the right to cross-roads P6 b on left. This was completed without	
		2.15 pm	opposition about 2.15 pm. Orders then received to advance on Q9 Central. Rough objective WERVICQ – GHELUWE Road from Q15 a 6.0 to Q9 d 70 99. 'D' Coy on right, 'C' Coy on left, supported by 'B' & 'A' Coys. Diamond formation was formed	
		4.15	on the high ground just east of AMERICA ROAD. attack commenced about 4 pm, & fighting was severe. Stubborn defence by enemy machine guns in Q9 c and Q15 a. Brig. Gen. G.H. JACKSON, CMG, DSO,	[initials]

(A9375) Wt W2358/P360 600,000 12/17 D. D. & L. Sch. 52a. Forms/C2118/15.

(9)

Instructions regarding War Diaries and Intelligence Summaries are contained in F. S. Regs., Part II. and the Staff Manual respectively. Title pages will be prepared in manuscript.

WAR DIARY
or
INTELLIGENCE SUMMARY.
(Erase heading not required.)

Army Form C. 2118.

Place	Date	Hour	Summary of Events and Information	Remarks and references to Appendices
Near	Sept. 30		personally led the right half of the Battn. and greatly inspired all ranks	
GHELUVELT			by his gallantry. At dusk the line ran from N. to S:– Q.2.d.2.4 to	
	?		Q.8.b.3.7, thence E. to Q.8.a.2.2. Bn. HQ. in farm Q.8.b.2.4. 'B' Coy	
			(assisted by 7 M.G's) and 'C' Coy. on left, 'A' & 'D' on right. Touch	
			obtained with LANC FUS. on left on road at Q.7.d.4.8. Very	
			heavy rain throughout operations & during the night. Enemy M.G's	
			very active. Pack mules being unable to reach the Bn., men	
			had to eat their iron rations. Relief promised at dusk by	
			2 Coys. K.O.S.B. Captures on 30th:– 1 M.G. & 3 prisoners.	
			Casualties on 30th 3 officers wounded; other ranks killed,	
			wounded missing.	
			Casualties during Tour.	
			Officers. Other Ranks	
			Killed – Killed. 24	
			Wounded 4 Wounded. 97	
			CAPT. W.F.H. CHAMBERS, M.C. (30th) Missing. 5	
			LT. H.D. LEES M.C. (30th)	
			2/LT. A.P. PENNINGTON (29th) Total. 126	
			J.W. CRAIG (30th)	

(A9173) Wt W2358/P566 650,000 12/17 D. D. & L. Sch. 52a. Forms/C2118/15.

(10)

Army Form C. 2118.

Instructions regarding War Diaries and Intelligence Summaries are contained in F. S. Regs., Part II. and the Staff Manual respectively. Title pages will be prepared in manuscript.

WAR DIARY
or
INTELLIGENCE SUMMARY.
(*Erase heading not required.*)

Place	Date	Hour	Summary of Events and Information	Remarks and references to Appendices
			Variation Return for week ending 27: 9: 18.	
			Increase. Decrease	
			OR OR	
			Rejoined from hospital 2 To hospital 17	
			Transferred to R.A.F. 1 Officer 2/Lt J L Finlayson	
			10: 10: 18. J H Smith ?/Lt. A/Adj. 1st. Border Regt.	

(A9175) Wt W2358/P360 600,000 12/17 D. D. & L. Sch. 52a. Forms/C2118/15.

SECRET

1st Bn The Border Regt

War Diary for Month ended 31st Oct 1918

Serial 42.

1st Borders
October 1918

WO 31

Instructions regarding War Diaries and Intelligence Summaries are contained in F. S. Regs., Part II. and the Staff Manual respectively. Title pages will be prepared in manuscript.

WAR DIARY
or
INTELLIGENCE SUMMARY.
(Erase heading not required.)

Army Form C. 2118.

Place	Date	Hour	Summary of Events and Information	Remarks and references to Appendices
Near GHELUWE	1	05.00	Owing to intense M.G. fire, daylight relief was quite impossible. Brig. Genl., Lt. Col. BURNE, D.S.O., R.A., & Lt. Col. G.E. BEATTY-POWNALL, D.S.O. visited Bn. in morning. Col. BURNE killed by sniper near Bn. H.Q. About mid-day, LANCS FUS. withdrew on left, leaving certain elements in our posts.	
		13.00	EAST SURREYS (41st DIV) attacked on right. No progress made.	
		15.30	EAST SURREYS again attacked under intense M.G. fire & made slight progress.	
		16.00	Our guns put down a barrage which fell short, & the attacking party was again forced to retire to our lines. About 70 men collected at Bn. H.Q. & taken under C.O.'s command.	
		18.30	New attack launched by 41st Div. This succeeded and our Bde. advanced through our lines in face of intense M.G. barrage fire.	
		19.30	Orders from Bde for Bn. to withdraw after dark, leaving EAST SURREYS covering the front.	
KRUISEECK	1/2	04.00	~~[illegible]~~ withdrawal completed by 04.00 & Bn. moved to old enemy hutment camp about P5a 0.9	
			Casualties during tour 27.9.18 to 2.10.18.	
			OFFICERS: Killed – Nil; Wounded – 4 {Capt. W.F.H. CHAMBERS, M.C.; Lt. H.D. LEES, M.C.; 2/Lt. CRAIG; " A. PENNINGTON.}; Missing – Nil; Total 4. Other Ranks: Killed 19; Wounded 89; Missing 21; Total 129	[initials]

(A9175) Wt W2355/P565 600,000 12/17 D. D. & L. Sch. 52a. Forms/C2118/15.

2

Army Form C. 2118.

Instructions regarding War Diaries and Intelligence Summaries are contained in F. S. Regs., Part II. and the Staff Manual respectively. Title pages will be prepared in manuscript.

WAR DIARY
or
INTELLIGENCE SUMMARY.
(Erase heading not required.)

Place	Date	Hour	Summary of Events and Information	Remarks and references to Appendices
KRUISEECK	3/4		Bn. resting & reorganising. Camp shelled on afternoon of 4th. No casualties.	
			Variation Return, week ending 4. O. R	
			INCREASE — O. — O.R. — DECREASE — O. — O.R.	
			Draft from Base. — 2 — - — Killed. — - — 19	
			(2/LTS. T. - M. N. CLAYTON) Wounded. — 4 — 89	
			Rejoined from Hospital. — — 2 — Missing — — 21	
			Reported missing now rejoined. — — 1 — Sick to Hospital. — — 2	
			Total — 2 — 3 — Total — 4 — 131	
WESTHOEK	5		Bn. moved to bivouacs & pillboxes at WESTHOEK.	
	6		Light training. Lt. Col. H.R. FESTING, D.S.O. admitted to hospital (sick). MAJOR H. W. SUT-	
			CLIFFE, M.C., assumed command of the Bn.	
YPRES	7	14.30	Bn. moved by march route to billets in YPRES, taking over from 7/LEINSTER RGT.	
	8		Coys. bathing. Light training.	
	9		Bde. inspected by Corps Commander, Lt. GENL. SIR C. JACOBS, K.C.B., in field	
			at H 10 c central near GOLDFISCH CHAU	
	10	12.30	Bn. moved by march route to Bde support area in BECELAERE in old	
			Boche huts & bivouacs. 3 of our observation balloons brought down by	[initials]

(A9175) Wt W2358/P565 650,000 12/17 D. D. & L. Sch. 52a. Forms/C2118/15.

3

Army Form C. 2118.

Instructions regarding War Diaries and Intelligence Summaries are contained in F. S. Regs., Part II. and the Staff Manual respectively. Title pages will be prepared in manuscript.

WAR DIARY
or
INTELLIGENCE SUMMARY.
(Erase heading not required.)

Place	Date	Hour	Summary of Events and Information	Remarks and references to Appendices
BECELAERE	10		E. A. which was later driven down by our planes.	
POTTERIJEBRUG	11	15.30	Bn. moved to support Bn. area at POTTERIJEBRUG. Accomodated in bivouacs.	
			Variation Return for w. e. 11.10.18	
			INCREASE. — O. / OR. ; DECREASE. — O. / OR.	
			From hospital — . / 1 ; Killed — 1	
			Drafts from Base — 5 / 41 ; Wounded — 2	
			LT. M. A. ASHLEY, 2/LT. E. R. RAINE, 2/LT. C. A. WATTS, 2/LT. L. V. LITTLE. HON. LT. & QM. H. BROWNING. ; Missing — 2 ; Sick (LT. G. B. D. CARGILL, 2/LT. W. E. KING) — 2 / 10	
			Transferred to 7/S.W.B. — 1	
			Total. — 5 / 42 ; Total. — 2 / 16.	
BEFORE COURTRAI	13/16.		Bn. in the advance to INGELMUNSTER - COURTRAI RY. See appendix.	I.
SALINES.	17		Bn. cleaning up & refitting.	
	18		Light training. Draft of 2 officers & 94 OR. from Reception Camp, MENDIGHEM. also 10% personnel.	
			Variation Return for w. e. 18. 10. 18.	
			INCREASE — O. / OR. ; DECREASE. — O. / OR.	
			Draft from Base (CAPT. R. E. S. JOHNSTONE, M.C.) (LT. J. R. MORRIS) — 2. / 81 ; Killed — 14	
			; Wounded — 3 / 79	
			From hospitals — 7 ; Missing — 12	
			Reported missing now rejoined — 5 ; Sick — 24	
			wounded — 1 ; To Base. (LT. & Q.M. BROWNING.) — 1 / –	
			2 / 94 ; 4 / 129	

WAR DIARY
or
INTELLIGENCE SUMMARY.
(Erase heading not required.)

Instructions regarding War Diaries and Intelligence Summaries are contained in F. S. Regs., Part II. and the Staff Manual respectively. Title pages will be prepared in manuscript.

Army Form C. 2118.

4

Place	Date	Hour	Summary of Events and Information	Remarks and references to Appendices
SALINES	19		Light training in morning. Refitting for line.	
	20		Bn moved by march route at 13.00 as advanced Guard to Bde., (which was in Divisional Reserve) across the LYS, to billets at I 27 c & d.	
	20/21		area shelled throughout the night.	
	21		Shelled by heavy hows. Lt. J R MORRIS wounded. A Coy moved to dug in in front of Bn. HQ.	
		14.30	Moved back to billets in area I 26 c & d & 32 a & b. 1st day	
	22		Story of Battn attached. 7 prisoners. Casualties:- Killed 1 O. 0 OR; wounded; missing } Total	
STEENBRUGGE	23		Battn relieved about 22.00 by 20th D.L.I. & moved back to billets about H 16, S. of HARLEBEKE. Bn. HQ. at I 25 a 9 9 N. of STEENBRUGGE. Lt. Col. J. FORBES-ROBERTSON, V.C, D.S.O, M.C, assumed command of Battn.	II
	24		Rest and re-organisation. Draft of 196 other ranks arrived.	
	25		Do. Baths.	
	26		Training.	
MOUSCRON	27		Bde march by stages to ST. ANDRE near LILLE. Left STEENBRUGGE at 07.45 marching via COURTRAI and reached MOUSCRON about 11.30. Bn. billetted in a hospital.	[initials]

(A9175) Wt W2358/P565 650,000 12/17 D. D. & L. Sch. 52a. Forms/C2118/15

5

Army Form C. 2118.

Instructions regarding War Diaries and Intelligence Summaries are contained in F. S. Regs., Part II. and the Staff Manual respectively. Title pages will be prepared in manuscript.

WAR DIARY
or
INTELLIGENCE SUMMARY.
(Erase heading not required.)

Place	Date	Hour	Summary of Events and Information	Remarks and references to Appendices
ST. ANDRE.			LT. Col. J. FORBES-ROBERTSON, V.C., D.S.O., M.C. assumed command (temporarily) of 86th Inf. Bde. MAJOR A.W. SUTCLIFFE, M.C. assumed command of Battn.	
	28		Bde march resumed. Bn left billets at 10.00, marching via TOURCOING, MOUVEAUX to ST. ANDRE, reaching billets at 14.00. Border Rgt & K.O.S.B. billetted in ASYLUM. Very good billets	
	29		Training. Practice ceremonial Parade. Brig. Genl lectured to all officers of Bde.	
	30.		Training.	
	31		Practice Bde ceremonial. Arroyo dos Molinos celebrated (impossible on 28th owing to move). 29th Div. Troupe performed at night. Regimental dinner at Bn. HQ.	

Variation for week ending 25.10.18.

INCREASE	O.	O.R.	DECREASE	O.	O.R.
Drafts from Base (CAPT. N.D. WILLIAMS)	1.	200.	Killed.		6
From Hospital.		13.	Wounded. (CAPT. R.E.S. JOHNSON, M.C. LT. J.R. MORRIS. 2/LT. L.V. LITTLE.)	3	90
Rejoined to take command.	1	-			
Previously reported wounded now at duty.		2.	Missing.	-	14
" " missing now rejoined		7	Evac. sick.		11
	2	222		3	121

(A9175) W1 W2358/P360 600,000 12/17 D. D. & L. Sch. 52a. Forms/C2118/15.

ADJT.
1st. BN. THE BORDER RGT.

1st Battn. The Border Regt.

Ref. Map. Sheets 27 and 29

I

Report on operations from 14th to 16th October, 1918 resulting in the capture of the area from LEDEGHEM (excl) to CUERNE (excl)

PRELIMINARY MOVES. On the afternoon of October 10th, 1918, the Battn. moved by march route from the RAMPARTS, YPRES to the Brigade support area in BECELAERE, square J.12.d., being accommodated in huts and bivouacs. The 87th Bde moved into the line on the afternoon of the 11th with 2nd S.W.B and 1st K.O.S.B. in the line near LEDEGHEM and 1st BORDER REGT. in support at POTTERIJEBRUG, with Btn. H.Q. at FORMAL FM.

At 2300 on the 12th gas projector attack was carried out by the special coy. R.E. on the enemy defences round LEDEGHEM, and DADIZEELE HOEK. No special signs from the enemy pointed to much success.

The Battn. dug assembly positions for 1st K.O.S.B. and 1st BORDER REGT on the following day, in square J.11.b. just North of the HEULEBEEK and DADIZEELE. Owing to a heavy ground mist the work was not observed by the enemy and was not interrupted by artillery fire. The positions were completed by 16.00

The Battn. left the POTTERIJEBRUG area at midnight 13th and occupied the assembly positions dug during the day. The 2nd S.W.B. and 1st K.O.S.B. withdrew to their assembly positions, being relieved by the 86th Bde on the left and the 88th Bde on the right.

About ~~02.00~~ 05.00 on the 14th the enemy put down a counter preparation barrage on the front line and supports, getting two direct hits on Bn H.Q. at the A.D.S. pill-box at SCORER JUNCTION, causing a few casualties, and setting fire to 4 motor ambulances.

Barrage fell exactly at zero, 05:35, and the enemy intermittently shelled the Brigade area from 2 mins after zero onwards. At 07.00 a telephone message was sent from Bde. ordering the Battn. to advance. As the advanced Battn. of the Bde, two routes were allotted to the Battn. They moved, A & B coys by the Southern and "C & D" coys by the northern, along the following routes:-

Southern Route: From assembly position past HOOLEY HOUSE by the old enemy track as far as KANTER HOEK, thence by the main road running east through LEDEGHEM STATION.

Northern Route: By the cross-country route by Bde H.Q. (TRIUMPH HOUSE) to WHITWORTH JUNCTION and thence through LEDEGHEM STATION

Battn H.Q. proceeded with Bde H.Q. in advance of the leading coy. On reaching a point about 600 yds east of LEDEGHEM STATION,

H

along the LEDEGHEM–[illegible] Rd. A very dense fog was encountered which made it impossible to see more than a distance of 100 yards. Guides were sent forward to LEDEGHEM STATION to bring the Coys along the LEDEGHEM–[illegible] Rd, as cross country work was practically impossible, and Battn H.Q. moved on to IVESON FM L.[illegible].6.6. Here, the atmosphere was clearer and it was observed that elements of the leading Brigades were still in the vicinity of [illegible], and fighting could be heard just in front. The [illegible] assembled in the vicinity of [illegible] until such time as the ground in front became clear. The Battn was then deployed along the hedges of the enclosure round IVESON FM. and picquets were put out to protect the right flank and the front, and patrols sent forward to gain touch with the Brigades in front. This [illegible] was from about 09.30 until 12.00. The Battn was ordered to move out into diamond artillery formation to cover the whole divisional front from the north edge of SOVEREIGN WOOD, L.10.d.92. to OLIVER FM. L.10.[illegible].6.6. Coys were reported in position by 13.00. It being reported that the 86th and 88th Bdes were roughly along the grid line between squares G.8. and G.9, the Brigade was ordered to move forward into a close support position. 1st BORDER REGT. to take up positions in artillery formation in squares G.8.a. and c. The Battn moved about 14.30 to accomplish this, "A" Coy on the right supported by "B" Coy, protecting the flank, and "D" Coy on the left supported by "C" Coy, Bn. H.Q. being in the centre of the diamond. About 16.15 the Bttn was in the vicinity of a line N & S. through G.7.c.11, with scouts about 300 yds in front, who reported that they were in touch with the support Bn of the 88th Bde, and a reconnaissance established the fact that the firing line ran approximately N. and S. through G.8. central, running sharply back on the right flank in the direction of MOORSEELE. A considerable amount of M.G. fire was experienced about this time and the Bttn was therefore withdrawn under orders from G.O.C. 87th Bde and dropped in close billets as follows:

"A" Coy in the farm L.12.c.9.9.
"D" " " farms round L.12.a.6.4.

with the support Coys "B" & "C" in farms near MUSEL HOEK. Bttn H.Q. was established with Bde H.Q. in POODLE FM, L.11.b.5.1.

Rations, [illegible] and watercarts were guided up to the Coys that night and the troops made as comfortable as possible.

At 21.00 G.O.C. 87 Bde held a conference & issued orders for the 87th Bde to attack under a barrage at 09.00 the following morning 15th inst; 1st BORDER REGT attacking on the Southern half of the Divisional front from about G.14.a. central to G.8.[illegible].5.9 with the 2nd S.W.B. attacking on the left.

A Battn conference of all Officers was held at 22.30 & details of the attack explained. Coys. were ordered to form up in diamond formation. "A" and "D" Coys in front, "B" and "C" Coys in support occupying positions as follows:-

"A" Coy in the vicinity of G.13.b.2.9.

"D" " G.7.d.1.6. with "B" Coy about L.18.a.1.9. and "C" Coy about L.12.c.3.6. Battn H.Q. about L.12.c.1.2. to be in position by 08.00.

2nd S.W.B. conformed on the left and at 08.15 the two Battns moved simultaneously until the leading platoons were on the line N & S through G.8.a.7.0. The Battn then halted and lay down in position to wait for the barrage. This was the disposition at about 08.40. as the barrage was to fall at 09.00.

The enemy apparently observed the movement and opened bursts of fire with numerous M.G.s. Several enemy aeroplanes flying over in formation also directed a certain amount of artillery fire on the assembly area, but very few casualties were inflicted.

4 mins before zero the barrage fell on the front of the 36th Div. on our right and our own barrage commenced 3 mins later, and the troops advanced to the assault passing through the front line of the 86th & 88th Bdes.

The Bn. immediately came under heavy M.G. fire and a certain amount of T.M. and artillery fire inflicting several casualties, but they pressed on and carried the enemy's first line of resistance. A second line of resistance behind a broad belt of wire running through G.9. central in a North Easterly and Southern direction offered considerable opposition, but was eventually captured by about 09.35.

At 09.45 "A" Coy reported the capture of the Village of SALINES.

At 10.15 front line ran through G.16.b.5.3, CULLEGHEM was, however, holding up the right flank. "B" Coy - right support Coy - therefore formed a defensive flank 300 yds East of SALINES, and the two Vickers Guns attached co-operated.

At about 10.40 CULLEGHEM was cleared and touch was established with the 36th DIV. and the advance continued. At 10.40 the front line Coys attacked the houses and enclosures on the northern outskirts of HEULE in G.17. a & c. and at 11.00 the left flank Coy. reported themselves in HEULE. The BOIS D'HEULE had not by this time been captured and enfilade fire was experienced by our left flank. "C" Coy under Capt. B.R. DURLACHER, M.C. formed a defensive flank facing North towards the BOIS D'HEULE.

At about 12.15 the BOIS D'HEULE having been taken and the troops on the left flank having come up, the advance was continued, and at 12.47 the Battn had captured the COURTRAI-INGLEMUNSTER Rly. from G.18.b.0.2. to G.12.d.3.4.

Enemy Machine Guns were enfilading the right flank from HEULE, which had not been taken, and "B" Coy again formed a defensive flank on Hill 20 facing South. Consolidation of this line was at once commenced, "A" & "D" Coys digging in in front of the Railway, "B" Coy on the defensive flank facing South, and "C" Coy in support West of the Railway in the vicinity of G.18.b.1.9.

At 13.45 touch was gained with the 36th Div. at G.18.a.30.00. and "A" Coy & "D" Coy proceeded to exploit forward of their line of Consolidation and by 14.00, Coys had taken up dispositions as follows:

"A" Coy with outposts in the vicinity of G.18.b.9.5.

"D" " outposts in H.13.a.4.8.

– With supports about G.18.b.9.8. and H.13.a.3.9. respectively.

"B" Coy in support through G.18.b.2.9. & "C" Coy in support in G.12.d.3.5.

Battn H.Q. which had originally been at G.8.c.3.7. moved forward on report being received that SALINES was captured, about 10.15, to G.9.d.5.4. and at 12.00 moved forward to G.16.b.1.9.

About 15.30 the Brigadier informed the C.O. that the KOSB were moving up to push through with a view to exploiting, and if possible, seizing the crossings of the HEULEBEEK. While the 9th Div. on the left of the Brigade were pushing forward to endeavour to capture CUERNE, the C.O. was ordered to put in one Coy to work in conjunction with One Company S.W.B., to maintain touch with K.O.S.B. left and the 9th Div. right.

The C.O. therefore went forward and personally arranged this. "C" Coy moved out and accomplished this at 16.20.

After proceeding about 500 yds, however, information was received from LIEUT COL. G.T. RAIKES, D.S.O., Commanding 2/S.W.B. that the services of this Coy were not required and it was, therefore moved back to its old position in support.

The Battn remained in the Dispositions given above that night. On the K.O.S.B. seizing the canal crossing between WATERMOLEN & CUERNE, & the 9th Divn. capturing CUERNE, Coys moved into billets in the houses in the vicinity of the trenches which they were holding, putting out Coy picquets.

The night was very quiet and the ~~next day the 16th inst.~~ the Bn. was relieved by the 4th WORCESTER REGT. and moved back into billets at SALINES.

The officers taking part in the attack were as follows:

MAJOR	A.W. SUTCLIFFE, M.C.	C.O.
2/Lt.	J.H. SMITH M.C.	Adj.
LIEUT	H.K. CLUCAS M.C.	I.O.
"	C. HELM, M.C.	Sig. Off.
Capt.	F.J. GIMMELL-SMITH	O.C. "A" Coy
Lt.	W.H. YOUDALE	
"	E. OXLEY	
2/Lt.	M.N. CLAYTON	
LIEUT	G.E.H. SLATER	O.C. "B" Coy.
"	R. RAE	
2/Lt.	C.H. DAVIES	
CAPT.	B.R. DURLACHER M.C.	O.C. "C" Coy.
2/Lt.	T. CLAYTON	
"	C.A. WATTS	
"	E.R.W. RAINE	
CAPT.	J DUGGAN, M.C., DCM	O.C. "D" Coy.
2/Lt.	G.H. BLACKBURN	
"	L.V. LITTLE	
LIEUT.	M.A. ASHBY	

The following casualties were suffered by the Battn:-

2/Lt. G.H. BLACKBURN - Wounded
" C.H. DAVIES "
" M.N. CLAYTON "
LIEUT. G.E.H. SLATER Wounded (Remained at duty)

Other Ranks:-

Killed - 14
Wounded 80
Missing 10
104

Prisoners and material captured during the operations were:-

150 Prisoners
1 - 4.5 Howitzer
5 - M.G.s

Several other M.Gs were captured of which no record could be kept owing to the pace of the advance.

Throughout the attack the enemy resisted with considerable vigour and it was a continuous running fight. The enemy artillery fire was never very heavy and seemed to come from several moving guns, chiefly "whizz bangs" and 4.5s. The defence consisted of a large number of heavy & light M.G.s. which were very difficult to locate owing to the enclosed nature of the country and the large number of farms and cottages scattered about & grouped into hamlets.

The country was rolling agricultural country with several transverse streams. The ground around these streams was of a sodden, spongy nature, but otherwise the going was good.

The Bn, thus, in a little over 3 hours, accomplished an advance of about 4.500 yds. on a frontage of about 750 yds, capturing the village of SALINES & the northern half of the village of HEULE.

[signature]

MAJOR.

Commdg. 1st. Bn. "The Border" Rgt.

19.X.18.

[illegible]

II

Narrative of operations 20/22 October inclusive

On the 19/10/18 the Bn was billeted in SAINTES [illegible] was notified that 88th Inf Bde. on night 19/20 would endeavour to break [illegible] between COURTRAI & CUERNE and establish bridge heads; and that an attack would be made on the [illegible] by the Division from the general line held [illegible] the [illegible] in a S.E. direction with the ultimate object of gaining approximately the line of the ESCAUT from AVELGHEM inclusive [illegible] inclusive.

For this operation the 87th Bde would be in reserve and would probably [illegible] approximately VIERKEERHOEK & INGOYGHEM. [illegible] objectives, etc were only approximate and dependent upon the situation.

At [illegible] from Bde. putting the Bn. on half an hour's notice from 08.00 on the 20th.

At 11.30 the Bn. received orders to move at 1300 to the area just west of CUERNE & moved off at 1300 for this purpose. En route the Bn was halted near WATERMOLEN and ordered to [illegible] pending further instructions.

At 15.15 G.O.C. 87th Bde informed C.O. 1st Border R. that as a result of the attack the 86th Bde were roughly on a line running N. & S. [illegible] village of KROTE & W. of ST. LOUIS that the right flank of the [illegible] was completely exposed & nothing was known of the situation on the Western bank of the canal, and that in consequence C.O. 1/Bor. R. [illegible] with G.O.C. 86th Bde & form a defensive flank along the E. bank of the canal to [illegible] enemy attack from the West.

1/Border R. was therefore ordered to move forward to L.25.a & the C.O. went forward to reconnoitre and at this time 8 M.G.s were placed under orders [illegible]
[illegible] that the [illegible] were [illegible] a line E. of ST. LOUIS through [illegible] possibly a footing on WOLFSBERG hill & were held up from [illegible] which was strongly held by the enemy.
G.O.C. 86th Bde had only [illegible] 2 fresh [illegible] from [illegible] hand, no assistance [illegible] the right flank [illegible]
[illegible]
[illegible]

This [illegible] shelling [illegible] suffered and several casualties [illegible]

At 23.20 [illegible] message [illegible]

III

from 87th Bde stating 86th Bde would move forward about 09.00 on the 21st to attack on to the objective from O.23 central to P.8 central, 87th Bde would be prepared (a) to pass thro' 86th Bde on this line to exploit or (b) to support the attack throughout but would only move under orders [illegible]
At 10.00 on 21st a message was received from 87th Bde stating attack by 86th Bde would probably not materialise for some time, and units were informed they would only move under orders G.O.C. 87th Bde. [illegible]

As the area occupied by the 1/Border R. had been consistently shelled [illegible] the Bn was moved to billets on northern outskirts of ESSCHER in order to avoid further casualties at 11.30

86th Bde attack developed in the afternoon about 15.30 & was reported to have reached the general line O.5. central. O.11.d, O.17 central.

At 19.15 situation report was received stating BAN HOUT BOSCH was captured. Probable line of departure of 87th Bde for attack on the 22nd was given as I.35.a.0.0, O.11. central O.17 central.

O.C. 1st Border R. was ordered to get in touch with Roy. Fusiliers 86th Bde with a view to attacking through their line on 22nd but no detailed orders regarding the attack would probably be available till after midnight.

At 03.00 on 22nd G.O.C. 87th Bde visited O.C. 1st Border R., described the situation, [illegible] Bn boundaries and objectives, informing him of the intentions of the troops on his flank to attack simultaneously, [illegible] on right, 1/KOSB on left and giving him particulars regarding barrage etc.

The attack was to take place on a 2 Bn front, 1/Border R. on the right 1/KOSB on left, 2/S.W.B. in reserve [illegible] their own supports. Div. boundaries were as [illegible] from O.9. central S.E. to P.34.c.0.0. Div. N. boundary through I.35 central to O.6. central, thence due East to P.[illegible] thence S.E. to O.17. central. Inter-Bn boundary between 1/Border R. & 1/KOSB was from O.11. central due E. [illegible] thence S.E. to P.19.d.0.0.

1st objective from O.24 central to P.3 central. 2nd objective the line AVELGHEM [illegible] MEERDE. The attack was to take place on a barrage which was to fall at 09.00 [illegible] O.17.a.4.0. through O.12. central to O.6. central where it would dwell for five minutes & then [illegible] rate of 2 minutes per 100 yards until O.24 central was reached and [illegible] would dwell for 50 minutes while the barrage stepped up on the left onto the line of the 1st objective then it would [illegible] 30 minutes [illegible] then cease.

CO arranged in conjunction with OC 4 [illegible] to move out from [illegible] at [illegible] [illegible] in the area O.10.d, O.16.b, [illegible] conforming on the left.

At 11.30 am a conference of Coy. Cmdrs, Trench mortar Officer & M.G. Officer [illegible] [illegible] [illegible] the attack explained.

Owing to the limited amount of time available no written orders were issued by the Bn.

The Bn moved [illegible] [illegible] [illegible] in diamond formation of [illegible] in the area specified, with B Coy on the right flank under Lieut. SLATER, C Coy on the left [illegible] under Capt. A.E.S. JOHNSON MC, A Coy under Capt. F.C. [illegible] SMITH in support to R. Coys, D Coy under Capt. DUCKHAM MC, [illegible] in support [illegible], the Bn being in position about 08.30.

The leading Pl. of A Coy was detailed under 2/Lieut. A.S. SMITH DCM, to act as flank Pl. to [illegible] the right flank. 2 MGs were allotted to work with this Pl. under Sjt. THOMPSON [illegible].

Bn HQ was established at O.10.a.7.5.

The assembly was observed by the enemy when the Bn was in the vicinity of O.10.a.1.6 so that the last 400 to 1000 yds had to be done under M.G. fire from hill 66 in O.23 [illegible] and from [illegible] of KATTESTAART [illegible] O.18. & several casualties were sustained. It was however, only due to the skilful handling of Coys & Pls by their officers that [illegible] casualties were not much heavier. The assembly area was also lightly searched by shell fire from 08.15 onwards.

At 9 am the [illegible] [illegible] [illegible] [illegible] [illegible] [illegible] [illegible] [illegible] [illegible] MG fire from [illegible] [illegible] KATTESTAART. They [illegible] pressed on [illegible] [illegible] [illegible] [illegible] [illegible] [illegible] the [illegible] [illegible]. At 09.45 C Coy formed a defensive flank towards hill 66 running roughly from [illegible]. A Coy [illegible] endeavoured to [illegible] down the MG fire from hill 66 by L.G. & MG fire. This was [illegible] [illegible].

Owing to the heavy fire [illegible] [illegible] flank from an [illegible] [illegible] [illegible] M.G.s, the [illegible] [illegible] [illegible] [illegible] [illegible] absence of any [illegible] the [illegible] was never [illegible] [illegible] [illegible] [illegible] held up by about 1000 and [illegible] [illegible] L.G.s [illegible] [illegible] [illegible] [illegible] to get forward [illegible] [illegible] houses in KATTESTAART [illegible] [illegible] [illegible] close [illegible] [illegible] of the general line O.18.d.3.7. to O.18.c.5.5. ... was reached. The left support Coy. ... reinforced the left firing line Coy which sustained heavy casualties by about 11.30. Conspicuous good work was done during the time by 2/Lt E.W. CHICKEN D.C.M. M.M. Cmdg the T.M. section & also by Lieut McGREGOR M.C. with his M.Gs. This officer, who had moved his guns forward on a limber to a sunken portion of the road near O.16.b.7.9 having reconnoitred the situation went back to his limber and galloped the limber from the cover of the sunken road into the open & over the rise into the cover of a slight bank in front, lying on top of the limber to do so. He was subjected to heavy concentrated M.G. fire but succeeded in winning thro' & subsequently getting his guns into action. About an hour later this very gallant officer was killed while directing the fire of his guns.

About this time 12.00, the situation was obscure & several officers endeavoured to clear it by personal reconnaissance. They were however prevented from getting contact with the front line troops owing to M.G. fire and similarly the front line troops were prevented from getting information back, several orderlies becoming casualties in the attempt. From observation points, forward of BAMHOUT BOSCH however, fighting could be seen going on for KATTESTRAATE the N. end of which had been cleared of the enemy. About 14.00 it was established that the general line held by the Bn. ran from O.18.d.3.5 to O.18.c.5.5. to O.12.c.7.1 with a combined post of Border R & KOSB. at O.12.d.8.7. At 14.25 a message was received from O.C. "B" Coy stating that at 13.16 the enemy had deployed in the vicinity of O.18. centre & had attempted a counter attack but had been repulsed by L.G. fire inflicting considerable casualties. O.C. "A" Coy reported similarly at 13.55. Reorganisation & consolidation of the line held was therefore carried out & during a slight lull communication was established and S.A.A. sent up to the front line. Touch was also gained with the flanks.

At 16.15, O.C. B Coy reported that in conjunction with the 41st Div on the right who made a 2nd attempt to take hill 66, he had endeavoured to go forward again about 14.15. His left flank was unable to do so. Nos 5 & 6 Pls on the right however succeeded in getting through between the two points of resistance of the enemy in O.23 & O.18, to a depth of 1500 x reaching the road in P.19.a.c. led by Lieut G.H. SLATER O.C. B Coy. By this time these Pls were reduced to a few [illegible] of 19 who were therefore withdrawn to original [illegible] on O.[illegible] & O.[illegible]. The Bn [illegible] this line & were relieved by [illegible] S W B, relief being completed by 21.50

all casualties were evacuated. Total casualties sustained by the Bn were 5 Officers wounded (2 remained at duty)

6 O.Rs killed, 88 wounded, 5 missing. The opposition encountered throughout the operations was of the strongest. It was established from observation & from prisoners statements that it consisted of an extraordinary large number of heavy & light M.Gs, manned by 5 or 6 men & commanded by an officer in each case.

These officers fought their guns gallantly & skilfully & [illegible] directing operations, several being [illegible] by our men while doing so, other officers were seen dashing about behind the enemy's line on horseback.

The position held by the enemy was of great natural strength & [illegible] to the defensive tactics employed by the enemy. It consisted of a series of spurs the crests of which were dotted with numerous [illegible] & enclosures with low hedges. The ground before the [illegible] was bare agricultural land almost entirely devoid of cover of the slightest description. This ground, chiefly consisting of plough, was sodden, & the [illegible] heavy rain further added to the discomfort & difficulties of the attacking troops.

It is estimated that at least 20 [illegible] German M.Gs were [illegible]

The Bn was commanded by Major A W SUTCLIFFE MC.

H Qr officers were:

Capt F.L. HOLLAND [illegible]
Lieut H.R. CLUCAS MC [illegible]
C HELM MC [illegible]

A Coy
Capt F [illegible] SMITH [illegible]
Lieut MORRIS
2/Lt [illegible] SMITH [illegible]

D Coy
Lieut G.F.H. SLATER
2/Lt W.W. CRAIK
[illegible] CLAYTON

[illegible] Coy

Volume 43.

Instructions regarding War Diaries and Intelligence Summaries are contained in F. S. Regs., Part II. and the Staff Manual respectively. Title pages will be prepared in manuscript.

WAR DIARY
or
~~INTELLIGENCE SUMMARY.~~
(Erase heading not required.)

Army Form C. 2118.

1st Border Regt

Vol 32

Place	Date	Hour	Summary of Events and Information	Remarks and references to Appendices
	NOV.			
St. ANDRÉ	1		Training	1
			Variation week ending 1.11.18	
			INCREASE O. O.R. — DECREASE O. O.R.	
			Drafts from Base 2 18 — Evacuated Sick – 2	
			(2/Lt. G.M. HOWE & W. COTTERILL (?))	
			From hospital – 1	
			2 19 — – 2	
	2		Ceremonial Parade & inspection by Lt. GEN'L SIR BEAUVOIR DE LISLE K.C.B., D.S.O., commanding XV Corps.	
	3		Divine Service. Played 1/2 MONMOUTHS at rugger in afternoon.	
	4		Training.	
	5		Do – M.O.'s Inspection. Q.M.s re fitting. Very wet day.	
	6		Do – Inspection & testing of S.B.R. in gas hut.	
TOURCOING	7		Bn. moved by march route from St. ANDRÉ to TOURCOING, leaving at 10.00 and reaching new billets at 1400. Very good billets. 87th Bde. in support to 88. Bde. who took over line near POTTES (on L'ESCAUT)	
	8.		Bde. march resumed. Bn. moved out at 08.00 (?) to billets at	

(A9175) Wt W2358/P360 600,000 12/17 D. D. & L. Sch. 52a. Forms/C2118/15.

Instructions regarding War Diaries and Intelligence Summaries are contained in F. S. Regs., Part II. and the Staff Manual respectively. Title pages will be prepared in manuscript.

WAR DIARY
or
~~INTELLIGENCE SUMMARY.~~
(Erase heading not required.)

Army Form C. 2118.

Place	Date	Hour	Summary of Events and Information	Remarks and references to Appendices
PETIT-TOURCOING	8		PETIT TOURCOING. Raining during march. German delegate arrived at French G.H.Q. and given until 11.00 on the 11th to accept armistice terms.	2/
			INCREASE. Variation Return for w.e. 8.11.18. DECREASE	
			Drafts from Base ×9 O. 72 O.R. Transf. to Base. O. – O.R. 9	
			From Hospital 3 Evac Sick (Lt E. OXLEY, M.C.) 1 11	
			× Lt C. R. HOWITT. 2/Lt G. TURNER, " C. W. SMITH. " J. WATSON. " F. T. CAMPION. Lt E. HALLAM. 2/Lt J. T. C. ROBERTS. " G. CRAIG. " E. J. CALVERT. — 9 75 — 1 20.	
DRIES.	9		CAPT. J. W. HOOD, M.C. & 2/Lt. A. J. SMITH, D.C.M. awarded D.S.O. C.O.'s conference at 10.00. Bn. at 1 hour's notice. Enemy reported to be evacuating. 88th Bde forced L'ESCAUT and GRAND COURANT. Bn. moved at 14.00 to billets in DRIES. Kaiser abdicated and Crown Prince renounced right to throne.	
Near CELLES	10.		Bn. moved at 08.00 across L'ESCAUT to billets just beyond CELLES. Cavalry moved up. 88th Bde. at ST. SAUVIEUR unable to get touch with enemy.	
	11.		Orders received at 01.00 to move at 09.00 forward. At 08.30 news came through that hostilities were to cease at 11.00 as enemy had accepted terms of	JW

(A9175) Wt W2535/P360 600,000 12/17 D. D. & L. Sch. 52a. Forms/C2118/15

Army Form C. 2118.

WAR DIARY
or
~~INTELLIGENCE SUMMARY.~~
(Erase heading not required.)

Instructions regarding War Diaries and Intelligence Summaries are contained in F. S. Regs., Part II. and the Staff Manual respectively. Title pages will be prepared in manuscript.

Place	Date	Hour	Summary of Events and Information	Remarks and references to Appendices
Near CELLES	11		armistice. "A" Coy working on roads, filling in craters from 09.15 to 17.15.	3
			C.O's conference for all officers at 17.00.	
	12		Battalion Ceremonial Parade. Divisional Cards presented by Brig	
			Gen JACKSON CMG DSO Commanding 87th Bgde.	
	13		Battalion moved by march route to St SAUVEUR. The C.O.	
			Lieut Col J. FORBES ROBERTSON VC DSO MC rejoined Battalion after	
			commanding 88th Bgde during absence of Brig Gen Comdg 88th Bgde	
			on leave in England.	
St SAUVEUR	14		Move continued by march route to OGY. Battalion left at 08.00	
			and arrived at new billets at 13.30. News came to Bn that 29th	
			Division was to be part of army of occupation in Germany.	
			Small parties of British prisoners of war coming through all day,	
			having been released by the Boche. They marched well & were in good	
			spirits.	
OGY	15		Cleaning Equipment & training. C.O's conference at 17.30.	[initials]

(A9175) Wt W2358/P360 600,000 12/17 D. D. & L. Sch. 52a. Forms/C2118/15.

Army Form C. 2118.

Instructions regarding War Diaries and Intelligence Summaries are contained in F. S. Regs., Part II. and the Staff Manual respectively. Title pages will be prepared in manuscript.

WAR DIARY
or
~~INTELLIGENCE SUMMARY.~~
(Erase heading not required.)

Place	Date	Hour	Summary of Events and Information	Remarks and references to Appendices
			Variation Return for week ending 15/11/18	
OGY	15		Increase 0. O.Rs — Decrease 0. O.Rs	4/
			From Hospital 3 — To England on duty 1 – 0	
			" Brigade 1	
			" Base 1 — 2nd Lieut J H Smith M.C	
			Lieut & QM E. Hodgson 1 - 4 — 1 – 0	
	16		Cleaning equipment & training. All surplus stores called in from Coys returned to DADOS. Ammunition reduced to 60 rds per man. Two motor lorries received by Bn for use during march.	
	17		Bn moved by march route to ISIERES and took over billets from 14th Bn ROYAL HIGHLANDERS. The weather was fine. Good billets.	
			The following important orders were received:— (a) In accordance with the terms of the Armistice the occupied areas of FRANCE, BELGIUM and LUXEMBOURG are to be evacuated by the enemy by November 26th.	
			(b) A further withdrawal to the RHINE will take place on a later date.	
			(c) The 29th Division will advance in the first echelon on the right of the II Corps. (d) The 87th Infantry Brigade will advance in the first	H.B.

(A9175) Wt W2358/P360 600,000 12/17 D. D. & L. Sch. 52a. Forms/C2118/15.

Instructions regarding War Diaries and Intelligence Summaries are contained in F. S. Regs., Part II. and the Staff Manual respectively. Title pages will be prepared in manuscript.

WAR DIARY
or
~~INTELLIGENCE SUMMARY.~~
(Erase heading not required.)

Army Form C. 2118.

Place	Date	Hour	Summary of Events and Information	Remarks and references to Appendices
OGY	17		echelon on the right of the 29th Division. (e) A Canadian Division will be advancing on the right of the 87th Infty Bgde and the 88th Infty Bgde on the left. (f) The advance will be covered by Cavalry advancing one days march ahead.	5 /
ISIERES	18		Bn moved by march route to GRATY. Distance about 10 miles Very good billets.	
	19		Training, & inspection of boots & equipment.	
	20		Bn moved to HORRUES starting at 2 p.m. & arriving at 4 p.m.	
HORRUES	21		Bn marched to HAUT-ITTRE a distance of about 15 miles. There was some difficulty with Transport owing to frosty weather & hilly roads	
HAUT ITTRE	22		Bn turned out for short cross country run, otherwise resting. The following were sent to represent the Bn at the celebrations of the King of Belgium's triumphal entry into BRUSSELS:— 2nd Lieut Smith A.J. DSO DCM. RSM. Windeler, Sgt Sheerer DCM bar MM. Sgt Moulding MM 2 bars Sgt Weber, MM 1 bar. Sgt Clegg DCM. Cpl Ferguson, DCM, MM. Cpl Wright MM 2 bars Pte Pharoh DCM, MM. Pte Adams, Pte Blylow DCM Pte Dunn DCM Pte Fookill MM 2 bars Pte Lee MM. Pte Smith (90) MM Pte George MM Pte Cundy.	WRC

Instructions regarding War Diaries and Intelligence Summaries are contained in F. S. Regs., Part II. and the Staff Manual respectively. Title pages will be prepared in manuscript.

Army Form C. 2118.

WAR DIARY
or
~~INTELLIGENCE SUMMARY.~~
(Erase heading not required.)

Place	Date	Hour	Summary of Events and Information	Remarks and references to Appendices
			Variation Return for week ending 22/11/18	6
	22		Increase — O. ORs / Decrease — O. ORs	
			From Base — 2, 18 / To Hospital — 39	
			Lieut G.H.S. McDonald	
			" G.B. Cox	
			From Hospital — 5	
			Total — 2, 23 / — 39	
	23		The Bgde group moved to BOUSVAL area. The Bn found the Advanced Guard for the Bgde and moved to SCLAGE north east of BOUSVAL. On arriving the Bn put out Outposts covering the Bgde front. Length of march about 12½ miles.	
SCLAGE	24		Bn moved to WALHAIN St PAUL Distance about 12 miles. Marching was very difficult owing to frost and hilly roads, but no men fell out.	
WALHAIN St PAUL	25		The 87th Bgde moved forward covering the whole Divisional front. The Bn moved south east to GRAND-LEEZ a distance of about 5 miles. Good roads and easy march. On arriving Bn put out Outposts for its own protection.	[initials]

(A9175) Wt W2357/P360 600,000 12/17 D. D. & L. Sch. 52a. Forms/C2118/15.

Army Form C. 2118.

Instructions regarding War Diaries and Intelligence Summaries are contained in F. S. Regs., Part II. and the Staff Manual respectively. Title pages will be prepared in manuscript.

WAR DIARY
or
~~INTELLIGENCE SUMMARY.~~
(Erase heading not required.)

Place	Date	Hour	Summary of Events and Information	Remarks and references to Appendices
GRAND LEEZ	26		Bn resting. Inspection of Kits. Iron rations &c.	4/
	27		Bgde moved forward passing through Cavalry screen. The Bn marched to SERON SERRESSIA area, acting as Advanced Guard for Bgde. Distance about 12 miles.	
SERON	28		Bn moved to STREE area. Length of march about 17½ miles	
STREE	29		Bn moved to COMBLAIN-AU-PONT distance about 11 miles, country very hilly but roads good. Very good billets.	
			Variation Return for week ending 29th/11/18	
			Increase — O. ORs. — Decrease — O. ORs.	
			From Base — 2. — — To Hospital — — 5	
			2nd Lt W. J. Devereaz, Lt G. Cargill — England Lieut A G Campion — 1	
			2 — 0 — 1 — 5	
COMBLAIN-AU-PONT	30		Bn marched to BASSEDESNIE and DESNIE area and acted as Advanced Guard for Bgde. Length of march about 13 miles	

W.R. Clucas Lieut
for LT., COLONEL,
COMMANDING 1st BN. THE BORDER REGT.

(A9175) Wt W2358/P560 600,000 12/17 D. D. & L. Sch. 52a. Forms/C2118/15.

1st Bn The Border Regiment

WAR DIARY

for

month ending December 1918

VOLUME 44.

Volume 44

Instructions regarding War Diaries and Intelligence Summaries are contained in F. S. Regs., Part II. and the Staff Manual respectively. Title pages will be prepared in manuscript.

WAR DIARY

or

~~INTELLIGENCE SUMMARY.~~

(Erase heading not required.)

Army Form C. 2118.

Place	Date	Hour	Summary of Events and Information	Remarks and references to Appendices
BASSE DESNIE	Dec. 1		Bn marched to area CHENEUX-MISTA-HAUSTA Distance about 13 miles, passing through SPA where the Boche Armistice Commission were billeted.	
MISTA AREA	2		Resting and cleaning	
	3		Training and Fitting equipment etc	
	4		Bn marched over the frontier into GERMANY with the Brig. Gen G.H.N. Jackson and the C.O. Lt Col J Forbes Robertson at the head, the Drums playing "John Peel". Bn took over billets at ELSENBORN.	
ELSENBORN	5		Bn moved to MOUNTJOIE + acted as advanced guard for Bgde.	
MOUNTJOIE	6		Bn moved to BOICH	
			Variation Return for week ending 6/12/18	
			Increase — O. ORs. — Decrease — O. ORs	
			From Hospital — 2 — To Hospital — 30	
BOICH	7		Bn marched to GLADBACH. A guard of 2 Offrs + 40 men was sent to 2nd Corps H.Q. for duty at DÜREN	
GLADBACH	8		Bn moved to BRUGGEN	

(A9175) Wt W2355/P360 600,000 12/17 D. D. & L. Sch. 52a. Forms/C2118/15.

Instructions regarding War Diaries and Intelligence Summaries are contained in F. S. Regs., Part II. and the Staff Manual respectively. Title pages will be prepared in manuscript.

WAR DIARY
or
INTELLIGENCE SUMMARY.
(Erase heading not required.)

Army Form C. 2118.

Place	Date	Hour	Summary of Events and Information	Remarks and references to Appendices
BRUGGEN	9		Bn moved with Bgde to assembly positions on western outskirts of COLOGNE taking over billets in KRIEL area.	
KRIEL	10		Fitting and cleaning.	
	11		do do	
	12		do do Guard of Honour of 2 offrs + 50 men sent to meet Lt Gen SIR CHAS FERGUSSON. Military Governor of COLOGNE at the Central Rly Station COLOGNE.	
	13		Bn march through COLOGNE, passed the 2nd Army Commander and crossed the RHINE and proceeded to BERG GLADBECH	
BERG GLADBACH			Variation Return for week ending 13/12/18	
			Increase — O. ORs. / Decrease — O. ORs.	
			From Hospital — 5 / Evacuated from Div area — 64	
			Accidentally wounded — 1	
			Off strength to England Capt B R Durlacher M.C — 1	
			Total: Increase 5 / Decrease 1 65	
	14		Bn Resting	[signature]

Instructions regarding War Diaries and Intelligence Summaries are contained in F. S. Regs., Part II. and the Staff Manual respectively. Title pages will be prepared in manuscript.

WAR DIARY
or
INTELLIGENCE SUMMARY.
(*Erase heading not required.*)

Army Form C. 2118.

Place	Date	Hour	Summary of Events and Information	Remarks and references to Appendices
BERG GLADBACH	15		Bn marched to HILGEN doing Advanced Guard for the Bgde	
HILGEN	16		2 Platoons of "B" Coy took over POST No 4 from the 4th DRAGOON GUARDS at the FORK ROADS north of K in KREMIN Reference SHEET GERMANY 2 L Officer in charge of POST Lieut G.H. SLATER	
	17		Training	
	18		A Colour Party consisting of 2nd Lieut C.W. SMITH 2nd Lieut C.A. WATTS Sergt LURKIN Cpl WRIGHT L/Cpl FIELD proceeded to ENGLAND to escort the Bn Colours to the Bn.	
	19		Training	
	20		Variation Return for week ending 20/12/18.	
			Increase — O — ORs; Decrease — O — ORs	
			From Hospital — 9; Evacuated from Div Area — 16	
			To Hospital 1 (Lieut E.A. Hodgson)	
			Increase total: — 9; Decrease total: 1 — 16	
	21		Training	

(A9175) Wt W2358/P360 600,000 12/17 D. D. & L. Sch. 52a. Forms/C2118/15.

[signature] Lieut

Instructions regarding War Diaries and Intelligence Summaries are contained in F. S. Regs., Part II. and the Staff Manual respectively. Title pages will be prepared in manuscript.

WAR DIARY
or
INTELLIGENCE SUMMARY.
(Erase heading not required.)

Army Form C. 2118.

Place	Date	Hour	Summary of Events and Information	Remarks and references to Appendices
HILGEN	22	1030	Church Parade. The C.O. lectured the Battalion on the "Old Comrades Association".	
	23		Bn Bathing	
	24		Training	
	25		Xmas Day. Church Parade 1130.	
	26		Training	
	27		-Mo- Variation Return for week ending Dec 27/18.	
			Increase: O. — O.R. / Decrease: O. — O.R.	
			From Base: — 4 / To U.K. 2nd Lt A/ Smith D.S.O. D.C.M.: 1. —	
			Hospital: 1. 1. / Evac from Divl Area: — 2	
			Lieut Qm. E. Hodgson: 1. 5. / 1. 2.	
	28.		Training.	
		0630	First draft for Dispersal One to Shorncliffe Area, two to Ripon Area.	
		1130	Second draft for Dispersal 39 - Oswestry "	

(A9175) Wt W2354/P560 600,000 12/17 D. D. & L. Sch. 52a. Forms/C2118/15.

[signature]

Army Form C. 2118.

Instructions regarding War Diaries and Intelligence Summaries are contained in F. S. Regs., Part II. and the Staff Manual respectively. Title pages will be prepared in manuscript.

WAR DIARY
or
INTELLIGENCE SUMMARY.
(Erase heading not required.)

Place	Date	Hour	Summary of Events and Information	Remarks and references to Appendices
HILGEN.	29	0630	One man to Ripon for Dispersal	
		0930	Divine Service.	
		1115	Lieut. General Sir A. G. Hunter-Weston K.C.B. D.S.O. inspected all Officers and Other Ranks who served with him on Gallipoli. Total 4 Officers 54 O.Rs. Officers present Lieut. Col: A. J. Ellis D.S.O. Lieut: Col: J. Forbes-Robertson V.C. D.S.O. M.C. Captain J. A. Proctor M.C. 2nd Lieut: W. G. Demesey M.C.	
		1130	33 Other Ranks left for Dispersal to Oswestry Area under the command of Lt. A. R. Clues M.C.	
		1200	Brigade Area readjusted. 1st Border Regt remain at HILGEN. The Detachment at VIERING-HAUSEN withdrawn on 1st K.O.S.B moving in position at KREUTHHOLL, Detachment joining Battalion at HILGEN by march route.	
	30		Training	
			Lieut: Col: A. J. Ellis assumes command of the Battalion vice Lieut. Col. J. Forbes-Robertson V.C. D.S.O. M.C. who assumes command of the 1/5th Bn. The Border Regiment. Authy A.G. 2158/8876(O)	
			Five Other Ranks joined the Battalion from the Base.	
			Seven Other Ranks to Ripon Area for Dispersal	[illegible]

(A9175) Wt W2355/P360 600,000 12/17 D. D. & L. Sch. 52a. Forms/C2118/13.

Instructions regarding War Diaries and Intelligence Summaries are contained in F. S. Regs., Part II. and the Staff Manual respectively. Title pages will be prepared in manuscript.

WAR DIARY
or
INTELLIGENCE SUMMARY.
(Erase heading not required.)

Army Form C. 2118.

Place	Date	Hour	Summary of Events and Information	Remarks and references to Appendices
HILGEN.	31st		Training.	
		0630	34 Other Ranks to Ripon Area for Dispersal. One O.R. 'Watford Details' to Watford.	DOD [illegible]

A. J. Ellis Lieut. Colonel
Comdg 1st Bn. The Border Regiment

(A9175) Wt W2359/P560 650,000 12/17 D. D. & L. Sch. 52a. Forms/C2118/15.

SOUTHERN (LATE 29TH) DIVN.
67TH INFY BDE

1ST BN BORDER REGT

JAN - APR 1919

Volume 45

29

1 Border Regt

Army Form C. 2118.

Instructions regarding War Diaries and Intelligence Summaries are contained in F. S. Regs., Part II. and the Staff Manual respectively. Title pages will be prepared in manuscript.

WAR DIARY
or
~~INTELLIGENCE SUMMARY.~~
(Erase heading not required.)

Place	Date 1919	Hour	Summary of Events and Information	Remarks and references to Appendices
HILGEN	January 1st		Training	
	2nd		Training	
	3rd		Training. 6 Other ranks to England for Dispersal. One Other Rank rejoined Bn.	Yarmouth Depot W.E.3 [illegible] App: B
	4th		Training. The "Colours" of the Battalion arrived i/c of the following "Colour Party" and were duly handed over Lt C.W. Smith & Lt C.A. Watts. Sgt Larkin Corpl Wright M.H. & L/Cpl Field.	see Appx "C"
	5		Divine Service. 2nd Lt W.W. Craik M.C. and 3 Other Ranks to England for Dispersal	
	6		Bn Training. At a meeting of "The Old Comrades Association" the following were selected to officiate for the Battalion. Hony Treasurer 2nd Lieut W.G. Dennany M.C. Hony Secretary. R.S.M. A. Windeler.	Jan-Apr 1919
	7		Training. A Ceremonial parade was held to receive the "Colours" Officers i/c of "Colours" Lieut A. Chicken & Lieut C.A. Watts.	
	8		Training. The Divisional Commander Major General D.E. Cayley C.M.G. inspected the Battalion at 1330 and presented Medal Ribbons see appendix (A) 1 Sergt 1 Corpl 1 Bugler 6 Privates to Divisional H.Q. Divisional Guard.	
	9		Training	
	10		do 8 Other ranks proceeded to England for Dispersal.	[illegible signature]

(A9175) Wt W2358/P560 600,000 12/17 D. D. & L. Sch. 52a. Forms/C2118/15.

VOLUME. 45

Instructions regarding War Diaries and Intelligence Summaries are contained in F. S. Regs., Part II, and the Staff Manual respectively. Title pages will be prepared in manuscript.

WAR DIARY

or

~~INTELLIGENCE SUMMARY.~~

(Erase heading not required.)

Army Form C. 2118.

Place	Date	Hour	Summary of Events and Information	Remarks and references to Appendices
	1919 January			
HILGEN	10	1130	The Army Commander General Sir H C O Plumer. G.C.B. G.C.M.G. G.C.V.O. visited 84th Brigade Headquarters and saw all Battalion Commanders.	Variation Report W.E. 10-1-19 Appx "B"
	11		Training. Lieut General W.R. Marshall K.C.B. K.C.S.I. Commanding British Troops in Mesopotamia sent his best wishes and greetings to the 84th Brigade, which he formerly commanded.	
			12 Other Ranks proceeded to England for Dispersal.	
	12		Divine Service. 3 other ranks proceeded to England for Dispersal	
	13		Training	
	14		do	
	15		do Major C.V. Fox D.S.O. Scots Guards lectured at Y.M.C.A. Cinema Hall BURSCHEID on "Demobilization and Reconstruction" 7 Officers + 100 O.R. attended.	
			Lieut: J.T.C. Roberts and 34 Other Ranks proceeded to England for Dispersal	
	16		Training. HONOURS AND AWARDS	
			D.C.M. No 6776 Sergt (A/C.S.M.) Blunt G.E. No 8456 Sergt Rowe, J. authy: London Gazette 1st January 1919.	

D. D. & L., London, E.C.
(A7883) Wt W809/M1672 50,000 4/17 Sch 52a Forms/C/2118/14

VOLUME 45

Instructions regarding War Diaries and Intelligence Summaries are contained in F. S. Regs., Part II. and the Staff Manual respectively. Title pages will be prepared in manuscript.

WAR DIARY
or
~~INTELLIGENCE SUMMARY.~~
(Erase heading not required.)

Army Form C. 2118.

Place	Date	Hour	Summary of Events and Information	Remarks and references to Appendices
	1919 Jany			
HILGEN	16		Belgium CROIX-DE-GUERRE.	
			Lieut (A/Capt) E.L. HOLLAND. No 4406 R.S.M. A. WINDELER No. 33692 Sgt A. APPLETON	
			No. 32047 Pte. H. BARBER. No. 34007 Pte. CHRISTIAN T.	
			The Divisional and Brigade Commanders congratulations have been received	
	17		Training.	
	18		do The Commanding Officer lectured the Bn on Re-enlistment	
			Five Other Ranks left for Cologne prior to Dispersal	
			Variation Return for Week Ending 18th January 1919.	

Increase.	O.	ORs.	Decrease.	O.	ORs.	
From England	*1.		Granted extension of leave	1.		2/Lt. G.H. LOWE.
" Hospital		19	To Concentration Camp for Dispersal	1.	55	Lt. J.H.C. ROBERTS.
*Capt B.R. DURLACHER, M.C. joined 13-1-18.			" England serving soldiers with 2 yrs or over to complete		5	
			Evac: from Divl Area		3	
Totals	1.	19	Totals	2.	63	

D. D. & L., London, E.C. (A7853) Wt W809/M1672 50,000 4/17 Sch. 52a Forms/C/2118/14

Instructions regarding War Diaries and Intelligence Summaries are contained in F. S. Regs., Part II, and the Staff Manual respectively. Title pages will be prepared in manuscript.

WAR DIARY
or
~~INTELLIGENCE SUMMARY.~~
(Erase heading not required.)

Army Form C. 2118.

Place	Date	Hour	Summary of Events and Information	Remarks and references to Appendices
	1919 Jany			
HILGEN.	19		Divine Service 27 Other Ranks left for Cologne prior to dispersal	
	20.		Training. 13 Other Ranks left for Cologne for dispersal	
	21		do. Lieut. A CHICKEN proceeded to Cologne for duty with Dispersal Draft	
	22		do. One Other Rank proceeded to Cologne for Dispersal	
	23		do. Mr. MASTERMAN SMITH lectured on "ALSACE LORRAINE" and "The GERMAN MENTALITY" at BURSCHEID 6 Officers and 110 Other Ranks attended.	
	24		Training. Variation Return for Week Ending 24-1-19.	

Increase	O.	O.Rs.	Decrease	O.	O.Rs.
From Hospital		5	To Cologne for Dispersal		44.
" Base		3.	Gtd Extension of leave pending demobilization		1
			S. of S. Authy O.B. 2176/E *3. II Corps 14/2 E.T. d/6/1/19		
Total		8	Total	3.	45

* A/Capt. E. TOWLE, A/Capt. W. H. YOUDALE, Lieut. G. E. H. SLATER

W.H.Y. Capt.

D. D. & L., London, E.C. (A7883) Wt W8c9/M1672 50,000 4/17 Sch 52a Forms/C/2118/14

Army Form C. 2118.

WAR DIARY
or
INTELLIGENCE SUMMARY.
(Erase heading not required.)

Instructions regarding War Diaries and Intelligence Summaries are contained in F. S. Regs., Part II, and the Staff Manual respectively. Title pages will be prepared in manuscript.

Place	Date	Hour	Summary of Events and Information	Remarks and references to Appendices
	1919 Jany			
HILGEN	25		Training. The C.O. inspected 'D' Company's Billets. 8 Other Ranks proceeded to Cologne for dispersal. Honors and Awards:- Meritorious Service Medal. No 10178 Sergt. TOMKINS. W. Authy:- London Gazette 18th January 1919. The Brigade Commander has remitted the suspended sentence of 1 year I.H.L. in the case of No 10320 Pte. J. NOLAN. Reason for remission "For conspicuous gallantry in action near COURTRAI on the 14th October 1918. Private NOLAN volunteered to carry some messages under very heavy fire, these messages he delivered correctly and up to time thereby rendering invaluable service. He again showed great gallantry and courage on the 23rd October in volunteering, under heavy fire, to carry important messages to a flanking unit."	
—	26.		Divine Service. Lieuts M.A. ASHBY and C.A. WATTS proceeded to Cologne for duty with dispersal drafts. 20 Other Ranks proceeded to Cologne for dispersal.	—
	27		Bn Bathing. Training. Captain J. DUGGAN. M.C. D.C.M. and 21 Other Ranks proceeded to Cologne for dispersal.	[signature]

D. D. & L., London, E.C. (A7883) Wt W809/M1672 50,000 4/17 Sch. 52a Forms/C/2118/14

VOLUME 45

Instructions regarding War Diaries and Intelligence Summaries are contained in F. S. Regs., Part II, and the Staff Manual respectively. Title pages will be prepared in manuscript.

WAR DIARY
or
INTELLIGENCE SUMMARY.
(Erase heading not required.)

Army Form C. 2118.

Place	Date	Hour	Summary of Events and Information	Remarks and references to Appendices
HILGEN	Jany 1919 28.		Training.	
	29		Training. The Official Photographer visited the Battalion and groups were taken as follows:- Officers. Original 1st Battalion who landed at HELLES on 25th April 1915. W.O.s & Sergts. Colours. Drums. Battalion on Parade. A. B. C. D & HQrs Coys. Transport. It is proposed to have a book of the above which has been put in hand.	
			Captain B. R. DURLACHER. M.C. took over Command of 'D' Company.	
			Lieut. Colonel A. J. ELLIS. D.S.O. took over command of the 86th Brigade	
			Captain J. W. HOOD. D.S.O. M.C. assumed command of the Battalion.	
	30		Training. One O.R. to Cologne for dispersal, Repatriation WINCHESTER	
	31		Route March. Variation Return for Week Ending 31st January 1919	

Increase	O.	O.Rs	Decrease	O.	O.Rs	Remarks
From Hospital		1	Concentration Camp for Dispersal	1.	51	Captain J. F. Duggan M.O. O.C.[illegible]
" Base		1	Evac from Hosptl		1	
			To W.O. G.S.O.3.	1.		Major H.E. FESTING D.S.O.
Total		2	Total	2.	52	[illegible]

[illegible] Lt. Col. [illegible]

(A7883) Wt W8c9/M1672 50,000 4/17 Sch 52a Forms/C/2118/14
D. D. & L., London, E.C.

Volume 45 War Diary Appendix (A)

[illegible] Roll of recipients of awards [illegible] presented [illegible] ribbons and bars tomorrow.

BAR to D.S.O.

Brig Gen [illegible] C.M.G. D.S.O.

BAR to D.S.O. and CROIX DE GUERRE

Major [illegible] D.S.O.

D.S.O.

Capt [illegible]

Bar to MC & Croix de Guerre – Major J C Ogilvie MC.

M.C.

Capt J [illegible]

Lieut [illegible]

2/Lieut [illegible] Clayton

BAR to D.C.M.

C Coy No [illegible] Sergt [illegible]

D.C.M.

B Coy No 4089 C.S.M. [illegible]

" " 26557 Sergt Clagg [illegible]

BAR to M.M.

A Coy No 27411 Sergt Graham R

B " 202660 Pte [illegible] A.

M.M.

A Coy No 20661 Sergt Armstrong V

B " 18579 Bell A

C 9097 [illegible]

C " 11740 [illegible]

D 33629 [illegible]

A 14777 Cpl [illegible]

B 33767 [illegible]

B 18358 [illegible]

C 10525 [illegible]

A [illegible] [illegible]

B [illegible] [illegible]

B 25249 L/Cpl Russell [illegible]

B [illegible] [illegible]

C 11534 [illegible]

C 32049 [illegible]

A [illegible] [illegible]

C 9554 [illegible]

B 30[illegible] Pte Lee W

B [illegible] [illegible]

A 26[illegible] [illegible]

C 33490 [illegible]

C 332[illegible] [illegible]

C 330[illegible] [illegible]

D [illegible] [illegible]

CROIX DE GUERRE

2/Lieut A Chicken

A Coy No 9701 Cpl Field J S

Volume 45

Instructions regarding War Diaries and Intelligence Summaries are contained in F. S. Regs., Part II, and the Staff Manual respectively. Title pages will be prepared in manuscript.

WAR DIARY
or
~~INTELLIGENCE SUMMARY.~~
(Erase heading not required.)

Army Form C. 2118.

Appendix B

Place	Date	Hour	Summary of Events and Information	Remarks and references to Appendices
	1919 January			
HILGEN	3		Variation Return for Week Ending 3-1-1919.	
			Increase. O. O.Rs. — Decrease O. O.Rs.	
			From England (Lt.Col. A.J. Ellis D.S.O.) 1. – — To England for Dispersal 105	
			" Base 5 — Committed to Prison 1	
			" Hospital 3. — Transferred to Eastern Cmd. England. 1	
			Evac from Div! Area 1 15	
			To 1/5 Border Regt (Lt.Col. Forbes Robertson V.C. D.S.O. M.C.) 1 –	
			Totals 1 – 8. — Totals. 1-122	
– " –	10		Variation Return for Week Ending 10-1-1919.	
			Increase O. O.Rs — Decrease O. ORs.	
			From Base 8 — To England for Dispersal 1 – 9	2nd Lt. W.W. Craik. M.C.
			" Hospital 20. — Evac from Div! Area 5	
			Senior Officers Course A'shot. 1 – 1	Major A.W. Sutcliffe D.S.O. M.C.
			Total 28 — Total 2-15	
				[signature]

D. D. & L., London, E.C. (A7883) Wt W8o9/M1672 50,000 4/17 Sch. 52a Forms/C/2118/14

VOLUME 46

Instructions regarding War Diaries and Intelligence Summaries are contained in F. S. Regs., Part II. and the Staff Manual respectively. Title pages will be prepared in manuscript.

WAR DIARY
or
INTELLIGENCE SUMMARY.
(Erase heading not required.)

Army Form C. 2118.

35

Place	Date	Hour	Summary of Events and Information	Remarks and references to Appendices
	1919 Feby			
HILGEN	1st		Training The C.O. visited Billets of C Company at 1030	
			Cross Country Run. 1st 2/Lt. R.H. JONES. 27min 2nd Sgt. R. GRAHAM. 27-30 min.	
			Winning Company D. 147 points. 2 O.R's to Cologne for Dispersal.	
-"-	2nd		Divine Service. Sergt. J. KERR granted 'LONG SERVICE and GOOD CONDUCT	
			MEDAL. Authority Army Order of 1-4-1918.	
-"-	3rd		Training & Bathing Educational Classes.	
-"-	4th		Training Educational Classes	
-"-	5th		Training 'The FRAGMENTS' gave a concert at 5-30pm. A good show.	
-"-	6th		Training 2nd LIEUT. J. WATSON and 2 O.R's to Cologne for dispersal.	
			Sgt Heppel G. joined Battalion and taken on strength.	
-"-	7th		Route March, March Discipline No. 9 Platoon, C Coy under the command	
			of 2/Lieut. T. CLAYTON. M.C. proceeded by march route to relieve Platoon 1st K.O.S.B.	
			at PREYERS MILL, F.8.7.2. frontier defences. Relief completed by 12 NOON.	
				W.G.D. Lt

D. D. & L., London, E.C. (A7883) Wt W809/M1672 50,000 4/17 Sch 52a Forms/C/2118/14

VOLUME. 46

Instructions regarding War Diaries and Intelligence Summaries are contained in F. S. Regs., Part II. and the Staff Manual respectively. Title pages will be prepared in manuscript.

WAR DIARY
or
INTELLIGENCE SUMMARY.
(*Erase heading not required.*)

Army Form C. 2118.

Place	Date	Hour	Summary of Events and Information	Remarks and references to Appendices
	1919 Feby			
HILGEN	7th		Variation Report for Week Ending 7th Feby 1919.	
			Increase. O. O.Rs. Decrease. O. O.Rs.	
			From Base. 1. To Cologne for Dispersal *1. 6.	
			" Hospl. 1. " Hospital 1.	
			" No10 Mily Prison 1. *Lieut. J. WATSON.	
			Total 3 Total 1. 6	
— " —	8th		Training Educational Classes. The C.O. inspected the Billets of Headquarter Company.	
			The Regimental Concert Party gave a performance at 5-30 p.m.	
— " —	9th		Divine Service	
— " —	10th		Bn Bathing. Route March & march Discipline. Educational Classes.	
— " —	11th		Training. Educational Classes. Captain J.W. HOOD. D.S.O. M.C. appointed a/Major from 21-1-19.	
— " —	12th		do do . The Regimental Concert Party gave a performance at 5-30 p.m.	
			. Lieut J. THORBURN proceeded to Cologne for Dispersal.	
— " —	13th		do . The Adjutant lectured the Battalion subject German Mentality.	[signature]

D. D. & L., London, E.C. (A7883) Wt W809/M1672 50,000 4/17 Sch. 52a Forms/C/2118/14

VOLUME 46

Instructions regarding War Diaries and Intelligence Summaries are contained in F. S. Regs., Part II, and the Staff Manual respectively. Title pages will be prepared in manuscript.

WAR DIARY
or
INTELLIGENCE SUMMARY.
(Erase heading not required.)

Army Form C. 2118.

Place	Date	Hour	Summary of Events and Information	Remarks and references to Appendices
HILGEN	14th		Training & Educational Classes LIEUT BOWMAN lectured on "Mental Efficiency"	
			LIEUT. R RAE 3rd Bn Royal Scots Fusiliers attached proceeded to Cologne for dispersal	
			Variation Report for Week Ending 14-2-19	
			Increase. 0. O.R. Decrease. 0. O.Rs	
			From Hospital 1. To Cologne for dispersal *1. 2	
			Demobilized in England *1. 2.	
			Evac from Div'l Area. 2	
			Total 1. *Lieut. / Thorburn Lieut. C Helm. Total 2. 6.	
	15th		Bn Wiring. HUNGER. Lieut: G.H.S. McDONALD took over command and payment of C Company.	
	16th		Divine Service	
	17th		Bn Bathing. Educational Classes 2nd Lieut: E.W. CHICKEN. M.C. D.C.M. M.M. and 2 Other Ranks rejoined from 87th Trench Mortar Battery.	
	18th		Bn wiring under C.O. Educational Classes. Lt Col Stevens D.S.O. R.A.M.C. lectured all officers on V.D.	
	19th		Bn Wiring under Capt. F.J.G. SMITH. Educational Classes.	[signature]

D. D. & L., London, E.C. (A7883) Wt W809/M1672 50,000 4/17 Sch 52a Forms/C/2118/14

VOLUME 46

Instructions regarding War Diaries and Intelligence Summaries are contained in F. S. Regs., Part II, and the Staff Manual respectively. Title pages will be prepared in manuscript.

WAR DIARY
or
INTELLIGENCE SUMMARY.
(*Erase heading not required.*)

Army Form C. 2118.

Place	Date 1919	Hour	Summary of Events and Information	Remarks and references to Appendices
HILGEN	Feby 19th		Lieut: J. PATTINSON proceeded to POPPLESDORF for course of Agriculture.	
			Lieut: C. HELM. M.C. rejoined Battalion and taken on strength.	
— " —	20th		Field Works. Lecture by Mr. MASTERMAN. SMITH. Subject:- 'France, Alsace-Lorraine and the danger arising from the deceitful mentality of the German Nation.	
			The following officers having proceeded on leave to United Kingdom for two months are struck off strength on the dates stated against their names.	
			Capt. J. H. PROCTOR M.C. 17-2-19. Lieut: G. C. A. COX. M.C. 18-2-19. Lieut. H. J. HAYMAN-JOYCE. 19-2-19.	
— " —	21st	0900	Outpost at PREYERS. HILL. relieved by One Platoon 'D' Coy. LIEUT. D. CARGILL in charge. Relief complete 1200. Bn Wiring under Capt. N. D. WILLIAMS. Educational Classes.	
			Variation Report for week Ending 21-2-19	
			Increase. Or. O.Rs. — Decrease Or. O.Rs.	
			Rejd. from No. 5. M. Prison. — 2. — S off S. Auth'y A.G. 8658(C) 3x. -	
			" 8th T.M.B. — 2. — Dispersal to U. Kingdom 1x 6	
			" England *1. — -. — Evac from Divl. Area. — 3	
			*Lieut. HELM. M.C. Total 1 - 4 — Total 4 - 9.	
			x Capt Proctor M.C. Lt Hayman-Joyce. Lt. Cox M.C. " Rae	
— " —	22nd		Commanding Officers Conference. Experiments carried out at BURSCHEID by	[initials]

(A7883) Wt W8-9/M1672 50,000 4/17 Sch 52a Forms/C/2118/14 D. D. & L., London, E.C.

VOLUME 46

Instructions regarding War Diaries and Intelligence Summaries are contained in F. S. Regs., Part II, and the Staff Manual respectively. Title pages will be prepared in manuscript.

Army Form C. 2118.

WAR DIARY
or
INTELLIGENCE SUMMARY.
(Erase heading not required.)

Place	1919 Feby.	Hour	Summary of Events and Information	Remarks and references to Appendices
HILGEN	22nd		2nd Lieut. E.W. CHICKEN. M.C. D.C.M. M.M. Of new type of Universal Percussion Grenade.	
		1430	Cross Country Run. Winner 'C' Coy Pte HENDERSON. Winning Coy 'B' Coy.	
— —	23rd		Divine Service. Lieut. E. HALLAM. proceeded to England to attend course of instruction in Demobilization and Re-engagement.	
— —	24th		Bn Bathing. Educational Classes. C.O. attended Brigade Conference at 1030.	
— —	25th		Bn Wiring. Educational Classes No. 5578 C.S.M. RUSHFORD. W. posted to Battalion	
— —	26th		do do.	
— —	27th		do do. 2nd Lieut. E.W. CHICKEN. M.C. D.C.M. M.M. and 12 Other Ranks proceeded to STRASSEN for attachment to 84th T.M.B.	
			HONORS and AWARDS. MILITARY MEDAL. 10052 Sgt. PUCKETT. P. Authy Xth Corps A.L. 25/78/1 O/22-119	
			Brigade Commanders Congratulations Received.	
— —	28th		Bn Wiring. Educational Classes Variation Report Week Ending 28-2-1919.	
			Increase Os. O.R. Decrease Os. O.R.	
			84th T.M.B. 2 Demob on leave 2	
			" Evac from District 3	
			Total 2 Total 5	[signature]

[signature] Lieut. Col. Comdg 1/6 Bn. [illegible]

(A9175) Wt W2155/P.16 600,000 12/17 D. D. & L. Sch. 52a. Forms/C2118/15.

1st Border 29

Army Form C. 2118.

Vol 36937

Instructions regarding War Diaries and Intelligence Summaries are contained in F. S. Regs., Part II. and the Staff Manual respectively. Title pages will be prepared in manuscript.

WAR DIARY or INTELLIGENCE SUMMARY.

(Erase heading not required.)

Place	Date	Hour	Summary of Events and Information	Remarks and references to Appendices
	1919 MARCH			Ceased
HILGEN	1st		Educational Classes. Training. Result of Cross Country Run 1st Capt. D.R. DURLACHER M.C. 26 mins 2nd 2nd Lieut R.H. JONES. 27 mins. Winning Coy. 'D'.	
	2nd		Divine Service	
	3rd		Bathing and Educational Classes. Lieut C.R. HOWITT and F. MAXWELL struck off strength pending Demobilization 1-3-19 and 31-1-19 respectively. Lt. G. CRAIG admitted Hospital. Remission of Sentence. The Brigadier remitted the suspended sentence in the case of No 10626 Pte CLARKE. C. Sentence Death commuted to 5 years P.S. Reason for Remission. "For conspicuous gallantry in action near HEULE on the 15th October 1918. This man displayed great ability in handling a Lewis Gun and was instrumental in the capture of an enemy post (Authy: Brigade Routine Order 251 d/1/3/19).	
	4th		Wiring on Defences. Captain E.L. HOLLAND having proceeded to England on duty, struck off strength from 1-2-19. 2nd Lieut. W.G. DENEREAZ. M.C. to be acting Captain (additional) from 10-2-19.	
	5th		Training Educational Classes. Lecture by D.T. HOLMES. Esq. Subject "Industrial Peace after the War". Major. J.W. HOOD D.S.O. M.C and L/Cpl. Mr J. HODGSON admitted to Hospital. Captain F.J.G. SMITH assumed command of the Battalion.	[illegible] Capt

(A9171) Wt W2353/P36 500,000 12/17 D. D. & L. Sch. 52a. Forms/C2118/15.

Army Form C. 2118.

WAR DIARY
or
INTELLIGENCE SUMMARY.
(*Erase heading not required.*)

Instructions regarding War Diaries and Intelligence Summaries are contained in F. S. Regs., Part II, and the Staff Manual respectively. Title pages will be prepared in manuscript.

Place	Date	Hour	Summary of Events and Information	Remarks and references to Appendices
	1919 March			
HILGEN	6th		Training Educational Classes	
	7th		Wiring on Defences	
	8th		Training. Five Officers and 20 Other Ranks paid a visit to the 1/5th Battalion stationed at HENNEF. A football match was played which resulted in a win for the Battalion result 1–0. The visit was extended till Sunday and all had a very enjoyable time.	
	9th		Divine Service. Lieut G.H.S. McDONALD appointed Acting Captain (additional) 1-3-19.	
	10th		Variation Return Week Ending 7-3-19	
			Increase — Off. O.Rs. — NIL — / Decrease — Off. O.Rs. — To England for Demob. 2. 2. — Officers proceeding to England 1. — Total 3. 2.	
	10th		Bathing and Educational Classes	
	11th		Wiring on Defences. 4 Other Ranks proceeded on furlo after re-enlistment under A.O. IV of 19.	
	12th		Training Educational Classes	
	13th		do — do	
	14th		Wiring on Defences. T/Capt B.R. DURLACHER. M.C. A/CAPT. G.H.S. McDONALD. G.D. CARGILL selected as Volunteers for Army of Occupation and posted to the 1/5th Bn. The Border Regt	[signature]

(A9195) Wt W2358/P356 650,000 12/17 D. D. & L. Sch. 52a. Forms/C2118/15

Instructions regarding War Diaries and Intelligence Summaries are contained in F. S. Regs., Part II. and the Staff Manual respectively. Title pages will be prepared in manuscript.

VOLUME [illegible]

WAR DIARY
or
INTELLIGENCE SUMMARY.
(Erase heading not required.)

Army Form C. 2118.

Place	Date	Hour	Summary of Events and Information	Remarks and references to Appendices
	1919 March			
HILGEN	14th.		T/Capt B.R. DURLACHER M.C. proceeded to join 1/5th Bn The Border Regt.	
	15th.		Training. Lieut A ALLAM 1st Border Regt. Lectured. Subject "POST BELLUM ARMY".	
			The outpost Platoon at PREYERS. MUHLE. was reinforced by one Platoon of	
			1/5th Devon Regt. Reinforcement completed by 12 NOON.	
	16th.		Divine Service. Variation Report for Week ending 14th.	
			Increase. Os. ORs Decrease. Os. ORs	
			Rejoined from hospital 8. Soffs to 1/5th Border 1. –	
			To Tank Corps. 1.	
			To U.K. 20	
			Total – 8. Total 1-21.	
			9 other Ranks proceeded on furlo to U.K on re-enlistment under A.O. IV of 19.	
	17th.		Bathing. Educational Classes. Promotion. Officers. Major (A/Lt Col) A. J. ELLIS. D.S.O.	
			to be Tempy Lieut Colonel whilst Comdg a Battalion (Authy: London Gazette [illegible]/3/19).	
	18th		Bn Wiring on Defences. Educational Classes.	
	19th.		Training & Educational Classes. Capt. A J F DANIELLI appointed Claims Officer 29th	[signature]
			[illegible] Struck off Strength (Auty. A.G. Y911(O) C.R. No 12261/15-7.	

(A9173) Wt W2358/P361 600,000 12/17 D. D. & L. Sch. 52a. Forms/C2118/15.

Instructions regarding War Diaries and Intelligence Summaries are contained in F. S. Regs., Part II. and the Staff Manual respectively. Title pages will be prepared in manuscript.

WAR DIARY
or
INTELLIGENCE SUMMARY.
(Erase heading not required.)

Army Form C. 2118.

Place	Date	Hour	Summary of Events and Information	Remarks and references to Appendices
	March 1919			
AACHEN	19th		Lieut E.R.W. RAINE appointed for duty to D.A.D.R.T. Cologne, struck off strength (Auty:–	
			G.O.C. 2nd Army C.R. No. 35505/101/B of 30/3/19.	
	20th		~~Draft 1/5th Devons relieved Outpost Platoon A Coy [illegible] at PREYERS MUHLE.~~ [illegible]	
			Draft 1/5th Devons (2 Offrs 36 Other Ranks) established a New Post at ZURMUHLE known	
			as No 3 Post, and linked up with No 2 Post PREYERS MUHLE on right and Post of 52nd	
			Devon Regt on left. Post established by 12 Noon.	
			Training and Educational Classes.	
	21st		Training as [illegible] and Educational Classes.	
			Variation Return Week Ending 31st	
			[illegible] Increase Offrs O.R. Decrease Offrs O.R.	
			From Hospital 4. Struck off strength 2 –	
			Evac for Duties 2	
			Demobilized 10	
			Total 4 Total 2 12	
	22nd		Draft 1/5th Devons 1 Offr [illegible] O.R. relieved Outpost Platoon A Coy PREYERS MUHLE	
			Relief completed by 12 Noon. Training	[illegible] Capt

(A9175) Wt W2358/P360 600,000 12/17 D. D. & L. Sch. 52a. Forms/C2118/15.

Army Form C. 2118.

Instructions regarding War Diaries and Intelligence Summaries are contained in F. S. Regs., Part II. and the Staff Manual respectively. Title pages will be prepared in manuscript.

WAR DIARY
or
INTELLIGENCE SUMMARY.
(Erase heading not required.)

Place	Date	Hour	Summary of Events and Information	Remarks and references to Appendices
	March 1919			
HILGEN	23		Divine Service. 2/Lieut A. J. SMITH D.S.O. D.C.M. Struck off strength on being posted to 3rd Bn in England.	
	24th		Bathing & Route March.	
	25th		Bn wiring on defences.	
	26th		Draft of Retainables and Volunteers for Army of Occupation under Lieut D. CARGILL, H. H. [illegible] M.C. and 2/Lieut R. SCOTT proceeded to join 1/5th Bn The Border Regt. strength 3 offrs 199 Other Ranks. The following Officers & Other Ranks were transferred to [illegible] MAJOR J. W. HOOD D.S.O. M.C. Capt F. G. SMITH, A/Capt G. H. S. McDONALD Lieut [illegible] B. HODGSON Lieut E. HALLAM 2/Lieut F. R. FREW, R. H. JONES, W. COTTERILL and T. CALVERT and 104 Other Ranks. They were given a Hearty Send off.	
	27th		Battalion were relieved by 1st Devon Regt and entrained for MULHEIM, station at which reduction to Cadre commenced.	
MULHEIM	28th		41 O. Ranks proceeded to Concentration Camp for dispersal.	
— " —	29th		Lieuts R. H. C. LUCAS M.C. A. CHICKEN 2/Lts T. CLAYTON M.C. G. TURNER with remainder of releasable men proceeded to No 1 Concentration Camp for dispersal.	
	30th		CADRE Lt Col A. J. ELLIS D.S.O. in Comd entrained 0900 enroute for DUNKIRK.	[illegible]

(A9175) Wt W2358/P360 600,000 12/17 D. D. & L. Sch. 52a. Forms/C2118/15.

Instructions regarding War Diaries and Intelligence Summaries are contained in F. S. Regs., Part II. and the Staff Manual respectively. Title pages will be prepared in manuscript.

WAR DIARY
or
INTELLIGENCE SUMMARY.
(Erase heading not required.)

Army Form C. 2118.

Place	Date	Hour	Summary of Events and Information	Remarks and references to Appendices
	March 1919			
DUNKIRK	31st		'CADRE' arrived 2130 hrs, accomodated in 'A' Camp.	
—	APRIL 1st		'CADRE' moved to No 2 Embarkation Camp.	
—	3rd		'CADRE' embarked on H.M.H.T. ANTRIM at 1200 hrs. Boat sailed 1230 hrs very good crossing. Disembarked at 1615 hrs at Dover. Entrained for BROOKWOOD at 1700. Arrived BROOKWOOD at 2200 hrs. Met by Major G. E. WARREN. D.S.O. commanding Foreign Service Details and Band of 3rd Bn the Border Regiment. Marched to DETTINGEN Barrack. BLACKDOWN. The Sergeants 3rd Bn the Border Regt entertained Officers & other Ranks at the Sergeants Mess and gave all a good welcome home.	

W. C. Dennis(?) Capt
A/Adjutant
1/Border Regt.

A7092). Wt. W12839/M1297 750,000. 1/17. D. D & L., Ltd. Forms/C2118/14.